4th edition

The POLICE MANAGER

DATE DUE

Orange   da

since 1887

p.o. box 1576
cincinnati, ohio 45201
(513) 421-4142

The Police Manager, Fourth Edition

ISBN 0-87084-707-4
Library of Congress Catalog Number 94-70022

 The text of this book is printed on recycled paper.

Elisabeth Roszmann *Editor*
Kelly Humble *Managing Editor*

Cover illustration and design by Sharpe Grafik Works

Preface

The goal of the fourth edition of *The Police Manager: Professional Leadership Skills* continues to be to provide selected step-by-step procedures to help police administrators execute their duties and fulfill responsibilities more efficiently, effectively, and productively.

This book does not pretend to be a complete source for all the management information necessary to operate a modern police department. It should be read along with a number of other excellent books in the fast-growing field of criminal justice management.

This revision includes four new chapters: "Philosophy to Outcome" (Chapter 2), "Organizational Culture" (Chapter 4), "Productivity" (Chapter 12) and "Ethics for the 1990s" (Chapter 18). Other chapters have been updated with the latest theories, practices, and data. Objectives are now included at the beginning of each chapter and discussion questions are included at the end of each chapter.

Programmed instruments that are mentioned in the instructor's manual may be used to supplement this text. Sufficient flexibility is left to the individual instructor, who may wish to round out instruction with personal experiences.

I hope that readers will use techniques and theories discussed in this book to assist them on an individual basis. By joining theoretical understanding to practical application of the techniques, you should be better prepared to serve your communities and upgrade law enforcement as a profession.

I am in great debt to a number of experts in the law enforcement field for their kind assistance, dedication, and patience in helping to develop the techniques presented in this text. Every effort has been made to acknowledge the sources and to give credit when due.

I want to thank specifically the following individuals, not just for their contribution to the subject matter but also for the influence they have had in helping me mature and develop during my law enforcement career:

S. B. Billbrough
Regional Director, DEA Retired

George Murphy
Mobil Corp.
New York

John Vermilye
Former Director, Department of Public Safety
Lakewood, Colorado

Mike Swanson
Institute of Government
University of Georgia

Special thanks go to my friend and colleague Dick McMahon of the Institute of Government, University of North Carolina. The chapter on transactional analysis is the product of his thought and hard work.

Further special thanks go to G. Patrick Gallagher, Director of the Institute for Liability Management, Vienna, Virginia, for developing and writing the chapter on civil liability.

Also, special recognition to Dr. James P. Morgan for his chapter on productivity.

Special thanks to my colleagues at the Institute of Government:

Dr. Roger Schwarz
Dr. Kurt Jenne

Many of their ideas are in some way captured in the pages of this text.

Theories are only worthwhile when they are put into practice. The leadership practices of a special few police executives are also included in these pages. Thanks for their help, support, *and* friendship.

Chief Larry Hesser
Chief of Police
Georgetown, Texas

Colonel Ed Werder
Chief of Staff, St. Lucie Sheriff's Office
St. Lucie County, Florida

Chief Fred Heineman
Chief of Police, Retired
Raleigh, North Carolina

One person in particular—my wife, Anne—has helped me to adopt the life goal of understanding and helping people. Others have helped me grow and mature as a man and find ways of making my life worthwhile, but none was more demanding and supportive than my three children, Scott, Chris, and Stacy. The many "warm fuzzies" my family gave me during the time it took to carry the idea for this book to the point of publication have sustained me and helped me to overcome any doubts that I may have had.

Finally, a grateful thanks to God; without His blessings, none of this could have been achieved.

Ronald Lynch

Contents

4   Organizational Culture   **41**

5   Management Communication Behavior   **49**

6   Organizational Environment   **69**

11 Management by Objectives   147

12 Productivity   169

13 Fiscal Management   177

14 Time Management   185

19 Assessment Center Process

Afterword

Index

A History and Philosophy of Police Management ‖ 1

Objectives

1. The student will gain knowledge of the background and principles that make up today's police management.

2. The student will become aware of the integration of technical, behavioral, and functional factors with the purpose of achieving stated objectives.

3. The student will learn the four levels of organization and why they must work together toward stated objectives in order to justify the trust and respect of the community's citizens.

4. The student will recognize his or her role in achieving goals of the organizational unit through the most effective and efficient use of assigned resources—people, money, time, and equipment.

5. The student will become familiar with the three philosophies of management and how they are employed by police managers today.

Are the problems that confront police managers on a day-to-day basis very different from problems confronting managers in industry and government? Are these problems different from the ones occurring in schools, hospitals, or churches? If we examine materials geared specifically toward industry or government, the answer is an obvious and resounding *no*. The problems facing police managers are similar to those that concern business executives, social leaders, and university personnel. The purpose of the organization may differ greatly from agency to agency, but the management process remains quite similar.

What, then, distinguishes the successful and effective police organization from one that is poorly run and under constant pressure due to its ineffectiveness? What is it that causes one police department to be exciting, interesting, and challenging whereas another is dull, suffers from high turnover rates, and is losing its battle against crime?

The major difference between the effective and ineffective can usually be traced to the management of the organization and, more specifically, to a difference in the philosophies of management. The differences can be seen in the organizational structure and in the amount of decision-making power granted to captains, lieutenants, and sergeants. The difference is clearly reflected in the attitudes and managerial philosophies of top management personnel.

The Police Manager's Role

What do police managers do? They listen, talk, read, write, confer, think, and decide—about people, money, materials, methods, and facilities—in order to plan, organize, direct, coordinate, and control their research service, production, public relations, employee relations, and all other activities so that they may more effectively serve the citizens to whom they are responsible. Police managers, therefore, must be skilled in listening, talking, reading, writing, conferring, thinking, and deciding. They must know how to use their personnel, money, materials, and facilities so as to reach whatever stated objectives are important to their organizations.

A study conducted by the Harvard Business School identifies the three elements common to all successful managers in government and industry: (1) the will to power, (2) the will to manage, and (3) empathy.

This study defines the will to power as the manager's ability to deal in a competitive environment in an honest and ethical manner and, once this power is obtained, to use it to accomplish the goals of the organization. The will to manage is described as the pleasure the manager receives in seeing these objectives accomplished by the people within the organization. It is important to note that the third quality does not stress the manager's technical ability but rather the ability to relate to other people and determine how they can best be helped to develop their fullest potential.

The police manager's responsibility is to unify his or her organization. There are commonly four levels to an organization: (1) *the system*—the total organization and its environment; (2) *the subsystem*—the major divisions or bureaus; (3) *the event*—a series of individual activities of similar type (normally a patrol watch or detective unit); and (4) *the element*—the incidents from which service to the community is measured. These four levels of the police department should coordinate in order for the police to reach stated objectives and justify the trust and respect placed in their hands by the citizens of their community.

Many police departments today have more than these four levels of organization. As a result, there often is an overlap of the different levels—and lines of authority and responsibility become unclear. A common problem might exist where the division is commanded by a captain who is assisted by a lieutenant. The assistant chief in the organization might not be clear on his or her specific role within the division and might make decisions that belong to the captain and the lieutenant. As a result of this interference, the lieutenant might begin to make decisions that belong to the sergeant. The sergeant, in turn, might make line operation decisions that should be made by the police officer. The result is that very little decisionmaking is left to the individual police officer at the element, or bottom, level of the department.

Figure 1.1 **Organizational Levels**

Level	Organizatonal Unit	Primary Responsibility
System	Department	Chief, Assistant Chiefs
Subsystem	Bureau or Division	Majors, Captains
Event	Division, Section, Watch	Captain, Lieutenant
Element	Squad	Lieutenant, Sergeant, Police Officer

Community-oriented policing (COP) helps to maintain a balance among the four major levels within the police department. In agencies where COP has been successful, usually the only ranks required at the working level are the police officer, the investigator, or the special police officer, all of whom are members of the element level of the department. In a typical COP scenario, at the first-line supervisory level, the sergeant is designated as the individual responsible for the coordination of the team's activities. She is a first-line supervisor, making decisions at the event level but assisting at the element level. At the subsystem or team level, the lieutenant is designated as the commander. He is responsible for the individual team achievements but leaves the choice of method to the sergeants and officers involved. At the system level is the chief of police and a key assistant, who is called the captain or assistant chief.

Police departments are beginning to reorganize with a stronger emphasis on the reduction of levels between the top of the department (the chief of police) and the bottom of the department (the police officer). The typical pyramid hierarchy that has been prevalent in the past is slowly beginning to flatten, and this trend seems likely to continue in the immediate future.

The Management Process

Effectiveness in reaching the objectives of the organization depends on the management process. That process is composed of three major areas: (1) technical factors, (2) behavioral (psychological) factors, and (3) functional factors.

The technical factors comprise skills that are common to all police agencies. They include the ability to investigate crimes and accidents as well as to perform preventive patrol and execute other routine procedures. These skills are not a subject of this text.

In any organization, the behavioral factors involve the circular flow of verbal and nonverbal communication that is a part of everyday operations. These factors deal with human interaction and are essential skills in a law enforcement organization.

The functional factors are those involved in producing desired results. They are designed to assist the police manager in controlling the organization. These factors include planning, organizing, decisionmaking, problem solving, and managing by objectives.

The *management process* is the integration of all these factors, with the purpose of achieving stated objectives. Police managers must utilize both theory and tools so that they may more effectively use the functional factors and behavioral factors in unison with the technical factors, thereby raising the overall level of service provided to the community.

Figure 1.2 **Integration Through Management**

Technical Factors	**Behavioral Factors**	**Functional Factors**
Investigation	Leadership	Planning
Preventive patrol	Values	Organizing
Fingerprinting	Conflict resolution	Decisionmaking
Calls for service	Change process	Problem solving
Property management	Communication	Managing by
Record keeping		objectives
Personnel allocation		
Traffic control		

Results

History of Management

The history of management can be divided into three broad philosophical approaches and overlapping time periods:

1. scientific management (1900-1940)
2. human relations management (1930-1970)
3. systems management (1965-present)

The *scientific management* theory dominated the period from the beginning of the twentieth century to about 1940. Frederick Taylor, "the father of scientific management," emphasized time and motion studies.[1]

His study of determining how pig iron should be lifted and carried is one of the classics of the scientific management approach. His recommendations for faster and better methods of production, in this case in the shoveling of pig iron, stress the importance of efficiency of operation through a high degree of specialization. The "best method" for each job was determined, and the employees were expected to conform to the recommended procedures. Employees were seen as economic tools. They were expected to behave rationally and held to be motivated by the wish to satisfy basic needs.

Taylor theorized that any organization could best accomplish its assigned tasks through definite work assignments, standardized rules and regulations, clear-cut authority relationships, close supervision, and strict controls. Emphasis was placed entirely on the formal administrative structure, and such terms as *authority, chain of command, span of control,* and *division of labor* were generated during this time.

In 1935, Luther Gulick formulated the now famous PODSCORB. This acronym—planning, organizing, directing, staffing, coordinating, reporting, and budgeting—has been emphasized in police management for many years.

Gulick emphasized the technical and engineering side of management, virtually disregarding the human side. Any changes in management during this period were designed to improve efficiency; little or no thought was given to the effect that the change process would have on the officer.

The major criticisms of the scientific management theory as it relates to law enforcement are:

1. Officers were considered to be passive instruments; their personal feelings were completely disregarded. Any differences, especially with regard to motivation, were ignored. All employees were basically treated alike.

2. The employee was considered to be "an economic man" who could be motivated through wage-incentive plans or through the fear of job loss.

3. The focus was on technical efficiency and not on the effectiveness of the organization.

4. The efficiency of operation was to be obtained only through:

   a. the division of labor—the breaking down of the police task into its smallest components.

   b. the specialization of police activities, resulting in vertical and horizontal groupings that were each headed by a single supervisor.

   c. the orderly arrangement of administrative units into a simple but rigid structure of line and staff departments.

   d. the use of a small span of control whereby the managers supervised only a few subordinates.

Beginning in 1930, the negative features of the scientific approach began to outweigh many of the established principles and practices. Strong criticism was brought against the failure of police management personnel to recognize the necessity for instilling dignity and pride in their employees. The impetus for the *human relations management* approach came from studies conducted in the Hawthorne plant of the Western Electric Company by Harvard scholar Elton Mayo.[2] The studies were initially designed to improve the existing physical facilities that affected work output. These studies focused on finding ways to bring about changes in production by changing working conditions, such as the number of hours, the number of work breaks per day, and the physical environment.

One of the first studies involved the effect of lighting on the output of each worker. A research group and a control group were established, with the research group being introduced to varying levels of light. It was first believed that the stronger the light, the greater would be the output of the employee. As the researchers increased the light intensity, output did go up. However, as they lowered the intensity of light below the original base level, output continued to rise. It was this startling fact that led the researchers to examine more carefully the causes for the increased output.

The researchers then began initiating smaller research groups, and they worked very closely with the employees in revamping working hours, rest periods, and complaint procedures. They invited creative comments on the part of employees. The researchers soon realized that the organization had more than just the formal organizational structure. The informal organizational structure—consisting of the rumor process, cliques, and informal status systems—was soon recognized as being an important factor in the increase or decrease of productivity. The individual employees involved in the study began to feel a sense of belonging and felt they were being treated as more than just tools to be used in the completion of a task.

In the 1940s and 1950s, police departments began to recognize the strong effect of the informal structure on the organization. Police agencies began to use such techniques as job enlargement and job enrichment at all levels to generate a greater interest in law enforcement as a profession.

Police departments began to realize that the classical concepts of the formal structure, with strong separation of staff and line operations, were not adequately meeting the goals of law enforcement. The trend began to change, allowing staff personnel to have direct authority over some line functions, and community relations units were created within the administrative function of the department.

The communication process within police agencies became one of the major problems for the police manager. The span of control originally established as an aid to effective police operations soon became a massive problem. Levels developed within the organization that did more to thwart effective communication between the police manager at the top of the organization and the police officer at the bottom.

During this period, industry recognized the difficulties created by the scientific management approach and began to deemphasize the tall organizational structure. Sears Roebuck, for example, developed the flat organizational structure, which provided for fewer levels of supervision. This type of structure required the delegation of responsibilities and emphasized careful selection, training, and placement of new employees.

During the 1950s, the management structure began to shift toward the more democratic or participatory management that is familiar in law enforcement today. Studies indicated that the supervisor who was "employee centered" was usually more effective than the one who was "production centered." The behavioral sciences became a source of information for police managers.

The human relations management approach also had its limitations. With the emphasis being placed on the employee, the role of the organizational structure and its importance became secondary. The primary goal seemed to be social rewards, and little attention was given to the necessity for completion of tasks. Many police managers saw this structure as being unrealistic. Douglas McGregor pointed out in his studies that the "soft" approach to management in many instances led to an abdication of management authority. Employees began to expect more and give less in return.

Management professionals in all fields of government and industry soon recognized the need for developing a third management approach that would encompass the positive features of both the scientific management and human relations structures.

In the mid-1960s, the features of the human relations and scientific management approaches were brought together in the *systems management* approach. This approach fused the individual and the organization; it was designed to help managers use their employees in the most effective way while reaching the desired production goals.

The systems management approach emphasized the organization as a unit, rather than concentrating on one element such as the employees or organizational structure. The importance of the elements within any organization cannot be minimized, but the total system came to be seen in terms of definitive levels such as system, subsystem, event, and element.

The systems management approach recognized that (1) it was still necessary to have some hierarchical arrangement to bring about cooperation and coordination; (2) authority and responsibility were essential; and (3) overall organization was required. This approach went still further by recognizing that an organization can reach its stated objectives and goals only through the interrelationship of its parts. In 1950, Abraham Maslow developed his "hierarchy of needs," in which he classified the needs of people at different levels.[3] Studies by Frederick Herzberg reinforced Maslow's theories concerning the motivation practices that produce the most effective results in any organization.

Further studies by Douglas McGregor in the 1950s stressed the general theory of human motivation as developed by Maslow.[4] McGregor developed a set of assumptions about human behavior in which he showed how the scientific management approach was based on a specific set of assumptions, which he labeled Theory X. McGregor's Theory Y, on the other hand, comprised the assumptions of the systems management approach.

In 1964, R.R. Blake and J.S. Mouton emphasized two universal ingredients or concerns that each manager must have.[5] They defined these as the concern for production and the concern for people, using these as the basis for their "managerial grid." They identified, for example, the manager who was heavily production-oriented and minimally people-oriented as a "9, 1 manager." The reverse, the manager who had low concern for production but a very high concern for people, was a "1, 9 manager." As the theories developed by McGregor, Blake and Mouton, and others are carefully examined, it becomes obvious that under the systems management approach the concern for reaching objectives and performing assigned tasks requires more than an emphasis on control or autocratic behavior patterns. The police manager, in order to be effective, must have a sense of interdependence with others and the ability to recognize and deal with conflict and change.

The police manager must develop meaningful tools and methods to implement the latest theoretical approaches to the field of management. Tools are designed to assist the police manager to be effective and efficient in performing daily tasks. This means that the manager must possess more than simple knowledge of technical management skills. The ability to handle people is also a necessary part of the manager's day-to-day operation. Stated simply, it is the police manager's role to achieve the goals of the organization through the most effective and efficient use of the available resources—people, money, time, and equipment. The goals of the organization can only be reached through team cooperation, not by an individual. Police managers can best obtain these organizational goals through the police officers who work with them on a day-to-day basis.

How procedures will change course in the future is hard to predict. One direction, however, seems fairly obvious. Law enforcement personnel of both lower and upper levels will be more qualified to do their respective jobs in the future, and they will be increasingly rewarded for their abilities and production. These rewards will come not only in the form of pay increases and the upgrading of fringe benefits but also by virtue of the manner in which the agency itself is run. The people within the agency will have an opportunity to develop pride, to increase their skills, and to feel that they are achieving some form of success while working for a specific police department within the police profession as a whole.

Notes

1. Frederick W. Taylor, *The Principles of Scientific Management* (New York: Harper and Brothers, 1911).

2. Elton Mayo, *The Human Problems of an Industrial Civilization* (New York: The Macmillan Company, 1933).

3. Abraham H. Maslow, *Motivation and Personality* (New York: Harper & Row, Publishers, 1954).

4. Douglas McGregor, *The Human Side of Enterprise* (New York: McGraw-Hill Book Company, 1960).

5. Robert R. Blake and Jane S. Mouton, *The Managerial Grid* (Houston: Gulf Publishing Company, 1964).

Discussion Questions

1. In reference to the police manager's role, which is the most difficult for him or her to develop: the will to power, the will to manage, or empathy?

2. Among the four levels of an organization (system, subsystem, event, element), where, in your opinion, are most operational decisions made by police commanders in the average police agency?

3. In team policing, what is an effective method of bringing together the four major levels within a police department?

4. How does one go about developing technical, behavioral, and functional skills?

5. Where do most police departments seem to be in terms of philosophy—scientific management approach, human relations management approach, or systems management approach?

6. What do you think it will take to be an effective police officer and police manager in the future?

Philosophy to Outcomes ‖ 2

Objectives

1. The student will understand the terms *philosophy, values, belief,* and *principle.*

2. The student will identify his or her important values and beliefs that relate to the role of a police manager.

3. The student will understand the relationship of *principles to behavior to outcomes.*

Introduction

This chapter deals with translating intentions into success. It presents a simple model, in which the police manager's philosophy—his or her values and beliefs—can be expressed in stated principles that guide behavior through decisions, routine activities, standards, policies, and procedures. Figure 2.1 shows a diagram of the model, the components of which are discussed in turn.

Philosophy

A philosophy may be defined as the sum total of a person's values, beliefs, and principles. Values are a person's assumptions about ends worth striving for, whereas beliefs are a person's assumptions about what is true. Values and beliefs together can be developed into principles that can serve as standards or guidelines for how those in the police department should behave.

Values

Values are defined as the assumptions about ends worth striving for. Values combined with beliefs can be developed into principles that can serve as standards for others concerning what is important in individual police agencies.

Figure 2.1 **Philosophy to Outcomes**

We can speak of three types of values—*intrinsic values, extrinsic values,* and *values that are relevant to how the police department should operate.* Intrinsic values are those that guide the individual's actions, such as honesty, commitment, dedication, and sensitivity to others. Extrinsic values are the values pertaining to what the individual seeks to achieve for himself or herself. For example, a person's motivations in his or her career and personal life may be related to values such as commitment to family, need for financial security, desire for recognition. Figure 2.2 gives examples of intrinsic and extrinsic values.

Values influence police departments in two ways—first, through the values of the individuals and, second, through the values adopted by the department. A leader's personal values may influence the actions of all people in the department, because a person's values will be inferred from his or her actions. For example, a police manager who shows unfailing courtesy to everyone demonstrates that he or she sincerely respects all people. Those serving under him or her will see that they, too, are expected to show courtesy and regard for everyone. On the other hand, a chief who treats his or her own people with less than full respect, or one who makes unkind remarks about individuals or groups, implicitly gives license to those serving under him or her to also use such behavior.

Figure 2.2 **Values**

Intrinsic	Extrinsic
Honesty	Comfortable retirement
Loyalty	Exciting life
Commitment	Sense of accomplishment
Sensitivity	World at peace
Trust	Financial security
Creative	Success
Loving	Recognition
Forgiving	Self-respect
Patience	Freedom
Cheerful	Friendship
Ambitious	Wisdom

The success of a police department depends in part on the nature of the values that the department adopts, either formally or informally. Successful police departments are usually value driven. Examples of values that may be formally adopted in the policy manual include:

Honesty—truthful, sincere, forthright, straightforward

Integrity—principled, courageous, honorable

Commitment—reliable, law-abiding, involved

Justice—equitable, open-minded, admits errors, tolerant

Sensitivity—caring, kind, compassionate, helping, sharing

Excellence—maintains high degree of competence, informed, prepared, industrious

Accountable—accepts responsibility for actions, leads by example, safeguards reputation of department and profession

A police agency may value openness or detailed reports or sharp dress. These values are often rooted in tradition and may or may not be found in policies or procedures. They are usually emphasized in training programs and in the personal instruction of field training officers.

Beliefs

Whereas values are assumptions about ends worth striving for, beliefs are assumptions about what is true, or opinions formed from observations and experience. Values tend to be fundamental and unchanging, whereas beliefs change, depending on facts, circumstances, and situations.

There are three different types of beliefs that concern us. First, there are *beliefs regarding the world as it exists*. For example, the police manager may believe, based on observation and experience, that the department's employees are competent, dedicated, and honest. The second type of belief includes *beliefs about the future* (e.g., the next three to five years). For example, the manager may believe that, given the fiscal problems the city government faces, the department will have to meet increased demands without being able to hire additional personnel. The third kind of belief is called *management belief.* These beliefs would include the belief that if people are involved in the decision-making process they will have a greater commitment to implementing decisions.

The policy manual of the North Carolina State Bureau of Investigation provides examples of the beliefs adopted by one law enforcement agency:

We believe that:

1. Bureau employees are committed to making the world a better place to live and to pursuing excellence in all they do, unselfishly serving the public.

2. Employees develop a commitment to excellence when they participate in decisions about the management of their areas of responsibility.

3. The best way to provide efficient and effective service to the citizens of North Carolina is to hire talented people and then give them the opportunities for training and education they need to develop their talents and initiative to the fullest.

4. In fostering an environment that promotes creativity and encourages positive thinking throughout the Bureau that employees are effective. We plan Bureau work to be satisfying, productive, and challenging and encourage intelligent risk-taking without fear of failure.

5. Victims of crime and their families need special consideration after experiencing the trauma of losing a loved one, suffering a violation of their personal rights, or losing property.

6. The Bureau is responsible for treating victims of crime and their families in a manner which assures their dignity, self-esteem, and constitutional rights.[1]

Executives of the SBI, in making their decisions or evaluating those made by subordinates, compare the decisions against the criteria of the stated values and beliefs. As a result, major decisions made at the executive level consistently reflect the values and beliefs of the SBI and the principles developed from them.

Principles

A principle is a rule or code of conduct that policies, decisions, practices, and procedures should follow. Principles are developed by combining values and beliefs. Police department principles must be stated clearly so that the behavior of all people in the department can be consistent with them. If the chief wants to build a cohesive, consistent, and committed police department, he or she must ensure that everyone understands the principles that should guide behavior.

Principles are best stated in a policy manual. It might be helpful to divide the principles into categories. For example, principles dealing with leadership might state that (1) we shall advise personnel what is expected of them, or (2) we shall share expectations—our expectations of ourselves and expectations of others.

A few general principles are better than a long list of detailed principles because people can more easily understand and eventually adhere to a few. The development of many principles may create conflict between principles or uncertain definitions as to how one might fit with the others.

The North Carolina State Bureau of Investigation has developed principles derived from its values and beliefs:

We shall:

1. Do everything within our power and authority to prevent criminal behavior.
2. Promote an open and trusting flow of information within our organization.
3. Make decisions consistent with legal and ethical standards to guarantee justice for all.
4. Protect the constitutional rights of all persons.
5. Treat all persons with dignity, respect, courtesy, and compassion.
6. Always tell the truth.
7. Neither shirk from our assigned power nor use such power for personal gain.
8. Hold all persons accountable for the reasonable consequences of their behavior.
9. Sustain an organizational climate in which our people can succeed.[2]

Examples of the relationship of principles developed from beliefs are shown in Figure 2.3.[3]

Behavior

It is not sufficient that a police manager state the principles that follow from his or her values and beliefs. If they are to be successfully translated into results, principles must be reflected in actions and behavior, above all in the actions and behavior of the chief. Here we discuss four examples of how values, beliefs, and principles can be reflected in actions and behavior: daily decisionmaking, routine activities, standards, and policies and procedures.

Daily Decisions

The police leader's values and beliefs—and his or her commitment to the organization's values, beliefs, and principles—will be evaluated according to how he or she makes decisions. Do the daily decisions reflect his or her commitment to openness and trust, or do they reflect a desire to keep control tightly in his or her own hands? Does he or she demonstrate a commitment to the principle that personnel will operate as team members by insisting that decisions are made only after consultation with everyone involved? Does the manager truly believe that people are competent, allowing them to act on their own judgment, or does the manager insist that every action be approved by a

Figure 2.3 **From Belief to Principle**

Beliefs:	Principles—We Shall:
• Valid and relevant information enables people to make free and informed choices, which increases the likelihood that they will be committed to those choices.	• Share all relevant information.
• People support what they help to create.	• Involve people in decisions that affect them.
• Taking risks and understanding failure is necessary for originating effectiveness and professional growth.	• Support people in taking risks to achieve desired outcomes. • Use mistakes to learn, not to burn. • Take risks to achieve desired outcomes.
• We can't change other people's behavior directly; we may change it by changing our behavior in a way that others can respond to.	• Control our own behavior; manage others. • Behave in a way that lets others make choices about their behavior.
• All people have values and beliefs; everything they do stems from those values and beliefs. People ultimately infer your values and beliefs through what you do; consistency and congruence between stated values and beliefs and behavior are necessary for effectiveness, because that is one way people judge us.	• We should state our values and beliefs. • We should behave consistently with our stated values and beliefs. • We should continually check for consistency/congruence between our stated values and beliefs and our behavior.
• Trust is essential to organizational effectiveness; trust results when people make themselves vulnerable and ultimately experience positive consequences from it.	• Take personal risks. • Follow all other principles.
• Discounting our own or others' capabilities leads to the wrong person taking responsibility for actions; in so doing, learning is sacrificed and the effectiveness of the organization is diminished.	• Value people's capabilities and allow everyone to be acountable for his or her actions.

SOURCE: Management Group Institute of Government (Chapel Hill, NC: University of North Carolina, 1992).

supervisor? If new weapons are to be selected, does the chief make the decision alone, or does he or she delegate responsibility to those who will carry and use the weapons? How a manager makes decisions, whether they are major decisions or the many minor decisions that must be made daily, will tell personnel much about his or her values and beliefs and commitment to the principles that the organization has elected to follow. For example, assume that the police manager wants to examine the issue of shift schedules. If the manager elects to make decisions without input or assistance from other personnel, then he or she may be judged to mistrust people or to think people in his or her department do not have adequate decision-making skills. On the other hand, the manager who delegates the decision-making responsibility to a special task force, gives them guidance, and listens intently to their feedback demonstrates an approach that was formulated from a different set of values and beliefs.

Decisions that emphasize coordination as opposed to control and delegation as opposed to centralized decisionmaking give a clear message to all police department personnel that they are competent and trusted—that openness is an important value.

Routine Activities

The police leader will also be judged by how he or she conducts himself or herself in routine activities. When the chief holds or attends meetings, does he or she dominate the meeting or allow others to participate and contribute? Does he or she have an open-door policy—approachable and accessible to everyone—or does he or she stay in his or her office and summon those he or she needs to see? How a chief conducts a daily routine, and how he or she deals with people on a daily basis, tells much about his or her values, beliefs and commitment to principle.

Think of the police manager who says that it is important to be involved with the community—one who attends community meetings, is open to the press, and joins civic groups. An opposite example is the manager who states that agency personnel should share relevant information but refuses to attend roll call, will only share information with immediate commanders, and rarely answers memos from officers and clerks.

Standards

Standards are criteria imposed by an authority or adopted by consent that serve as the basis for evaluating actions or performance. There are four types of standards that concern us: legal, ethical, moral, and performance.

Legal standards are established by law. Because law enforcement officers are sworn to uphold the law, in an ideal world there would be no need to question the requirement that police departments adhere to legal standards. In practice, of course, whether police officers adhere to legal standards depends on the quality of training, the effectiveness of law enforcement officers, and the application of good judgment and just practices when police officers enforce the law. So, inevitably, how a police department fulfills its responsibility to meet legal standards depends on the values, beliefs, and principles that guide the actions and behavior of individuals.

Ethical standards govern professional conduct. Ethical standards for law enforcement have been developed by the International Association of Chiefs of Police. A state or local law enforcement agency may also develop its own ethical standards.

Moral standards pertain to right or wrong behavior as prescribed by the individual. These actions may be generally accepted standards such as "keep your promises," or they may be specific to individuals—whether we should pay for college education of our children or should assist them in paying for their first home. Moral standards in the police department may be whether one should accept the take-home car and if so, to what extent one would be allowed to conduct personal business in the car, assuming that there are no legal standards (rules and regulations) or ethical standards (agreements made between the police chief and his or her employees). Moral standards in many instances cannot be forced on subordinates by the chief of police. As a result, the chief must guard against attempting to control moral behavior through written policies, but must be able to deal with behavioral standards under a different category such as legal, ethical, or performance standards for the policy agency.

Performance standards are used to judge professional behavior. For example, there are standards for filing reports or for testifying in court, and most police departments have a set of performance standards used for recruitment and promotion. These standards are usually found in the procedure manual.

Policies and Procedures

A policy is a stated or written guide for action intended to encourage uniform and consistent action. Policies are especially important because they permit the chief to influence the department's direction in many different matters. Except instances in which, for example, retaining legal standards calls for precise, detailed procedures, procedures can also be used to ensure that day-to-day conduct conforms to the principles adopted by the department.

Policies should reflect the principles adopted by the department. Consider, for example, a principle that "we shall have an open and trusting flow of information." This principle can be reflected directly in policies regarding how information is shared, as when security levels are set for intelligence and internal affairs documents.

An ideal policy statement should involve three main features. First, it should state the purpose of the policy. Second, it should establish a general standard of conduct or behavior that can be applied to day-to-day decisions and conduct. Third, it should indicate how, and under what circumstances, discretion is left to the individual.

A procedure prescribes the actions that should be taken in a given situation. While no police department can operate without rules and procedures, police managers must understand that using procedures has both advantages and disadvantages—the key element being flexibility. Whenever exact compliance is required and situations can be foreseen, instruction in standard procedures and regulations saves both time and thought. Lack of flexibility, however, removes the opportunity for individual discretion, initiative, and judgment.

Written policies and procedures should be easily accessible to all. For example, a police department may have one relatively short policy manual, which contains policies covering constitutional rights, personnel resources, fiscal management, training and education, and news media relations. It may then develop several procedure manuals. One manual may cover behavior and administrative practices applicable to all department personnel regardless of their assignment, whereas another manual is created for each division of the department containing procedures specifically applicable to those departments (e.g., Division of Criminal Information, Division of Laboratory Services, and the Field Operation Division).

Outcomes

Leading based on a strong philosophy is a complex issue that incorporates numerous values, beliefs, principles, and behavior patterns. The following example is oversimplified. It does not capture the different and often conflicting values and beliefs that can guide a chief's behavior. But this example can give some understanding of how the chief's philosophy affects the final outcome.

This scenario involves two police chiefs. Chief A says that the values that are important for him are to be loyal to a set of principles and to see to it that people are committed, dedicated, trustworthy, and honest. His belief about the agency is that most of the personnel in this agency do not become involved in the use of drugs. The principle developed might state, "It is my responsibility to see to it that members of this police department are able to work in a drug-free environment."

As a result of this principle, based on values and beliefs, this chief implements this principle through behavior. The chief emphasizes in speeches praising personnel that he trusts his officers and states how serious the drug problem might be, but that in his police agency there are committed professionals who never become involved in using drugs. In meetings the chief emphasizes to his key executives that they should also spread this message throughout the agency and the community. The chief then develops a written policy that says "Police officers shall be drug tested only if there is some reasonable suspicion that an officer may be using drugs. Such testing shall adhere to legal and ethical standards."

Chief B has the same stated values as Chief A. However, she believes that only a few police officers, perhaps only 5 percent, are using drugs during off-duty time. The chief states the same principle as Chief A: "It is the responsibility of the chief to create and to maintain a drug-free work environment." This chief uses stronger control, seeing to it that personnel do not take excessive leave time. In routine meetings the chief emphasizes the need for drug testing and sees to it that the department develops appreciation for a drug-free police agency. Again, this police chief, like the first, adheres to the legal, ethical, and moral standards of the agency. This chief, however, develops a different policy, which says "This agency shall have random drug testing of all police officers."

As police officers from each department get together to discuss their respective drug testing policies, an officer from Department A might say that her police chief is easy to work for because the chief trusts the officers. She uses as an example of this trust the policy concerning drug testing only upon reasonable suspicion. A second officer, from Department B, might agree that his chief also trusts officers but obviously not as much as the first chief. The second officer might go on to state that his chief does not praise them enough and, in fact, is somewhat suspicious of the officers in the department because of the random drug testing policy.

The outcomes might be different also. For example, in Department A, because of the emphasis on trust and the beliefs that such trust can and will be practiced in the department, that agency might develop team management practices more easily, may become involved in work groups, and perhaps, together as a team, may have open communication including exposure and feedback. Members of that agency may be willing to discuss successes and failures.

The outcome in Department B may be one of a conservative approach to management. Department B may require a taller organizational structure, further development between two ranks that work with each other such as officer to sergeant and sergeant to lieutenant, but not necessarily between all ranks of the agency. The outcome might involve more centralized decisionmaking, slower involvement of personnel, and less respect and commitment to the directions and visions created by Chief B.

As this example shows, there can be numerous outcomes stemming from values, beliefs, principles, and behaviors. Some of these outcomes may be planned, but some may be totally unexpected.

Conclusion

While developing principles, police leaders should obtain input from all department personnel. This can be accomplished through the use of special task forces, through meetings with department personnel, through formal contacts with members of the department, and through daily informal contacts, some of which may carry a greater weight than any of the other aforementioned methods.

The police manager can guarantee success if he or she develops a policy statement that clearly delineates the values and beliefs that are most important. Then employees can have an understanding of the direction being endorsed by the manager. The police manager can establish eight to ten principles that can guide the behavior of all personnel. Each person can then call on the principles to guide his or her growth.

The police manager can use different techniques to implement the values, beliefs, and principles. The first is to put them in writing and distribute to all personnel, sworn and nonsworn. The leader then must act consistently with these principles, administering praise for behavior that reflects them and dealing quickly with behavior that is inconsistent.

The leader can take advantage of everyday situations to give guidance and understanding. Reiteration of the principles at attended roll calls and staff meetings emphasizes their importance. The manner in which the leader spends his or her time also reflects the importance of the principles. By being available and responding in a sincere and honest manner, the police manager will go far to solidify an open flow of information within the police agency.

Notes

1. Policy Manual, North Carolina State Bureau of Investigation, Raleigh, NC, 1992.

2. Ibid.

3. Developed by Management Group, Institute of Government, University of North Carolina at Chapel Hill, NC 1992 (Roger Schwarz, Dick McMahon, Peg Carlson, Kurt Jenne, Ron Lynch).

Discussion Questions

1. Identify your intrinsic and extrinsic values.

2. Develop one management belief and one principle consistent with that belief.

3. Develop an effective set of management beliefs and principles for a police department.

4. Select an established police agency policy and procedure and define the principle behind the policy.

Behavioral Aspects of Police Management || Part One

The police manager's role demands a knowledge and understanding of the psychological aspects of management—an awareness of the effect that operations have on the people within the police department.

Part One deals with the organizational environment facing the police manager. Included is a discussion of the various theories about people in organizations, including police departments.

Chapter 3 discusses leadership behavior styles and shows the varied behaviors available to a police manager. This chapter also considers the qualities necessary to be a successful police manager and places strong emphasis on use of the managerial grid. This section provides criteria that may be used in helping police managers decide which style of leadership is best for them within their own given environments.

Chapter 4 is designed to assist the student in recognizing the culture of a police agency. It helps unite this part with the first two chapters.

Chapter 5 deals with management communications. It attempts to clarify and explain the styles of communication available to the police manager and to demonstrate the consequences of each approach. Special attention is given to the processing model called the "Johari window."

Chapter 6 talks about Maslow's hierarchy of needs, Herzberg's motivation-hygiene theory, and the relationship between these two theories and Douglas McGregor's Theory X-Theory Y.

Chapter 7 deals with the latest techniques available to management concerning the issue of human behavior. This chapter on transactional analysis will not only help police mangers analyze their personal behavior but also give them tools with which to gain insight into the behavior of others. Through the implementation of some of the techniques mentioned in this chapter, police managers will eventually gain a greater insight into themselves and will thus be in a better position to help bring about changes in their departments.

Chapter 8 deals with another human behavior model that can help the police chief to understand department personnel. Such understanding can, of course, allow for smoother operations and easier implementation of policies and goals.

In short, the psychological aspects of management discussed in this section provide a base on which police managers can build specific procedures and techniques to be implemented within their own agencies.

Leadership
Behavior Styles ‖ 3

Objectives

1. The student will be aware of the numerous styles of leadership.

2. The student will understand how choosing a leadership style will help the police manager become aware of departmental goals and purposes of the organization.

3. The student will understand the principles underlying the "learning" police department.

4. The student will understand the five disciplines that help create an innovative learning agency.

The qualities of leaders and the processes of leadership have long been considered important areas of inquiry. Early speculation about the personality traits and qualities of a successful leader has given way to the study of leadership behavior and analysis of situational factors such as the type of group and the nature of the group's task.

Several scholars have studied leadership behavior and have sought to classify the different approaches to leadership and the different ways of exercising the leadership role. The style of leadership chosen by a manager largely depends on what he or she intends to accomplish.

Police managers must understand that their subordinates will follow their leadership for one or a combination of four reasons:

1. Fear of their authority and the manner in which they control, direct, and plan.

2. Personal liking.

3. Personal respect, based on the manager's actions, values, and consistent manner in dealing with subordinates.

4. Trust, based on the manager's professional competence and proven ability to make decisions and manage conflict and change.

Trust is a result of numerous personal contacts between the manager and the people he or she supervises directly. This kind of leadership is the most lasting and the most effective.

Qualities of a Successful Police Manager

Managers need to exhibit certain qualities in order to be successful, regardless of the style of management behavior they use. The following qualities, when exhibited by managers, have helped the individual to reach success in day-to-day operations.

1. *Patience*—managers must be calm and steadfast, despite opposition to their beliefs, opinions, and attitudes.
2. *Wisdom*—managers must have the ability to judge fairly and equitably the behaviors and actions of subordinates.
3. *Virtue*—managers must show moral excellence, not only by word of mouth but also by everyday actions in dealing with departmental problems and personal issues.
4. *Empathy*—managers must learn to accept and understand the feelings of their subordinates, always being prepared to see others in a positive light.
5. *Kindness*—managers must try to be kind and gentle in all their dealings with others.
6. *Trust*—managers must develop confidence in subordinates, not just respecting their position or knowledge but also allowing them to achieve their personal goals as well as those of the organization.
7. *Knowledge*—managers must constantly attempt to upgrade their knowledge of technical matters, the management theories being developed and implemented in government and industry, and facts as they occur within their own departments.
8. *Self-control*—managers must be able to restrain their emotions.

Police managers can develop these qualities by:

1. Showing a high frustration tolerance.
2. Encouraging full participation of subordinates.
3. Emphasizing the subordinate's right to express another point of view.
4. Understanding the rules and acts of ethical competitive warfare.
5. Expressing hostility tactfully.
6. Accepting victory with controlled emotions.
7. Never permitting setbacks to defeat them.
8. Knowing how to "be their own boss."
9. Continually seeking success.
10. Being experts in their fields.

Styles of Leadership

Leadership can be defined as the role of the manager in influencing subordinates to work willingly to achieve the stated objectives of the organization. In essence, leadership involves accomplishing stated departmental objectives through other people in the department. Therefore, leaders have two major concerns: they must be concerned with purpose and they must show concern for people.

Many writers have attempted to define styles of leadership. Writers emphasizing the scientific management approach of the 1920s argued that the primary function of the leader was to set up and enforce performance criteria to meet the goals and objectives of the agencies.[1] The manager's main concern was for purpose or production, with very little concern for the needs of the employees within the agency.

With the human relations movement, initiated by Elton Mayo, the function of the leader was to focus on the individual needs of employees and not on those of the organization itself.[2]

In essence, the scientific management movement emphasized concern for purpose or task and the human relations movement stressed concern for people. Leaders who were concerned primarily with tasks were said to be "task-oriented" or "authoritarian" leaders, whereas those who emphasized the concern for interpersonal relationships were said to be "people-oriented" or "democratic" leaders. The style chosen by the leader depended on the assumptions he or she made concerning the members of the department. The police manager who felt and believed in Theory X assumptions was predominantly an authoritarian leader. The police manager who believed in Theory Y assumptions was more democratic. In 1958, Robert Tannenbaum and Warren H. Schmidt suggested that leadership varies along a continuum from boss-centered at one extreme to subordinate-centered at the other.[3] Based on this analysis, they defined four styles of leadership—tell, sell, consult, and join (see Figure 3.1).

Under the *tell* style of leadership, the manager makes his or her own decisions and announces them to subordinates, expecting them to be carried out without question. An example of this type of leadership would be a police chief who makes all the decisions in the daily operation of his or her agency—establishing schedules, assigning personnel, giving specific orders on how each crime must be investigated, choosing who should attend what training program. After reaching all these decisions, the chief advises his or her immediate subordinates—the middle managers—who, in turn, advise supervisors, who advise the officers. In essence, there has been no input by any member of the department below the chief's level, and the chief has made his or her decisions based on personal experiences.

The manager who chooses the *sell* style of leadership makes all the decisions but, rather than simply announcing them to subordinates, attempts to persuade them to accept the decisions. Recognizing the potential for resistance on the part of subordinates, the manager concentrates on selling them ideas.

Under the *consult* style of leadership, the manager does not make any decision until the problem has been presented to members of the group and until he or she has listened to their advice and suggestions. The manager still makes the decision, but not until after consulting with members of the staff.

Figure 3.1 **Continuum of Styles of Leadership**

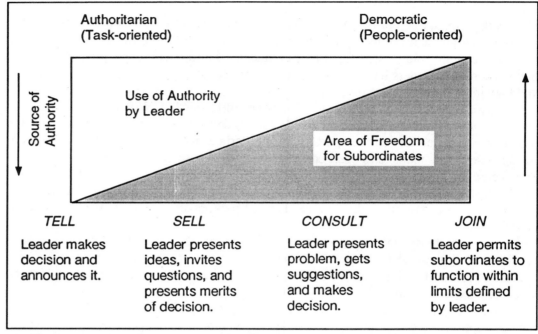

Adapted and reprinted by permission of *Harvard Business Review.* Exhibit 1 from "How to Choose a Leadership Pattern," R. Tannenbaum and W. Schmidt, March/April 1957.

The manager who uses the *join* style delegates the authority for making decisions to subordinates. He or she may reserve the right to be part of the decision-making process, but views his or her primary function as one of helping to define the problem and to indicate the limits within which the decisions must be made. After the problem has been freely discussed by the subordinates, either a consensus or majority opinion will bring forth the final decision. There are three major disadvantages to the join type of leadership. First, it is time-consuming; second, it is frustrating; and third, it calls for mature subordinates who have the ability and willingness to arbitrate and arrive at some form of agreement.

Leaders who are at the tell end of the continuum are primarily concerned with purpose or task; they attempt to influence the subordinates by use of the power delegated to them by the organization. Leaders at the other end of the spectrum are more group-oriented and allow a greater amount of freedom to subordinates in accomplishing their assigned tasks. The join type of leader must be aware of the fact that it is easy to carry this type of leadership to the point where decisions are not being reached and the members of the department are not gaining any personal satisfaction. In such instances, people are left to rely on their own initiative, and there is no attempt to influence anyone's behavior. This scenario is not included in the leadership continuum because it is really an absence of leadership as opposed to a leadership style. The police manager must be constantly aware of the decision-making process within the department, and not allow his or her personal behavior to be interpreted as an abdication of leadership.

Another method of viewing leadership is the grid model, originally developed by R.R. Blake and J.S. Mouton, which represents a two-dimensional view of management behavior.[4] In the grid, the emphasis is on the two most basic concerns that any manager is believed to have: (1) the concern for production, and (2) the concern for people.

The police manager will adopt a fairly specific set of behavior patterns in dealing with these two major concerns, and these behaviors will be considered a specific style of management most prevalent for the individual manager.

Under the managerial grid, five styles of management are suggested (see Figure 3.2). According to the grid concept, the concern for production and concern for people have been rated on a scale of 0 to 9. The five predominant styles have then been identified as 9, 1—authority compliance; 1, 9—country club; 1, 1—impoverished; 5, 5—middle of the road; and 9, 9—team.

Figure 3.2 The Leadership Grid® Figure

SOURCE: The Leadership Grid® Figure from *Leadership Dilemmas—Grid Solutions,* by Robert R. Blake and Anne Adams McCanse (formerly the Managerial Grid Figure by Robert R. Blake and Jane S. Mouton). Houston: Gulf Publishing Company, P. 29. Copyright © 1991, by Scientific Methods, Inc. Reproduced by permission of the owners.

The 9, 1 (or authority compliance) manager believes that efficiency in operations comes from arranging work conditions in such a way that interference by human elements is minimal.

The 1, 9 (or country club) manager pays thoughtful attention to the needs of people on the theory that satisfying relationships lead to a comfortable, friendly organizational atmosphere and work tempo.

The 1, 1 (or impoverished) manager exerts the minimum effort to get the required work done and is concerned with people only to the degree that sustains organizational membership.

The 5, 5 (or middle-of-the-road) manager believes that adequate organization performance is possible through balancing the need to accomplish tasks with maintaining a satisfactory level of morale.

The 9, 9 (or team) manager believes that work is accomplished through the interdependence of people who are committed to organizational purposes. This interdependence leads to relationships of trust and respect.

Police managers of the 9, 1 type make decisions and expect these decisions to be treated as final. They stand for ideas, opinions, and attitudes, even though this may sometimes appear offensive to other people. When conflict arises, such managers cut it off or allow it to continue only if they feel they are going to win with their position. When operations within the department become confusing, they defend, resist, and counterargue any kind of change that may threaten their individual position. These police managers have a tendency to drive themselves and others, thereby creating stress within themselves and sometimes promoting stress and burnout in others.

Managers of the 9, 1 type sometimes seem too strong and tend to overwhelm other people within the police department, especially those who do not have the same level of knowledge. When holding meetings, they may attempt to control by monopolizing the conversation and correcting points made within the meeting that they feel are not correct, no matter how trivial such points might be. In most meetings, 9, 1 types attempt to structure things so that only *how*, as opposed to *why*, questions are discussed.

Managers of the 1, 9 type, on the other hand, support decisions that promote good personal relations, embracing the opinions, attitudes, and ideas of others rather than attempting to push their own. They avoid conflict, but when it appears, attempt to sooth people's feelings.

Such managers value acceptance and tend to say things they believe others want to hear. They dread the possibility of mentioning information that might be interpreted as negative and are continually striving, in meetings and elsewhere, to please people. The result is that productivity tends to be low or may even come to a halt.

The 1, 1 manager is indifferent to others and normally accepts the decisions of both superiors and subordinates. Such managers avoid taking positions and are not likely to reveal their opinions, attitudes, or ideas. They strive for neutrality. Because they remain uninvolved on issues, they rarely show feelings of approval or disapproval and may seem indifferent to the processes within the police department.

In a management sense, such people appear passive. In meetings, they have a tendency to let others lead the conversation. They volunteer little or no information; when asked direct questions, they tend to give short answers and to avoid elaborating on any additional information. In some meetings they may appear to be bored.

Managers of the 5, 5 type search for workable, if not perfect, decisions; they are willing to meet halfway people who hold opinions, ideas, and attitudes different from their own. When conflicts arise, they try to negotiate them away through compromise.

In meetings, they try to impress others regardless of their status, reputation, or prestige. When they are asked questions, they tend to be tentative; they prefer to avoid giving direct answers until they understand everyone else's position fully. This caution may sometimes look like fear of being wrong, but it is actually a way of testing and probing the positions of others in order eventually to support the majority viewpoint.

A 9, 9 manager places a high value on creative decisions that result in understanding and agreement. Such managers listen for and seek out ideas, opinions, and attitudes different from their own. They have strong convictions but are willing to respond to sound ideas and are more than willing to change when such ideas tend to achieve the purpose of the police department and are acceptable to the personnel within the agency. When conflict does arise, the 9, 9 manager attempts to identify the reasons for the conflict and seeks to resolve underlying causes, thereby reducing the number of conflicts that may eventually arise within the agency.

In meetings, 9, 9 types command the respect of others by their behavior. They seem to enjoy the give-and-take processes within meetings but are usually geared toward keeping the meeting focused on its original purposes. They listen keenly and are able to distinguish fact from opinion.

In attempting to determine whether his or her management style is affected more by the scores on a managerial grid instrument or those on the Johari window, individual managers place more weight on the grid scores. In reality, subordinates have a tendency to describe the police manager's communication style more accurately; therefore police managers who are aware of both their managerial grid and Johari scores are more likely to be among those whose style is accurately described by subordinates. This is especially true when the subordinate is at least two levels away from the manager's present position. For example, sergeants identify the styles of captains more quickly and more accurately than they do the styles of higher level managers.

When the managerial and communicative style are identical, little confusion will arise. However, when managerial style, which might be 9, 9, is confused with communication style, which might appear to be closer to 9, 1, the manager must be aware of these differences as perceived by subordinates. Only through a more open communication process will subordinates be able to identify both the management and communicative styles accurately. Effective police managers strive for consistency in these respects.

The Learning Police Agency

According to Peter Senge, organizations that place an emphasis on learning are sometimes referred to as the *double loop learning* by Chris Argyris.[5] Leaders in these organizations demonstrate behaviors of openness, systematic thinking, creativity, self-confidence, and empathy. By contrast, *adaptive,* or *single loop learning,* focuses on solving problems in the present without examining how these problems may affect the entire police department or the effect they may have on the future.

Senge believes that there are five specific disciplines that tend to create a police department that will be an innovative learning agency. According to Senge, "Though developed separately each will, I believe, prove critical to the others' success just as occurs with any ensemble. Each provides a vital dimension in building organizations that can truly learn, that can continually enhance their capacity to realize their highest aspirations."[6] The five disciplines are systems thinking, personal mastery, mental models, building a shared vision, and team learning.

Systems Thinking

This discipline recognizes that multiple levels of understanding, explanation, and issues develop in any complex situation. For example, systems thinking requires a complete look at all four levels as described in Chapter 1. Explanations at the element level explain "who did what to whom" and dooms the individual police leader to a reactive stance. Examination at the event level, which defines a pattern of behavior, focuses more on seeing some longer term trends and assesses what effect they would have on the police department. This level begins to be responsive to issues that may be more complex. In systems thinking the question raised is: What has caused our pattern of behavior? As a result, a careful analysis is made of the entire issue. An example would be in a training program, the instructor and a member of the class, such as a patrol officer, have a difference of opinion as to whether the training is appropriate for the job to be performed. An examination at that level would solve the conflict between the instructor and the officer. However, examining the pattern of behavior would begin to evaluate whether other officers either act consistently or inconsistently with the teachings. A systemwide approach would examine whether there is a need to provide this training and how much input has been received from the patrol officers who may be responsible for implementing the ideas that are presented within the program itself.

Personal Mastery

Personal mastery infers a special level of ability on the part of the leader. This discipline starts with clarifying the issues that really matter to the police department. The police leader becomes interested in joining together personal learning and organizational learning.

Mental Models

Mental models are deeply ingrained assumptions, values, beliefs, generalizations, and images that have an effect on how we understand our responsibilities in the world around us. This discipline starts with being able to look inward first and then examining "pictures" of what the police department is and whether or not they are accurate. Personal mastery allows members of the police department to feel free in exposing their own ideas in a way that allows others to think and learn.

Building a Shared Vision

When a genuine vision for the future exists, the members of the police department will learn and make decisions consistent with that vision. They will support the vision, assuming that the leaders in their individual behaviors also support this vision. Building a shared vision is more than just providing a vision statement. It is the opportunity for people to develop this vision and to find ways in which it can be achieved. A police leader who has a vision that his or her agency would be considered the most progressive in his or her geographical area and constantly brings about innovative changes within the department is attempting to implement practices that are consistent with the vision on a day-to-day basis. When this vision is shared with all members of the department, they, too, may commit to the same vision. By allowing these persons to interact with other agencies and learn that their agency is one of the most professional in the area, they, too, will assist in building this shared vision.

Team Learning

Team learning means that information is constantly shared between members of the department. It means a dialogue, which is a Greek term for the free flowing of meaning through a group. The creation of task forces to deal with all issues within the department leads to consistent team learning. In addition, when these teams spend time developing an answer to the specific issue and a set of guidelines for future behavior, team learning begins to take place.

These five disciplines form a developmental path for the police leader so that he or she can acquire the necessary skills, competencies, and techniques to assist him or her in achieving great personal success as well as assisting the department. A police leader may find that each member of the agency has a different level of innate ability to practice and understand each of the five disciplines. Therefore, the police leader should use people to assist others so that they too can develop a skill level in each of the disciplines equal to the best that each has to offer.

The major difference between the five learning disciplines and other management practices is that these disciplines are personal.

Is There a Best Style?

Emphasizing that the police manager has two primary concerns—for people and for production—is there really a best style for effective direction, planning, and control of a police agency?

Research conducted in industry indicates that the manager who is able to balance both concerns is more effective than the manager who deals with only one. Likewise, successful police managers must contribute to the specific objectives of the police department while also helping individuals within the agency to achieve their personal goals.

Rensis Likert did extensive research in analyzing high-production, as opposed to low-production, managers.[7] His studies indicated that the managers who focused primary attention on the human aspects while building effective teams were more successful than managers who were job-centered. The manager who achieved high production used general rather than close supervision of subordinates.

Even though Likert's studies suggest that the employee-centered, democratic leader is most successful, his findings leave some doubt as to whether a single style of leadership behavior can or should apply to all situations. The recommendation for using a single style of leadership leaves to chance the cultural or traditional differences that may exist and does not provide clear explanations of the effect of education and standard of living on the employees. Therefore, most studies indicate that the effective leader does not use a single style of leadership behavior but instead takes into consideration numerous existing variables.

Adaptive Leadership

Police managers are often trained to seek an ideal leadership behavior pattern that they can employ to maximize the effective operation of their individual agencies. In reality, however, the effective police manager is one who is able to integrate all the available styles and adapt to meet each given situation. In essence, police managers who are able to change their style of leadership according to the situation and the needs of their employees are those who will be most effective in attaining both personal and organizational objectives.

In choosing a leadership style, the police manager must consider three major variables:

1. Personal relationships with members of the department.
2. The degree of structure in the task that the agency has been assigned to perform.
3. The authority, power, and responsibility provided by the manager's position within the organization.

The effectiveness of the leadership style chosen by the police manager will depend on the closeness of the relationship between the manager and subordinates, the degree of structure in the task, and the authority of the manager. In essence, the more flexibility given to the manager, the higher the possibility for effective decisions.

For example, the police manager who is assigned the task of eliminating corruption and unethical conduct within an agency will find that a democratic leadership style or an attempt to develop team decisionmaking will be the most ineffective method of controlling the situation. Under such conditions, the manager who is more autocratic and has a high regard for production will be more successful on a short-term basis. Another example is the police manager who is faced with a riot or emergency condition. His or her success will depend on an immediate response to the issues. He or she may not have time to explain the situation to subordinates and engage in team decisionmaking. Once the crisis is over, however, the manager may find a different leadership style much more effective.

Reality Leadership

Reality leadership focuses on the realities in a given situation. The police manager must develop the best kind of executive behavior for each administrative situation. The most effective manager will advise subordinates ahead of time regarding which conditions will produce which style of leadership. For example, a police chief may employ group decisionmaking in general while reserving the authority to make all decisions concerning promotions of key personnel.

Police managers must realize that their leadership style must be judged in the light of the departmental goals and purposes of the organization. Furthermore, depending on its nature and its location within the agency, a group may need a particular kind of leadership. For example, the police manager may find an open, team style of management most effective in dealing with units composed of intelligent, mature employees. However, in other units in which the tasks are mundane in nature, such as basic filing, the police manager may find that an autocratic style would be more effective. Police managers must always realize that they, as leaders, are only as effective as their subordinates will allow them to be, and in most group situations the entire group is really responsible for the success or failure of the stated objectives.

Deciding How to Lead

In reaching decisions, police managers are affected by (1) forces within themselves and (2) forces in the situation.

Police managers, in deciding which style of leadership or management is most applicable, are affected by their value systems, by the amount of confidence they have in their subordinates, and by their leadership inclinations that have been brought about by the success that they have already achieved within their organizations. For example, if they have been successful by being heavily autocratic in leadership style, chances are that they will continue this style, regardless of the levels they reach in the bureaucratic structure. In situations that have an element of uncertainty, managers will not jeopardize their own security by delegating too much responsibility and authority to subordinates.

Subordinates usually will receive greater freedom if they have clearly demonstrated the need for independence and have exhibited a readiness to assume responsibility. In choosing a leadership style, the manager will consider the amount of interest shown in the problem by subordinates. For example, when the first-line supervisor has received the necessary knowledge and experience to deal with the situation, understands the goals of the organization, and has learned to share in the decision-making process, the chances become greater that the style of leadership chosen by the manager will be more democratic.

Different forces in the total situation greatly affect the leadership style employed by the manager. The effectiveness of the group itself in its past decision-making processes gives some indication of how much freedom it should be given in each individual situation. If the organizational structure is highly bureaucratic in both principle and policy, with numerous levels between top and bottom, the chances of effective group decisionmaking are greatly reduced. The problem itself and the pressure of time also affect the style of leadership that can be employed.

The effective police manager should choose a style of management that attempts to bridge the gap between the management process and actual line operations. The manager must learn to be a "multicrat"—flexible enough to deal with each situation.

Consider the effective police chief who deals with the department's command operations and internal operations by employing techniques that bring about high-quality team decisions. However, in dealing with the political structure of the community, this chief becomes a more compromising manager. Depending on the demands of particular pressure groups, the chief may employ a different style of leadership and be most effective in bringing about peace and tranquility to the community.

Effective Leadership Practices

Police managers can become more effective by searching for opportunities and treating each assignment as a new venture regardless of the status of that assignment. They can constantly question the status quo and design new ways to improve the department. The effective police manager can find something that is broken and fix it. Many police managers find opportunities that add adventure to every responsibility they have and they make this adventure fun.

James Kouzes and Barry Posner believe that people are willing to both admire and follow leaders who are honest, are consistent in word and deed, are competent, have a winning track record, are forward looking, have a sense of direction and concern for the future, and are inspirational—that is, enthusiastic, energetic, and positive. They define five leadership practices that, when followed, would make the police leader an effective manager, thereby creating a more professional police department.[8]

These effective leadership practices are: (1) challenging the process, (2) inspiring a shared vision, (3) enabling others to act, (4) modeling the way, and (5) encouraging the heart.

Challenging the Process

Leaders look for ways to alter the status quo, for new processes, for ways to change the system operating within the police agency to one that will achieve its goals and objectives. Those who challenge the process initiate change, and the result of this is igniting enthusiasm in themselves as well as others. There are two commitments that leaders under this practice employ: (1) they search out challenging opportunities to change, grow, innovate, and improve, and (2) they experiment and take risks.

Inspiring a Shared Vision

The four attributes of a vision are (1) having a future orientation, (2) creating an image and actually seeing the future, (3) having a sense of the possibilities, and (4) taking pride in being a different police agency. Thereby, vision means invoking images with a strong future orientation, a standard of excellence, and a quality of uniqueness. The two major commitments of this practice include the ability to envision the future and to enlist others in a shared vision.

Enabling Others to Act

Police leaders must make others feel like owners of the police department—not hired hands. They strive for cooperation as opposed to competition—trying to do a good job and trying to beat others are two different things. Personnel of a police department are most likely to cooperate when they know that they will deal with each other again. The two commitments that these practices develop are the fostering of collaboration and the strengthening of others.

Police leaders who enable others to act always try to develop integrative solutions. They seek many outputs. They are willing to meet in teams as well as one-on-one. They keep all personnel in the department posted as to the progress being made and the direction. They seek specific and broad support. Collaboration has trust at its core. The foundation of trust is believing that the other members of the police department have integrity. This can be demonstrated by meeting commitments and keeping promises. Things that the police manager can do to foster collaboration include always saying "we," creating interactions between members of the department, creating a climate of trust to focus on gains rather than losses, involving people in planning and problem solving, and being a risk taker when it comes to trusting others.

Modeling the Way

The police manager must have a philosophy, a set of high standards by which the department is measured, a set of values and beliefs about how the employees—sworn and nonsworn—as well as citizens ought to be treated, and a set of strong principles that make the police organization unique and distinctive.

The police leader makes two commitments in modeling the way. The first is to set an example that is positive, and the second is to plan small wins. By setting the example, the police manager is asking all members of the department to observe a set of standards—the same standards by which the police leader will live. By planning small wins, the manager is continually involved in the growth process and personnel become committed to the overall goal. Some strategies to help facilitate this process include making a plan, taking one step at a time, reducing the cost of saying yes, and giving people choices and making these choices highly visible.

Encouraging the Heart

Successful leaders have high expectations of themselves as well as other members of the department. These expectations become very powerful. The police manager gives heart by visibly recognizing the contributions of members of the department to the common vision. They practice two commitments: The first is recognizing these contributions—that is, linking rewards with performances. Ways to recognize such accomplishments include developing tough, measurable performance standards, installing a formal systematic process for rewarding performance, being creative about such rewards, letting others design the nonmonetary compensations to make the recognition public, and finding members of the department who are doing things right. The second commitment includes celebrating accomplishments. One strategy here may include schedules of celebrations. The police manager could be a leader and a coach, and employ his or her internal values of trust, honesty, commitment, and above all, love.

Developing Organizational Teamwork

The police manager can bring about effective teamwork within his or her department by establishing systematic procedures. The manager must determine what is to be done, how it is to be done, who is to do it, and, eventually, how effectively it is being accomplished. This process of developing organizational teamwork can also provide a basis for reviewing the progress of change, for helping to identify problems, and for planning individual and group development.

The first step is to clarify the work requirements. The police manager must reach an agreement with subordinates as to the functions and responsibilities that are to be performed, the authority that will be given to the subordinates, and the expected results.

The development of functions-authority-results (FARs) is the key to the careful development of organizational teamwork between the manager and his or her subordinates. A simple three-column table, as shown in Figure 3.3, can easily be established. In the first column, both the subordinate and the manager agree on the tasks for which the subordinate is responsible. Next, the police manager must outline the authority he or she is willing to give to the subordinate. Authority may be broken down into three levels: (1) the subordinate may have to report before acting; (2) the subordinate may have the authority to act and then report to the manager; and (3) the subordinate may be given complete authority, meaning that he or she is responsible only for the overall results of his or her actions.

The police manager should recognize that the tasks may be quite similar for each subordinate but the levels of authority can be different. As a subordinate begins to exhibit the ability to accept responsibility, the level of authority can move from report-act to complete authority.

Once this major step has been clarified and agreement has been reached on the FARs, the manager can then divide his or her attention between the management of tasks and the management of subordinates. Under the broad category of management of personnel, the police manager should evaluate the performance of subordinates. This comes under the third column.

Figure 3.3 **Functions-Authority-Results (FARs)**

Functions	*Authority*	*Results*
Organizational structure	Act-report	Simplified structure
Budget preparation	Report-act	Prepared line-item budget
Assignment of personnel	Complete	Scheduled by incident
Robbery prevention programs	Complete	5% robbery reduction

The manager also must assess the potential his or her subordinates have for future development. Working with each subordinate, the police manager should plan a career-development program. This program should indicate possible paths or promotions and the acceptance of added responsibilities within the framework of the subordinate's present assignment. The purpose of this process is to guarantee the utilization of the abilities of the subordinate, ensuring growth for both the individual and the department.

In managing tasks, the second responsibility of the manager, he or she should review the work progress and the problems generated in attempting to carry out the FARs. Specific objectives must be set, and they must be carefully evaluated to determine whether they have been reached. It is important that problems be analyzed, that decisions be reached concerning the overcoming of obstacles, and that action be taken by both the manager and the subordinate to solve the problems in bringing about change.

Figure 3.4 indicates the process of organization for the manager. Through this process, the department is strengthened and the abilities of the individual within the department are developed to their fullest.

Approaches to the Organizational Development Process

Approaches to change fall into two broad categories, those oriented toward changing people and those oriented toward changing the structure or system.

People-oriented approaches include attempts to change the philosophies and attitudes of the individuals within the department. Many police agencies send key personnel to specialized schools with the hope that exposure to new information will enable them to perform assigned functions adequately. An agency may also provide consultants for the same purpose. But for the most part, this approach has not proved to be very successful for police departments.

In some instances it is necessary for the police manager to transfer individuals who hold key positions. By transferring personnel on a periodic basis, the manager can bring in "new blood" to initiate changes in day-to-day operations. These periodic changes in position can be seen as a challenge and often produce a commitment to implementing new procedures. This approach seems to be more effective than attempting to change the individual who is presently holding the position.

Another people-oriented approach to change is team development. Starting with the managers at the top level, team training programs can be implemented. Each unit forms a

Figure 3.4 **The Foundations of Management**

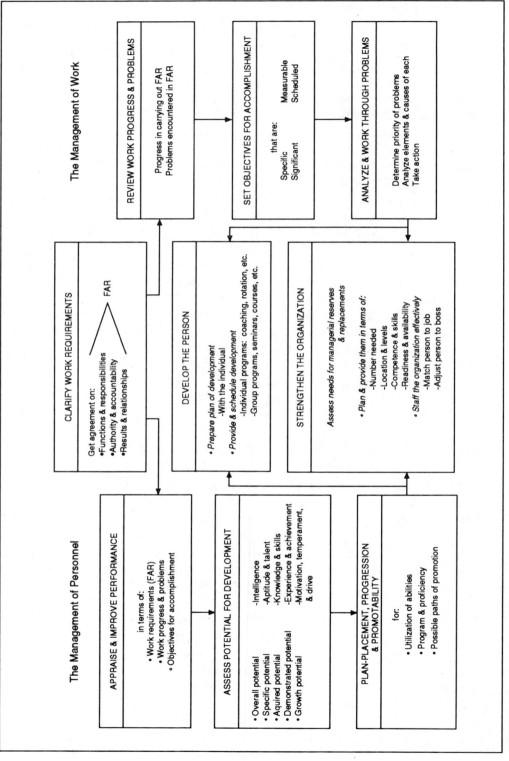

SOURCE: Lakewood, Colorado Police Department, 1971

cohesive team that forces evaluation of present practices and instills in the members a commitment to change and upgrade the department. The development of decision-making teams within an agency has proved to be an effective strategy for bringing about change.

Revising the present organizational climate as it relates to personal interactions is another people-oriented strategy for change. Such techniques as (1) projects designed to evaluate the feedback and exposure communicative processes and (2) sensitivity training are examples. Developing a new style of leadership or a new planning process can help to reduce resistance to change in department personnel.

Other people-oriented strategies, such as giving pay raises, creating rewards through an evaluation system, or initiating a strong control system that forces people to change have been the least effective strategies.

Structure-oriented approaches for change might include creating additional units within the department, dissolving present units, or combining them with already established divisions.

Another approach for structural change is instituting new procedures, rules, and regulations. By placing emphasis on enforcing the rules, changes can be implemented. Changes in technology and equipment are also tools for revising the system. The use of computers in decisionmaking has created changes in police agencies throughout the United States.

In deciding which approach to use, the manager should carefully evaluate the conditions in his or her own department. If, for example, the manager feels that the climate for change is positive, then changes that are directed toward people may prove more effective than those directed toward structure. In instances in which resistance to change may be high, the manager may begin the overall process by implementing structural changes such as reorganization, the development of computer systems, and the purchasing of new equipment.

No matter which approach the manager chooses, he or she should avoid becoming defensive about proposed changes and should not consider opposition to them as a personal threat. He or she should also avoid being unrealistic in the goals that he or she sets, the time frames, and the degree of commitment necessary on the part of the personnel within his or her command.

Finally, the police manager should not disregard the consequences of the change process. Whatever approach is employed, the manager must be aware of the major effects that the strategy will have on everyone involved. Initiating changes without any thought to how these changes will affect the rest of the police department may create serious difficulties in the implementation of programs for upgrading the department.

Notes

1. Frederick W. Taylor, *The Principles of Scientific Management* (New York: Harper and Brothers, 1911).

2. Elton Mayo, *The Social Problems of an Industrial Civilization* (Boston: Harvard Business School, 1945).

3. Paul Hersey and Kenneth H. Blanchard, *Management of Organizational Behavior*, 2d ed. (Englewood Cliffs, NJ: Prentice-Hall, Inc., 1972).

4. Robert R. Blake, Jacquelyn Mouton and Ashe Jane, *The Managerial Grid* (Houston: Gulf Publishing Company, 1991), p. 29.

5. Peter M. Senge, *The Fifth Discipline* (New York: Doubleday, 1990).

6. Ibid., p. 6.

7. Rensis Likert, *New Patterns of Management* (New York: McGraw-Hill Book Company, 1961).

8. James Kouzes and Barry Posner, *The Leadership Challenge* (San Francisco: Jossey Bass, 1987).

Discussion Questions

1. How may a police manager develop the necessary qualities to become an effective leader?

2. What style of management would be most appropriate for leading a police department?

3. If you were to take over a police department that was corrupt, inefficient, and ineffective, what style of management would you attempt to implement and why?

4. How can the five effective leadership practices be implemented?

5. Develop a vision. The questions that can be addressed to clarify this vision include: (a) How would you like to change the world for yourself, your department, or your division? (b) If you could invent the future, what future would you invent for yourself and your department or division? (c) What is your dream about your future as it relates to law enforcement? (d) What is your personal agenda and what do you want to improve?

6. What can a department do that indicates that the leaders are challenging the process, inspiring a shared vision, enabling others to act, modeling the way, and encouraging the heart?

Organizational Culture ‖ 4

Objectives

1. The student will understand why culture is important in a police department.

2. The student will understand how culture is developed.

3. The student will learn ways to identify the culture of a police department.

Introduction

Culture is a formal force that controls the behavior of department personnel. It is a combination of our assumptions, values, beliefs, traditions, and the role modeling of others we follow. Although the organizational culture of the individual police department is rarely, if ever, found in its writings, it is easy to observe from the actions of the department personnel who actually determine what is right or wrong for that individual police department.

There is a strong emphasis on the establishment of an organizational culture through role modeling the behavior patterns of its police executives. For example, the police manager who maintains that honesty is extremely important but will not answer inquiries from subordinates about incidents that may be going on within his or her area of responsibility creates a culture that is inconsistent with the one he or she has stated.

Why Culture is Important

Police departments react to calls for service. Some are major calls such as homicides, robberies, or injuries, and some are minor, such as theft of hubcaps, a loud party, or hot-rodders in the community. The way in which the individual officer deals with each of these incidents is controlled by his or her perception of the culture of their respective police department.

When there is a conflict between a sergeant and an officer or between a supervisor and his or her subordinates, they each rely on the culture of the department to make the right decision as to how such a conflict should be resolved. If the organizational culture is that conflict is not confronted directly, then the sergeant or supervisor may back down. However, if the sergeant and supervisor realize that they will be supported in their reasonable decisions, then they may take a completely different course of action in dealing with a conflict between themselves and a subordinate.

Organizational culture can be positive, and it can allow personnel to maintain high ethical standards with the need for only a few specific rules. On the other hand, the culture can be very negative, requiring multiple rules, close supervision, and eventually a police department in which trust is not considered an important part of the culture.

Culture is defined as a set of assumptions that sworn and nonsworn members of a police agency hold in common concerning the way that police department operates.

The culture of the police department shapes how decisions will be made. It will limit and encourage certain behaviors, will be used as a key to solving difficult problems, and in many ways, is the way in which police leaders shape the meaning of events in order to achieve the police mission and create the vision that they have for their individual police departments.

How Culture is Developed

The police manager will make a decision based on his or her values, beliefs, and principles. Members of the department—sworn and nonsworn—observe the police manager's actions. They then begin to interpret his or her beliefs, values, and principles. They can either accept or reject the police manager's beliefs, thereby forming a culture for the police department.

Culture can be developed through statements of values, beliefs, and principles. Once these are in writing, actions will be interpreted by personnel within the agency concerning whether the manager is consistent with the stated values, beliefs, and principles.

When a chief or police manager has an open door, talks to subordinates, and keeps personnel advised of actions that are pending and activities that are going on, they become more open to the public. If the officers do not agree and do something inconsistent with that openness but receive no consequences from the police manager, the manager's beliefs fail to become the agency's culture. If the officers are disciplined, the culture of openness is enforced.

Another force in the development of culture is to reward the openness. Allow the officers and personnel within the police department to share the flow of information and they will be honored for their behavior. It is important for the chief and for other police managers to understand the values and beliefs so that there can be consistency in the implementation of these principles.

Culture is developed from observing the actions of fellow officers in addition to the managers. The role of the training officer and the emphasis of a sergeant at a roll call also tend to develop and strengthen the department's culture.

Which beliefs, values, and principles become culture depends on the perception of the members of the police department, especially the way in which they perceive the chief's response to those values, beliefs, and culture. This is one reason why it is so very important for police managers to be consistent with their actions and their principles.

Identifying Your Police Department's Culture

The task of the newly appointed police manager, especially when coming from outside the agency, is to learn, understand, and work with the organizational culture. He or she must also make decisions about which part of the culture, if any, is to be changed.

When the new chief or the new manager comes from within the police department, he or she should be fairly familiar with the organizational culture. However, when being promoted from a mid-manager's position to an executive position in the police department, he or she may not be familiar with the values and beliefs of the chief. Only through personal daily contact and conversation about the police organization's culture can the culture be easily identified by the new police manager.

If the manager comes from another state, then his or her responsibility is to learn not only the culture of the police department but also the culture of the surrounding area. Think about a police chief who might come from another part of the country. Perhaps where he or she came from, the use of guns was something that was frowned on by the community. However, in the new community, there are many hunters and others who strongly believe in the right to legally carry guns. If the chief were to attempt to convince the city council to pass ordinances concerning control of weapons, he or she may be attempting to change the culture of the entire community—which might bring about dismissal.

To identify the culture, the new police manager can play the role of a good investigator. He or she can start with a review of the policies, rules, and procedures and then use task forces to analyze these procedures to determine whether they are still effective or acceptable. The manager would then examine many of the physical surroundings. For example, the condition of the uniforms, the condition of the rooms in which the people must work, and the condition of vehicles. He or she can further evaluate the educational level of personnel and can examine the culture of openness by looking at who is authorized to discuss with the media what happens within the police department.

Further examination should include the department rituals, such as always saluting a senior officer or special privileges for higher ranking officials. Then the new manager can identify the culture. Probably one of the most effective ways is by socializing in an informal atmosphere with members of the police agency and listening to "war stories" concerning past endeavors. These give good clues to the organizational culture of the police department.

There is a series of questions that the new police manager can ask in order to identify the culture. The first issue is reputation. The new police manager can check with sources external to the police department to answer this question. For example, a discussion with local merchants may disclose that the police department is viewed more as a night watch service or a service police organization rather than a crime fighting department. The external reputation of the department can also be examined through prior newspaper articles.

The second issue addressed is status, and this is an issue that deals with internal operations of the department. For example, is a detective held in higher esteem than a patrol officer, even though both positions may be of equal rank? Are any special considerations given to age? For example, are the older police officers viewed not only as more experienced, but also as those who can really assist you in finding ways to be effective? Another internal issue might be that, although there is no specific rule, emphasis on college-educated officers is shown by the fact that in the last five years only officers with a college education have been promoted above the rank of sergeant. As a result, the culture of this police agency is such that people joining the department who have not completed a college education strive to achieve this goal, fully recognizing that in a matter of a few years the agency may only be selecting college graduates for the position of sergeant.

A police manager can then look at the management style of his or her fellow leaders. Does the management style rely on control? Does the department perceive itself as a problem-solving organization? Does it see itself emphasizing coordination activities so that the department's goals are reached, or does it predominantly compromise any issue that may arise? How are decisions reached? Unilaterally, in small teams, are they reached by delegation alone, or is there very little delegation?

The next point to look at are policies of the police department itself. A good examination of the written policies can give the new manager an idea of the culture. However, many of the unwritten policies, norms, or customs also provide an excellent analysis of the police department's culture. If the police agency does not have anything written concerning a dress code for nonuniformed personnel, but all the investigators and nonsworn personnel you find working the building are wearing jackets, ties, or dresses, then a dress code is being enforced.

There are some questions that, if answered, can help a new police manager identify his or her unit's culture. How are the unit's common areas furnished and decorated? How about the work area's furnishings and decorations? Do they allow only certificates and plaques on the wall or are they allowed to hang items of a personal nature? If this police department had a T-shirt, what would the motto read? Are there special-interest groups that this agency pays more attention to than others? For example, Mothers Against Drunk Drivers, the local news media, or the Chamber of Commerce? During recruit school, what stories about the history of the department are told? Are there mistakes in this department, and if so, are they forgiven or carried forever? Where do people spend their time? If the leaders say that the personnel are extremely important, do they take the time to meet with them at roll call or visit the offices of the nonsworn personnel? Once the police manager has answered these questions, he or she can evaluate whether the values, beliefs, and principles on which these factors depend are consistent with those of the new police manager. Many times the answers to some of these questions bring about what are called the *artifacts*. The artifacts are products of the police department's past and are able to give a quick analysis of what their present culture may stand for. Discussions around the developed artifacts can determine the strength of parts of the police agency's culture. Such discussions will show the weight between honesty and loyalty.

A strong culture may be a great help to the police manager if he or she agrees with that culture, but it also can be an obstacle to change. The issue that the new manager must resolve is that of effectiveness and being trusted by the personnel of the department.

The police manager will find that there are cultures that are different from the police culture in other agencies within city government. With an issue of conflict, the personnel department may be less prone to deal directly with conflict and the city attorney's office may be much more prone to compromise, whereas a chief may believe that a conflict should be dealt with directly.

Trying to identify a police department's culture is difficult. The shared beliefs and the organizational values and how they are arrived at by officers sometimes can give different interpretations to the artifacts. Questionnaires are not always valuable and sometimes listening to espoused values and beliefs can be misleading. The best way to determine the organizational culture is to observe the behavior of the personnel of the department. Consider the police chief whose stated belief is that female officers are just as important to the police department as male officers and should not be treated any differently, but when assignments are observed, female officers are not assigned to some of the more critical areas of investigation or patrol.

Changing the Culture

To change the police department's culture a police manager must behave consistently with his or her own values and beliefs.

One way to begin to develop a new culture is to change the artifacts, or signs, of the old culture. If the police cars are old and dirty, purchase new ones; allow for take-home vehicles if possible and employ a different design. If promotions in the past have been based predominantly on seniority, strive for an assessment center approach, thereby creating a more open and trusting promotional system. A new police manager may have to maintain some signs of the old culture but change the way that they are interpreted. Staff meetings may be important but the new manager can change those from only a select few to opening them to more subordinates. Roll calls, although needed, may now be attended by executives, creating a more open flow of information.

Some of the direct methods that the police manager may use in changing the culture include identifying and discussing the operating beliefs and values of the police agency. The new police manager can then modify, remove, increase, or decrease the strength of these values, or change the priority of such values when necessary.

A police manager can explain to others how to make sense of individual actions and situations. The manager can role model and explain what he or she is role modeling so it is clearly understood. And finally, the manager can make use of situations that arise in day-to-day operations to explain how he or she would deal with similar issues in the future.

There are some indirect methods also. Police managers must allocate their time consistently with what they perceive to be important. They must ask for and share information on things that are important. They should measure and reward what they really believe in and what they really consider to be a true value. They must recruit, select, promote, and when needed, dismiss people based on a set of professional standards: legal, ethical, moral, and performance.

If they have the authority, they can structure the police department consistent with their beliefs. For example, a flat organizational structure may emphasize coordination on the role of all executives, whereas a tall organizational structure may emphasize control.

The new police manager must act consistently, especially in moments of truth. For example, what if there is pressure from a political body and outside sources to discipline a police officer for alleged misconduct, but the police manager believes that the conduct was reasonable on the part of the officer. This becomes a moment of truth. Does the chief bend to the pressures of council, press, and citizens' groups? Or is the chief willing to stand behind his or her officer, even at the risk of risk losing his or her present position?

An example of changing culture may be how the new police manager deals with the issue of conflict. Before his or her assignment, conflict may have been considered negative and was avoided. The new manager then discusses the reasons he or she believes in the value of openness and believes that conflict brings about growth and does not hamper overall operations. He or she develops a new principle—"we shall face all issues"—and then does not play referee but allows personnel to solve their conflicts. Assume that patrol and records have a problem concerning the time limits of information being analyzed and returned to the patrol force. Instead of the new manager ordering a certain solution to the problem, he or she plays the role of facilitator and allows them to join together.

The new police manager, once realizing that this new culture is beginning to take place, could then follow through with a training program in conflict and finally issue general policies and procedures that may assist in dealing with conflict throughout the police department.

This appears to be time consuming and frustrating to many people, and it will be. But in the long run it will be effective. Establishing a new or improved culture takes about 12-18 months; however, it will affect the level of behavior of police personnel for many years into the future.

Consider a new chief who takes over a corrupt, closed police department, opens communication, relies on trust, and prosecutes those who acted in an illegal manner. After a few years the department becomes a model and the values of trust, openness, and honesty are practiced long after the chief leaves or retires.

Conclusion

Culture comprises many values, beliefs, and principles. An effective culture that is developed by the police manager will allow that manager to be viewed as a strong leader and successful in almost all facets of his or her behavior.

On the other hand, the ineffective culture will make the police manager appear weak, not in control, unable to communicate, and unable to coordinate activities. Police managers who either instill or retain an ineffective culture will most likely fail.

Bibliography

Adapted from Roger Schwarz, "Understanding and Changing the Culture of an Organization." (Institute of Government 58, University of North Carolina, 1989).

Discussion Questions

1.   Visit a local police department and identify five activities that define its culture.

2.   Assume you are a new police chief. How would you develop your culture for the police department?

3.   List three techniques you believe would be effective in changing a police agency's culture.

Management Communication Behavior ‖ 5

Objectives

1. The student will recognize the importance of an open relationship among those involved in the communicative process.

2. The student will be aware that the development of effective communication in any police department requires a combination of exposure and honest, realistic feedback.

3. The student, in the use of feedback and exposure, will be aware of the negative tendency of people to neglect one and overuse the other, causing decreased effectiveness of communication.

4. The student will strive to achieve a *balanced arena* in order to equalize feedback and exposure.

5. The student will become familiar with the four basic communicative behavior patterns and become aware of when a communicative pattern is most appropriate for use in the daily decision-making process.

Communication has been defined in numerous ways, but the most appropriate definition is "behavior that results in an exchange of meaning." There are many examples of communication in an organization such as a police department, including facial expressions of police managers, spoken or written messages, the notices placed on bulletin boards, interactions in staff meetings, and the issuance of general orders. This varied output from the manager transmits the feelings, attitudes, and ideas of management to the other personnel in the department. The exchange between the sender, usually the management, and the receiver, usually the employees, carries meaning and intent.

When a misunderstanding or "communication misfire" occurs, it can generally be traced to either (1) the sender having conveyed unclear expressions, words, or ideas or (2) the receiver having misinterpreted the transmission or having been distracted while receiving it.

The critical question that the police manager should answer is, "What is effective communication for my department?"

Levels of Communication

The communication process in a police department involves two levels. The primary level may be observed or heard. It is a single transaction in the form of either a written or oral statement from one person to another. The second level of communication is determined by the prior history of interactions between the manager and personnel.

Consider the statement "I want you to make as many decisions as possible." If managers in two different police agencies were to make this statement, the agencies would have identical first-level communication. However, in one agency the true meaning, or second level of communication, may be that before implementing decisions, the subordinate must receive approval from the manager. In another agency, the same statement may mean that the individual has complete authority to act without seeking prior approval from the manager.

The police manager should constantly be aware of both levels of communication and should realize that actions taken on a day-to-day basis will have a greater effect on communication than will a statement made only once.

Hierarchy of Effective Communication

Through effective communication, a manager in any police organization attempts to establish a specific behavior pattern in subordinates. Effective communication may be described as a four-step process.

In the first step, information is exchanged between manager and subordinates. Step two involves the development of understanding. The manager may have to clarify a message to the subordinates so that they clearly understand the boundaries of their authority in making decisions on a daily basis. Again, such development of understanding requires openness, trust, and willingness on the part of each to talk and listen. The third step is the resolution of the issues communicated in steps one and two. If, for example, orders are clearly explained by the management and the subordinates understand but do not accept them, the goals of the communication process have not been achieved. For example, a manager may order subordinates to arrive on time for roll call, but the officers do not agree with the order, refuse to accept it, and continue to arrive approximately five minutes before roll call. In this case the communication process, for all intents and purposes, has failed.

The function of the fourth step is to produce appropriate behavior in both the sender and the receiver. In the example given above, the manager should stop, reevaluate the process, and either issue stronger orders with more control or reopen the communication in an attempt to develop understanding and acceptance.

Fact versus Inference

In organizational communication, confusion occurs when people are not able to differentiate between fact and inference. The police manager who makes an inference and is unaware of having done so will not be able to calculate the chances for failure involved in the process. A subordinate who acts on the inference made by the manager may be taking an unrecognized and unnecessary risk.

Certain characteristics distinguish statements of fact from statements of inference. Statements of fact should be based on the individual's firsthand observation, not on assumptions. Statements of inference, however, can go well beyond what the individual has actually observed; they are limited only by his or her imagination. Statements of inference involve probability as opposed to certainty.

The effective communicator sets specific behavioral goals that may be stated as follows:

1. To make all the inferences I want but know when I am doing so and to understand the difference between fact and inference.

2. To check my inferences, perceptions, and reflections, because appearances can be deceiving, and not to give them the same weight I give to my personal observations.

3. To try not to pass on inferences as if they are statements of fact and not to accept the inferences of others as facts.

4. To avoid acting on inferences as if they are facts.

5. To base my life on the assumption of probability, not on the assumption of certainty; to continually check my assumptions and be willing to say, "I don't know."

The Johari Window

The Johari Window is an information-processing model by which the manager can judge his or her effectiveness in dealing with the concerns of feedback and exposure.[1] The model is expressed graphically by a square (see Figure 5.1). This four-celled figure shows the interaction of manager and subordinates, and it lists the behavioral processes required in utilizing feedback and exposure.

The Johari Window may be viewed as comprising numerous pieces of information that the manager can use in establishing interpersonal and team relationships. The window represents all the available communicative processes. As shown in Figure 5.1, it is divided into four regions, each representing relevant information about the quality of the relationships. To fully appreciate the effect of each region and the manner in which they intertwine to create interpersonal and team effectiveness, the police manager should not only consider the size and shape of each region but also the reason for their presence within the total structure of the Johari Window.

As stated, the window deals with two kinds of communication—feedback and exposure—each of which is subdivided into categories that are known by the manager, unknown by the manager, known by others, and unknown by others.

Figure 5.1 **The Johari Window**

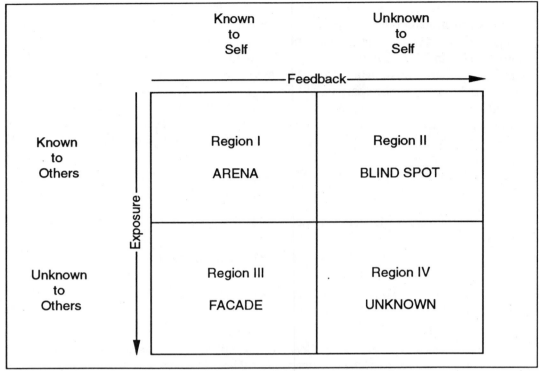

SOURCE: Adapted from Jay Hall and Martha Williams, *Personnel Relations Survey* (The Woodlands, TX: Teleometrics Int'l).

Region I, for example, represents open communication, in which information is shared equally and understood. This information, known by the manager and known by others, is the facet of the interpersonal communication relationship that controls interpersonal productivity. This region helps to develop an effective hierarchy of communication. The assumption behind this principle is that interpersonal effectiveness and productivity are directly related to the amount of information that is mutually held within the relationship. Therefore, as the police manager increases the size of Region I, his or her interpersonal and team relationships will become more rewarding, effective, and productive. Region I is called the *arena.*

In Region II, information is known by others but unknown by the manager. This situation handicaps the manager, because it is difficult for him or her to understand the behavior, decisions, and potential of others if he or she does not have the necessary data on which to base conclusions about their motives. The other person has the advantage in knowing his or her own reactions, feelings, and perceptions. Region II, because it is an area of hidden, unperceived information, is called the *blind spot.* More limited in scope than Region I, this is an area of inhibited interpersonal effectiveness.

Region III, the *facade,* also inhibits interpersonal effectiveness, but here the imbalance is in favor of the police manager. Most of the information is known by the manager but unknown by others. The manager may attempt to keep any information that is seen as potentially detrimental out of the communicative process. What happens, therefore, is that the manager operating under the assumptions of Region III develops a series of communication facades, which act as his defense. Facades are present in almost all relationships, but damage to the communication process depends on how extensively they are used. The police manager should decide how much conscious defensive behavior can be introduced into the communication process before the arena (Region I) becomes inhibited and interpersonal communication suffers, causing ineffectiveness in the police department.

Finally, Region IV constitutes the portion of the interpersonal relationship in which information is unknown by both the police manager and others. This "unknown" region, however, begins to shrink as the manager enlarges the arena (Region I).

The police manager should realize that the information within all these regions constitutes both primary and secondary level communication. At the secondary level, the manager should constantly be aware of how assumptions, prejudices, and attitudes relate to factual information. Furthermore, the Johari Window concept deals with data that is relevant to the decision-making process, and it is designed to examine only relevant information.

Basic Interpersonal Processes

The police manager should be aware that the development of effective communication in any police department requires a combination of exposure and feedback. It is up to the manager to encourage downward communication and at the same time to enlarge the feedback process in a horizontal direction. The police manager should understand that in order to develop a climate of mutual exposure, the necessity for honest and realistic feedback must be emphasized. The manager must also be willing to solicit such feedback by encouraging subordinates to expose their information.

To reduce his or her blind spot, the police manager must have the cooperation of subordinates. The manager's willingness to deal openly with issues will dictate the level of cooperation and trust that he or she is given by subordinates.

Police managers should realize that, theoretically, we all strive for a high degree of exposure and feedback, but we fail to achieve an optimum level within organizational communication. The police manager usually has a preference for either exposure or feedback and has a tendency to overuse one and neglect the other. Imbalance results, causing tension, frustration, and confusion, which impairs the effectiveness of the communication process. Figure 5.2 presents some commonly used approaches to the exposure and feedback processes.[2] Each process may be described as an interpersonal style, and each is associated with fairly predictable behavior patterns exhibited by the police manager.

Four possible behavior types are demonstrated in Figure 5.2.

Type A. Under type A, there is little use of either exposure or feedback. Here, the police manager is not very concerned about communication with subordinates. The "unknown" region dominates this type, and an analysis usually indicates that the type A individual withdraws from decisionmaking and does not emphasize creativity or risk taking. Type A police managers are usually only personally motivated to create safety and security for their present positions. These managers are usually rigid, aloof, and uncommunicative with their subordinates. The police manager who believes in the 1, 1 style as defined in the management grid would have a window similar to that of the type A.

Type B. The type B police manager has an aversion to exposure but also exhibits some desire for interaction with subordinates. The emphasis, however, is on feedback, to the extent that it is overused. Personnel and police managers with this type of communication window usually mistrust those with whom they come in contact; they believe in developing a facade behind which they can hide their intentions. The feedback, in many instances, may simply denote a probing on the part of the manager because of lack of trust in subordinates. Once this is realized by the subordinates, the manager's facade is easily recognizable, and effective communication ceases to exist.

Figure 5.2 **Exposure-Feedback Styles**

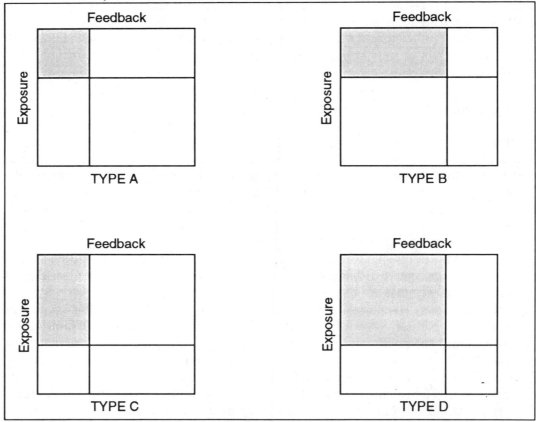

SOURCE: Adapted from Jay Hall and Martha Williams, *Personnel Relations Survey* (The Woodlands, TX).

Type C. In type C, exposure is overemphasized and feedback is neglected. The police manager within this kind of window is usually ego-striving and does not trust the people with whom he or she communicates. Such managers usually feel confident about their own values, opinions, and decisions and like to emphasize their authority. They are usually unaware of the impact of others in assisting in the decision-making process. A large blind spot usually results from this type of behavior. Persons with whom the manager communicates usually feel that their thoughts, ideas, and feelings are not being valued. This attitude often results in the subordinates feeling insecure, hostile, and rebellious. In many cases the personnel in the department will deliberately withhold important information from the manager or attempt to offer only the feedback that they feel the manager wants to hear. This results in decisionmaking that is based on insufficient information.

Type D. In the type D manager, exposure and feedback are balanced. The result is openness, trust, candor, and sensitivity to the needs of others. The arena becomes the dominant feature of the communication relationship; therefore, the productivity of the entire department increases. The police manager should be aware that attempts to increase the arena may lead some subordinates to react defensively. This is especially true if they are not accustomed to honest and trusting relationships with their superiors. Although managers who want to increase the size of the arena should be aware of such possible defensive behavior, they should continue to create and promote the trust and respect that is so important to effective communication.

Generally speaking, the larger the manager's arena, the more effective his or her relationships with subordinates, peers, and superiors will be. The manager should be aware that effectiveness is related not only to the size of the arena but also to its shape. The size of the arena is usually related to the quantity of production stimulated by the communication process. The shape of the arena is directly associated with the quality of the work produced as a result of interpersonal communication. A balanced arena is preferred, because this means that both the exposure and the feedback processes are equal or as close as possible to being equal. Such equality allows the manager to establish a foundation from which further enlargement of the arena may be accomplished.

Giving Useful Feedback

To have an effective police organization, the police manager should be concerned with growth and development and be able to devote time and effort to problem solving and decisionmaking within the department. Effective decisionmaking requires open relationships among those involved in the process. This type of open relationship—based on candor, honesty, and trust—allows individuals within the department to express their feelings freely; it also helps reduce existing barriers that hamper effective decisionmaking.

One way in which the police manager can develop open communication is through the effective use of feedback. The question the manager should ask before becoming involved in the process of feedback is, "Do I really feel that the information I am about to give to my subordinates can be used to help them improve and grow?" Police managers must first examine their own motives. If they find that they are only trying to unload a burden of hostility, then the feedback will do more harm than good. Three important criteria are:

1. The other person needs to understand the feedback information.
2. The other person must be willing to accept the feedback.
3. The other person must be able to change his or her behavior or otherwise act on the feedback.

The manager should realize that there will be times when it will be extremely difficult to demand that the subordinate accept critical and negative feedback. In attempting to gain acceptance of feedback, the manager should follow some general principles.

First, managers should develop a foundation of trust with their subordinates before beginning to use feedback.

Second, managers should be aware of the manner in which they discuss feedback with subordinates. They must constantly be aware of tone of voice, facial expressions, choice of words, and all behavior indicating second-level communication to the recipient of the feedback.

Third, managers should realize that their subordinates will be more likely to listen to negative feedback if they simply describe to a subordinate what they, as managers, have seen and what effect it has had on them. For example, a statement to the subordinate such as, "I think that's a nasty way to act toward people, and I think you ought to grow up," does not really help the subordinate to change and may bring out feelings of hostility. However, if the manager points to a specific situation and carefully describes his or her feelings about the incident, then the feedback, although negative in nature, is more likely to be accepted by the subordinate.

Finally, the manager should be careful to time the feedback correctly and be able to judge whether the subordinate is in a proper state of mind to receive negative feedback. For example, if the subordinate appears to be confused, angry, upset, or defensive, the feedback should be postponed. However, if the subordinate seems to be in an open state of mind, then the time is right and the feedback will have a greater chance of being accepted.

There are some general rules for establishing and understanding feedback. First the feedback should be specific rather than general. For example, if the police manager merely says that he or she feels that the subordinate does not produce quality work but does not state facts to support this criticism, then the feedback is not very useful to the subordinate. The manager should cite specific instances and examples to clearly show how the subordinate is not acting in a proper manner.

The second rule for establishing understanding is to use recent examples of the employee's behavior rather than old ones. It is not advisable to give feedback to the subordinate concerning alleged behavior of three or four months earlier. In many instances, police departments force themselves into this situation by completing performance evaluation reports only once or twice a year. Because these performance evaluations are the only feedback from manager to subordinates, the manager should begin the feedback process as soon as possible after a given incident so that the event is still vivid in the minds of both the manager and the subordinate.

The third rule states that the feedback must be conducive to being acted on by the subordinate. Frustration is only increased when the subordinate is reminded of a shortcoming over which he or she has no control. If the police manager feels that the subordinate is not acting with the degree of commitment necessary to perform his or her patrol duties effectively, then the manager should be able to give the subordinate specific instances that will help him or her to understand the feelings and opinions of the police agency. Merely stating that the officer does not adequately perform assignments and functions usually does not help to change his or her behavior. Whether the police manager elects to give negative feedback to a subordinate depends on the manager's estimate of the subordinate's ability to change the behavior.

The fourth rule states that feedback must be influenced by the needs of both the subordinate and the manager. Feedback can be destructive when it serves only the manager's need and fails to encompass the needs of the subordinate.

Fifth, the feedback should be solicited rather than imposed. Feedback is most useful when it is the subordinate who formulates the kinds of questions that the police manager, through observation, can best answer.

Last, the feedback should be checked to ensure effective communication. One way of doing this is for the subordinate to rephrase the feedback received from the manager to see if it corresponds with what the manager originally intended.

Receiving Feedback

To keep the Johari Window as open as possible, the police manager must also receive feedback. There are some overall criteria that should govern the manager's conduct in receiving feedback.

The police manager should make a sincere attempt to avoid being defensive. One of the surest ways to stifle feedback is for the police manager to insist that the subordinate does not understand him or her and that therefore the premises of the feedback are erroneous. Such a manager would end up receiving nothing more than reinforcement of his or her own thoughts and opinions. Within a short time, this manager would become isolated from the facts about the department.

If police managers do not clearly understand the information their subordinates are trying to offer, they are unable to help their personnel. On the other hand, an open response from the manager can help to clarify his or her behavior. Examples will sometimes zero in on the true issues brought about within the feedback process—for example, such statements by the manager as, "Remember when we met last Thursday and I did not allow all members of the staff to express their ideas? Is this the kind of behavior you are talking about?"

Once the feedback session has been completed, it is a good idea for the police manager to briefly summarize what has been said. This gives a final check and an opportunity to clarify any misunderstandings that may have occurred during the meeting.

Rules on Exposure

The police manager should be aware that there are rules governing exposure as well as feedback.

First, the exposure should come about as part of the ongoing relationship between police managers and subordinates. The exposure should be timed so that it fits into the existing realities of the department. Police managers should be aware of the effects that such exposure will have on them as well as their subordinates. As they drop their facade, managers will also reduce their blind spots in relation to their subordinates. Once the subordinates decrease their facades, the two-way communication process begins to be effective.

Exposure should also carry with it a reasonable but not overly high risk. Police managers should not be so open that they create a win-or-lose situation with subordinates. Constantly criticizing or downgrading subordinates may be a form of exposure, but the manager who does this runs the risk of never receiving any feedback from the subordinates.

Principles of Change in the Johari Window

Actions and interactions between individuals have definite effects on the size and shape of the Johari Window. Some of the basic principles of change operating within the Johari Window are as follows:

1. A change in one quadrant will affect all other quadrants. As the size of the arena increases, the facade, blind spot, and unknown begin to decrease.

2. It takes energy to hide, deny, or be blind to behavior involved in interaction. In other words, it becomes a sheer impossibility on the part of a police manager not to witness and give some interpretation of the actions of other members within the department, whether they are peers, superiors, or subordinates.

3. Threats tend to decrease awareness, whereas mutual trust tends to increase awareness. This principle emphasizes the necessity for the high degree of trust that must exist within any police agency in order for the police manager to partake in effective and open communications.

4. Forced awareness is undesirable. In the communication process, as in other processes, forcing someone to give exposure or feedback usually carries little long-term effect; in many instances it does more harm than good in the short term.

5. Interpersonal learning comes about through an increase in the arena. Only by having a moderate to large arena can a police manager expect to grow in technical, rational, and psychological skills. The police manager who emphasizes the autocratic 9, 1 approach to management will, in the long run, develop a fixed arena that, depending on the manager's position and authority, will very quickly cease to grow.

6. Working with others is facilitated by a large area of mutually shared information. The larger the arena, the easier it is for the police manager to work with superiors, peers, and subordinates. On the other hand, the smaller the arena, the poorer the communication process between the manager and other members of the department will be.

What Affects the Size of the Arena in an Agency?

The trust between management and subordinates strongly affects the size of the arena in any police agency. Consider what happens when police officers do not believe their superiors. In such a case, the only information flowing upward is that which the lower levels of the organization believe the upper levels want to hear. Very quickly, the police manager ends up in the proverbial ivory tower, not really aware of day-to-day activities within the department.

The rank and structure of the police agency also affect the size of the arena. If the structure contains five steps between the police officer and the chief, each level begins to filter out, accept, and reject information in different ways. The arena begins to shrink in such agencies, especially where superiors have only one or two people under their direct control.

Probably one of the most important factors in any police agency is the unwise use of power by the police manager. If the police manager feels obliged to make as many of the decisions as possible, continually attempts to justify his or her position, avoids conflict, and tries to guarantee that no mistakes will occur, less effective communication will take place within that agency. Usually communication will deal with nebulous problems or with social activities within the agency; they rarely address the more important issues that require team decisionmaking.

Police managers should be aware of the different types of information that they and others possess. First, they have different feelings about each other. They know different facts concerning a given issue and have separate sets of assumptions, prejudices, and opinions. Each person possesses skills that enable him or her to deal with issues and each has an individual way of confronting or avoiding conflict. All of these factors directly affect the size of the arena.

Patterns of Communication

There are four basic patterns of communicative behavior that the police manager can implement in influencing subordinates. *Influence* has been defined as the major process, function, or activity involved in the leadership role. The four basic patterns of influence available to the police manager are: (1) controlling pattern, (2) relinquishing pattern, (3) defensive pattern, (4) developmental pattern.

In Figure 5.3, the circle is divided into four quadrants indicating the four approaches to another person:

Style	**Approach**
Controlling	"I want to have most of the influence."
Relinquishing	"I want to give you influence."
Defensive	"I want to stay uninvolved and neither exert nor respond to influence."
Developmental	"I want to use my influence and yours to solve a problem."

Figure 5.3 **Patterns of Communication as They Relate to Influence**

SOURCE: From *Management Models—The Communication Process* (Westport, CT: Educational Systems and Designs, Inc., 1967). Reprinted with permission of Educational Systems and Designs, Inc.

Controlling Pattern

Under the controlling pattern, the police manager uses his influence to force his subordinates to do exactly as he, the leader, desires. Police managers who constantly try to lead by using sell techniques are exhibiting a control type of leadership behavior.

Police managers who rely on their power or threats to control their subordinates are indicating constraining behavior, and they attempt to maintain total influence over the decision-making process. The influence belongs solely to the leader, and he does not share with his subordinates. On some occasions, the police manager may not have stated authority but will attempt to use superior knowledge or threats of some negative consequence to influence the behavior of subordinates. For example, "If you don't follow this rule, I'll have you suspended," or "The chief says that you'd better get this done as quickly as possible," or "I'm sure the chief would want it done my way." These statements are typical of a police manager who is attempting to control the influence and not share with the subordinates in the decision-making process.

Relinquishing Pattern

Under the relinquishing pattern, the police manager is giving up part or all of her influence in making the decision. She wants her subordinates to accept her as a leader or is attempting to be "one of the boys."

The police manager may attempt to relinquish her influence by complying with her subordinates' point of view. She does not totally withdraw from the situation but is still involved through compliance. She offers little or no resistance to suggestions made by other people in the group, even though she may strongly disagree with their opinions or conclusions.

Managers who, in the decision-making process, make such statements as "Well, you're the boss, I gotta follow what you say, so I'll go ahead and do it" or "I'm sure we won't have any trouble if we do it exactly the way the officers want it" are really examples of the manager abdicating the leadership role.

Defensive Pattern

In the defensive pattern, the police manager or leader totally withdraws from the problem-solving process. He does not contribute or solicit ideas and usually avoids involvement with the problem. Statements such as "Well, I've done all I can, there's nothing else for me," or "That's not my job, let somebody else figure it out," are examples of defensive behavior.

Sometimes this withdrawal will be exhibited by emotional outbursts on the part of the police manager. He begins to move away from the problem and begins to attack other people involved in the decision-making process. Such statements as "That was a stupid thing to do" or "I'm tired of the way you've been behaving, and I sure wish you'd get yourself straightened out" are examples of withdrawal communicative behavior. The responses are really directed at other individuals within the group, not at the issue or problem at hand. Many times, these statements build hostility and cause other people to be defensive, and very little is accomplished in the problem-solving, decision-making process.

Developmental Pattern

Under the developmental pattern, the influence flows between the police manager and her subordinates. Each participant in the decision-making group is allowed to contribute opinions and ideas, and the group in turn attempts to draw out the ideas of all members involved in the decision-making process. The desire on the part of the leader is to find the best possible alternatives for the resolution of the problem. To accomplish this, the police manager must be willing to listen, explore, and test new ideas.

The developmental pattern consists of two types of action-reaction. First, the police manager can attempt to develop some course of action by developing commitment and understanding and by dispensing information to the other people involved in the decisionmaking process. Her role as a leader is one of stimulating discussion and interaction with other members of the decision-making group. Before entering decision-making discussions, the manager must plan how she can stimulate thinking, challenge the other people in her group, and decide what she can contribute to the growth of the group. Police managers may begin the discussion of issues with such statements as "I saw a report the other day that indicated that 20 percent of our population causes about 80 percent of our crime problem. I think this has real significance for us on how we are going to allocate our resources." By beginning the discussion with such a statement, the manager is attempting to develop alternatives, to bring in new facts for the knowledge and awareness of other people in the group, and to provide information from which the problem can be solved.

Second, the police manager who wants to implement such patterns of behavior can attempt to seek out the ideas and opinions of others in the agency. She should take the role of asking questions, reflecting opinions of others, giving support, and showing an interest in the others' points of view. Such responses as "How do you feel about this?" or "What is your opinion?" are ways in which the police manager can develop a developmental pattern of communicative behavior.

In essence, then, the influence in the decision-making process and the role of leadership is really a two-way process, being shared by the police managers with their subordinates.

Applying Patterns of Communication

The four patterns of communicative behavior and their relationship to the influence process have been described. Police managers must understand the four basic patterns of communication and, more importantly, they must be aware of when a given pattern of communication is most appropriate.

Controlling Pattern

The leader who chooses a controlling pattern of behavior uses his authority to apply pressure, and he attempts to persuade people to do what he wants. The issue for the police manager is whether this approach would ever be appropriate. The answer is yes.

If the manager wants to control his personnel so as to achieve his objectives, he must first have the facts, information, and experience to justify his adoption of the controlling pattern of behavior. For example, when the police manager is first assigned to a unit, he should not attempt to use the controlling pattern because he is not familiar with the qualifications of his subordinates.

Therefore, when the police manager is first given a new supervisory position within the police department and is unfamiliar with the job, the developmental pattern or even the relinquishing approach may prove more effective in problem solving. If, however, the police manager has all the facts, understands the situation clearly, and has the necessary experience and knowledge to make high-quality decisions, then the controlling approach is more appropriate.

In emergency or crisis situations in which action and direction are needed immediately, the controlling approach is the most appropriate pattern of communication for the police manager. For example, if a disturbance broke out during a specific tour of duty, it would be inappropriate for the manager to sit down with his superiors and subordinates and attempt to develop some course of action. Directive, specific controlling behavior is much more appropriate in such a situation. Usually, the police manager who shows presence of mind and knowledge in giving directions and organizing his people to fight the disturbance and control it is behaving in the most effective way. Therefore, in crisis and emergency situations, the controlling pattern of behavior is often appropriate.

Another situation in which the manager may choose this behavior pattern is where the joint commitment and motivation of the subordinates are unimportant and unnecessary. Any situation that is positive or useful from the subordinates' point of view can be handled effectively by the controlling pattern. For example, if the city manager's office allowed office personnel to leave early with pay, the joint decision-making process would be unnecessary.

Also, the manager must have some authority or control over the alternatives available for solving the problem. For example, when managers of equal rank attempt to use a controlling approach on each other, the approach rarely works. A police sergeant would not give a direct order to a fellow sergeant, especially when he has no authority or responsibility over the other's affairs. By the same token, when the police manager has no authority or responsibility over activities of subordinates, he would not use the controlling approach. Consider what would happen if the police manager attempted to dictate what church his police officers should attend or how they should deal with their private lives. In essence, the authoritarian or controlling approach would have no effect. Also, with the trend today of increasing the authority, responsibility, and freedom of subordinates, the controlling pattern is becoming less and less effective.

Police managers in some instances are legally restricted in the degree to which they can use controlling methods. As a result of such issues as mandatory collective bargaining, civil service rules and regulations, and threats of lawsuits, the police manager has lost much of the control that he had over his subordinates' activities in the past. Even in instances in which the police manager has legal or stated authority over the alternatives, he must always remember that he does not have complete control of the individual's motives, feelings, or attitudes. If the subordinate decides that the controlling pattern as exhibited by his manager is overcontrolling and overdirecting him, he will usually find a quiet, subtle way of resisting the orders. This passive resistance shows up in many police agencies. Police officers begin to perform only the amount of work necessary to keep from being dismissed or having charges brought against them. Therefore, the police manager, even though he has legal and stated authority over the alternatives, must always balance that against how much control he really has over the alternatives.

The controlling approach is probably most appropriate when resistance to change is low, because when resistance is high, controlling techniques are rarely effective. If they are, the effectiveness lasts for a short period only. When the police manager attempts to force a specific change on police officers who are vehemently opposed to the new course of action, rarely will commitment and self-motivation be developed by the controlling pattern. Usually the manager would have to take the time and effort to discuss the issue with the staff to develop understanding and get them personally involved.

This does not mean, however, that the police manager must never implement change against these forces. The real professional recognizes the management situations in which such difficult decisions must be made and in which the changes must be imposed, regardless of the resistance from internal or external sources. In many instances, when resistance is great, the manager would be required to use more controlling techniques than usual. Nevertheless, the police manager must always realize that the controlling pattern of leadership is not the best way of introducing new ideas into an organization.

In summary, the following ingredients must be present if the controlling pattern is to be effective:

1. The police manager must have all or most of the facts, experience, or knowledge related to the issue.

2. An emergency or crisis situation exits.

3. The manager must feel that joint commitment with subordinates is not necessary or important.

4. The manager must have full control of the alternative solutions.

5. The manager is not legally restricted from using this approach.

6. Resistance to change is low.

Relinquishing Pattern

The process of relinquishing means that the police manager gives up her influence and reduces her contribution or role in the problem-solving process. It occurs most often when the manager is concerned about losing acceptance. Unfortunately, in many situations, this pattern of communication is used to avoid unpleasant situations or keep subordinates happy. Rarely is this sufficient reason for a manager to relinquish influence and authority.

The police manager must always be concerned with the goals and objectives of the police department and with the various precedents she is in the process of establishing. In dealing with subordinates, the police manager cannot always act merely to keep her people happy but must be concerned with the total situation.

There certainly are some circumstances when the relinquishing pattern is appropriate. For example, when the police manager finds that her subordinates are in a highly emotional state, then this relinquishing of her influence may be the most suitable way to handle the issue. Even though the manager may feel that the subordinates are misinformed, she may be willing to go along with them until they calm down and can be approached logically. Remember, however, that it is dangerous to assume that emotional people can be handled effectively by relinquishing influence. However, if the subordinates are irrational, the police manager may find it more advantageous in the long run to allow them to express their personal feelings. After the emotional outburst, the manager may find it more appropriate to restrict the conversation to the issue at hand.

There is a second set of circumstances under which the relinquishing approach may be the most effective for the police manager. In situations in which the subordinates have all the information, experience, and facts necessary for the decision-making process, the manager may very well want to give up her influence in the decisions. In essence, the manager is exhibiting trust in her subordinates and in their ability to make the right and proper decisions. For example, if the police manager was required to approve the decision concerning which computer system to employ or which police radio to purchase, she may find it more effective to follow the advice of technically qualified subordinates.

In emergency situations, when the police manager first arrives at the scene, she may be willing to give up her influence in the decision-making process until she becomes more familiar with the facts. Under such circumstances, the relinquishing of influence would be only temporary. Once the facts are known to the police manager, she must decide whether to take the controlling pattern or the developmental pattern in reaching the remaining decisions.

Finally, when the police manager wants her subordinates to learn by experience, she may very well decide to give up her influence. This is especially true when the employee is highly motivated. For example, when the police officer approaches the police manager with a new program to reduce the number of armed robberies in a specific area of the community, then the police manager may, assuming the project is reasonable in nature, allow the officer to plan, implement, and evaluate the entire operation. In essence, she has relinquished her influence in the decision-making process concerning the development of the project itself. Obviously, if the subordinate's program is too costly, too dangerous, or inconsistent with department objectives, the police manager must take a direct role, denying permission to implement the project. Usually after a careful explanation, the subordinates would either accept the manager's decision or attempt to redesign their project to meet the specific guidelines outlined by the manager.

In review, then, when the following key factors exist, the police manager may find the relinquishing pattern to be appropriate:

1. When the other individual is highly emotional or disturbed by the issue at hand.

2. When the other person has most of the facts and experience related to the issue.

3. When the manager first arrives at an emergency situation and does not have all the facts yet.

4. When the subordinate is highly motivated and wants to implement a specific project.

Defensive Pattern

This pattern of communicative behavior is usually inappropriate. However, there are a few situations in which this approach might prove effective. In considering issues that are legal, moral, or ethical, the police manager may find it appropriate to withdraw from the issue. For example, when dealing with union agitators, the police manager may refuse to comment on a practice or procedure. In essence, he would withdraw from the situation and avoid involvement.

If a police manager is approached by either a superior or a subordinate and asked to engage in some practice that might be illegal, the manager may express a strong withdrawal action. He may become angry at the person rather than at the problem. Thus, there are circumstances in which this approach would be both understandable and even appropriate. These situations rarely emerge in most law enforcement agencies, but the police manager must also realize that managers, supervisors, and police officers are human. It is certainly desirable for the police manager to avoid losing his temper, but if he does, it may be better for him to withdraw from the situation. However, he must always be able to judge whether it is necessary for him to come back to the situation and try to achieve some solution with those involved.

Similarly, in dealing with others, the police manager must develop a tolerance for human reactions. He must realize that subordinates will become frustrated and, when they fail to understand the real issue, may also engage in withdrawal behavior.

In summary, although it is generally undesirable to use defensive patterns of communication, in the following situations this may be the most appropriate form of behavior:

1. When there is a legal, moral, or ethical issue.

2. When the individual is frustrated or does not fully understand the situation in which he or she is involved.

Developmental Pattern

In a majority of the situations faced by the police manager, she does not have all the facts. There are usually differences of opinion and a need to develop understanding through personal two-way communication. The police manager needs the ideas of her subordinates, she needs their commitment, and she needs them to be self-motivated. It is almost impossible, in running any police agency today, for the police manager to be completely unilateral in her decisionmaking.

If the police manager can answer *yes* to any of the following questions, then the developmental pattern would be the most appropriate pattern of communicative behavior for her to use:

1. Are there others who have additional facts, experience, or knowledge that can contribute to making a more effective decision?

2. Is joint commitment important?

3. Is there a difference of opinion among personnel who will be concerned with the implementation of this decision?

4. Is there a possibility of resistance to the decision?

5. Is there a need or opportunity for creativeness or innovation?

Summary of Communication Patterns

Police managers must always realize that whenever they interact with superiors and subordinates, their style of communication will fall into some behavior pattern. When speed is important, when they have the knowledge and experience to make effective decisions, the controlling pattern may be the most appropriate. Managers should use the controlling behavior pattern only when they are positive they are right and when there is no resistance on the part of the subordinates.

On the other hand, if someone else has more facts and knows and understands what is required, managers should relinquish their influence by adopting the relinquishing pattern of behavior.

Situations in which the defensive pattern of behavior would be appropriate are rare, but managers must realize that such behavior is normal, and they must be able to respond with understanding and guidance.

Finally, the developmental pattern has proved to be the most useful style of communicative behavior in situations in which the decisionmakers attempt to identify the causes of resistance to change, to work out some joint solutions to specific issues, to produce high-quality results, and to maintain a high degree of motivation among their personnel.

Notes

1.   Jay Hall and Martha Williams, *Styles of Management Inventory*. (The Woodlands, TX: Teleometrics Int'l.).

2.   Ibid.

Bibliography

Educational Systems and Designs. *Management Models—The Communication Process*. Westport, CT: Educational Systems and Designs, 1967.

Discussion Questions

1.   What problems exist in police agencies because people are not adequately trained in the use of effective communication methods?

2.   What might you do to be a more effective communicator?

3.   Can the Johari Window be applied to law enforcement?

4.   Using the Johari Window as a reference, what kind of shapes exist in the average police agency today?

5.   How might the communicative process best be strengthened within the police department, between the police commanders and other members of the criminal justice system, and between members of the police department and the community?

6.   Regarding certain managerial styles—such as 9-9, 5-5, and 9-1—what would be the appropriate communication practice to make each style of management most effective?

Organizational Environment | 6

Introduction

The study of organizational behavior is a search for answers to perplexing questions about human nature. What motivates people? How can the police manager make the best use of the behavior patterns found within organizations? Recognizing the importance of the human element in organizational behavior, this chapter will attempt to develop a framework for police managers that can help them understand their employees better, enable them to determine the "whys" of past behavior patterns, and, if possible, allow them to predict, change, and control behavior patterns.

Police managers, having different types of personnel within their departments, must attempt to mold their people into productive units so that higher objectives may be set and reached. Only through the understanding of human behavior as it relates to the organization can managers make the most effective use of personnel within their departments.

An issue continually faced by police managers is that of motivation. Many managers believe it is part of their job to help motivate subordinates; indeed, the author's own studies show that there are three essential aspects to developing motivated, highly productive officers. First, assuming that the officer has the ability, he or she needs time to grow and develop; such time can be granted by the police manager. Second, officers need knowledge. This can be provided by the police manager through individual and group training programs. The third and most important ingredient is desire, or motivation. This must come from within the individual. Without such motivation, the employee cannot be expected to grow and develop.

How, then, does a manager motivate employees? Usually we attempt, as managers, to serve as examples to our subordinates. Police managers must be keenly aware that their performance is linked to the goals they seek. However, these goals are also controlled by the officers' performance. For example, a police officer who wishes to work in a certain patrol unit to gain extra time for continuing education would have a high performance level because he or she is strongly motivated to gain the potential reward. The manager, in turn, might work closely with the officer, giving him or her additional responsibilities for the ultimate outcome of higher productivity within the patrol unit. Because the two goals—that of the officer and that of the manager—are consistent, the manager's goals will probably be met and the employee would be considered to be highly motivated. However, once the individual officer's goal ceases to be important—if, for example, the officer were to drop out of school, graduate, or possibly transfer to another shift where he or she cannot attend school—his or her performance level would probably drop. It is important for the manager to sit down with subordinates and discuss personal goals—that is, their reasons for working—and, whenever they are consistent with the manager's goals, help them to achieve these goals.

As stated previously the officer's individual performance depends on ability as well as the drive or desire to succeed. It is also influenced by the officer's attitude, experience, and training. Assuming that an individual has ability, there will be a direct relationship between the manager's performance and goals and those of the individual officers. If motivation comes from within each individual, the police leader can play an important role in helping individual officers to achieve their ultimate goals.

In addressing the issue of motivation, the police manager must be careful not to attribute false motives to the behavior of others. Normally, when new behavior is distinctive—that is, when an officer has performed well in the past but now suddenly changes his or her pattern of behavior—there is a tendency to attribute this change to factors within the officer. If, however, such a change in behavior is exhibited by several officers, the tendency would be to attribute this to external conditions and to take measures to improve the situation. Although it is possible to make certain assumptions about motivation, such assumptions must be tested by exploring them on a one-to-one basis. The police manager must understand that the greater the psychological difference between manager and subordinates, the more likely it is that motivational problems will be blamed on the officers. By being aware of individual differences, the police manager can check his or her assumptions and thus arrive at more effective final decisions.

Principles of Motivation

There are several motivational principles that the police manager should be aware of and understand. First, people cannot motivate other people. If a person is assigned a certain responsibility in the police department, three factors exist. The person needs knowledge to do a good job, the person needs time to grow and develop, and the person needs the internal desire to really want to perform. The police manager can provide the knowledge and the time, but the best he or she can do is to open the doors so that the desires of this officer can be achieved.

The second principle states that all people are motivated, but they act for their individual reasons, not necessarily for the reasons given by the police manager. The third principle is that a person's strength, when overused, may become their weakness. For example, a police captain may have a great sense of humor, but if everything becomes a joke he or she will not be respected as a true leader and much of the good knowledge he or she has to offer may be discounted by the members of the department.

The last principle can be stated in this way: If I know more about you than you know about me, I can control the flow of communication. However, if I know more about you than you know about yourself, I can control *you*. For example, if I understand that you are the kind of individual who does not like to interact very much with people on a daily basis, then I can assign you to a planning and research position that may not require that kind of activity. If I place you in an appropriate position, I can achieve high levels of success. Alternatively, I could assign you to a public speaking position in community relations and end up burning you out in a short period of time. You might not fully recognize exactly what my intentions as a police manager might be, but by knowing as much as possible about you and what it is that you desire, I can control your degree of success and how quickly you might burn out.

Hierarchy of Effective Communication

Dr. Abraham Maslow described human behavior in terms of human needs. He developed a five-step hierarchy outlining these needs and emphasized that this system is the source of all motivation. In essence, as the first need is satisfied, the person then moves on to the second, then to the third, to the fourth, and finally the fifth. If a manager wants to motivate his or her personnel, the manager's actions must fit the needs of the employee. According to Maslow, only the unsatisfied needs become sources of motivation. Furthermore, having satisfied one level of need to some degree, an employee will advance to the next level. Certain conditions, however, may cause an individual to go back to his or her primary needs. For example, if an individual is satisfied with his or her present income, then the basic and safety needs are being met. However, if that employee loses his or her job, then the basic needs become primary until a new job is found.

Maslow has suggested that people have five basic needs that account for most of their behavior (see Figure 6.1). He goes on to say that although the need may never receive total and complete satisfaction, there must be a degree of satisfaction before the need ceases to affect behavior. Once this minimum degree is reached, satisfaction is acquired and the person moves on to experience the potential associated with the next level.

Harris, Thomas H. *I'm O.K.—You're O.K.* New York: Avon Books, 1967.

James, Muriel. *The O.K. Boss*. Reading, MA: Addison-Wesley, 1976.

James, Muriel and Jongeward, Dorothy. *Born to Win*. Reading, MA: Addison-Wesley, 1971.

Jongeward, Dorothy, et al. *Everybody Wins, Transactional Analysis Applied to Organizations*. Reading, MA: Addison-Wesley, 1974.

Jongeward, Dorothy and James, Muriel. *Winning with People: Group Exercises in Transactional Analysis*. Reading, MA: Addison-Wesley, 1973.

Meininger, Jut. *Success Through Transactional Analysis*. New York: Signet Books, 1973.

Steiner, Claude. *Games Alcoholics Play*. New York: Ballantine Books, 1971.

_____. *Scripts People Live*. New York: Bantam Books, 1974.

Discussion Questions

1. What are some common statements heard around a police department?

2. Do these statements usually come from the parent, adult, or child ego state?

3. What kinds of transactions exist in the daily operation of the police department?

4. Which ego state is most commonly used by police managers and which ego state in their subordinates do they normally address?

5. Give an example of an ulterior transaction between a middle manager in a police department and the police chief.

6. What life position does most criminal behavior stem from?

7. What life position does most police behavior stem from?

8. What are some examples of negative strokes given in police work?

9. What are some examples of positive strokes that a police officer or police manager might receive?

10. What techniques might a police manager use to give as many positive strokes as possible?

11. Should a police manager ever give negative strokes?

12. What are some typical games that are played in police departments?

13. How do most police managers structure their time as defined by transactional analysis?

Figure 6.1 **Maslow's Hierarchy of Needs**

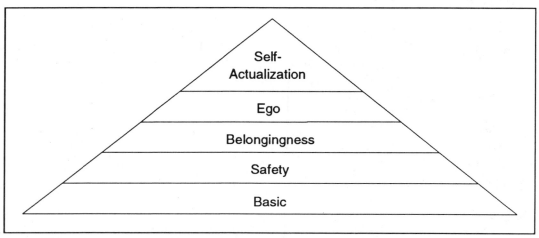

SOURCE: Abraham H. Maslow, *Motivation and Personality* (New York: Harper & Row, Publishers, 1954).

Basic Needs

The bottom level of the hierarchy refers to the need for food and shelter. These basic needs have, for the most part, been satisfied in contemporary society. As they pertain to employees within a police department, these needs are sometimes reflected in the desire for added personal property and an increased salary—both directed toward increasing comfort. Once the officers receive adequate satisfaction of their basic needs through wages sufficient to enable them to live comfortably, they begin to move upward in the hierarchy.

Most police departments today, especially those in and around major population areas, provide adequately for the basic needs of their officers. Many rural police agencies, however, are still struggling with sixty- and seventy-hour work weeks as well as with salaries that place their officers in lower income brackets. Until these problems are overcome, these agencies will have difficulty in progressing to professional standards.

Safety Needs

Once an officer has received adequate satisfaction of her basic needs, awareness of the safety need is developed. She focuses on security, protection, and avoiding harm and risk. Within the police profession, the officer becomes concerned with issues such as fringe benefits, hospitalization insurance, retirement and pension plans, and consistent performance standards. Officers concerned with safety needs are likely to be unimaginative, constantly complaining, and lacking in creativity in their work activities. They generally exhibit little or no flexibility. Strict adherence to rules and regulations is important to these officers. The police department and police managers who overemphasize the upgrading of fringe benefits are, in essence, attempting to motivate the officers by satisfying their safety need. If, however, the safety need of the majority of the personnel is adequately satisfied, a different form of motivation is necessary. This is not to de-emphasize the need or the necessity of satisfying it, but only to caution police managers not to devote all their motivation programs to the satisfaction of this need to the exclusion of the next three.

Belongingness Needs

The third level of the need hierarchy deals with the desire of the officer for membership within a department, for acceptance by fellow officers, and for the feeling of belonging to an organizational family. These needs are manifested in the officer's wish for friendly peers with whom he can develop personal relationships. The police manager is beginning to find that through the creation and implementation of team-type policing, this need to belong is satisfied in members of the department.

The officer will usually look first to the organization for satisfaction of this need. If, however, his need cannot be met within the department, he will then become involved with a formal or informal group established either inside or outside the agency. This need to belong or social need has often been satisfied through active participation in chapters of the Fraternal Order of Police or through other social groups closely related to the activities of the police department. By instituting activities designed to reach organizational goals, the police managers can often direct the enthusiasm and creativity of their personnel to benefit the department rather than losing these energies to outside interests.

Ego Status Needs

Once the officer has satisfied the need to belong, she generally demonstrates interest in achieving some special recognition or status for her contribution to the department. Some police departments have attempted to satisfy this need through the creation of such systems as the "officer of the month," by special commendations and awards, or by giving the officer added responsibility. This ego status need usually drives the officer to find opportunities to show her competence, hoping that she will reap recognition from peers as well as achieve some material reward. These factors motivate the officer to contribute as much as possible to the organization in order to be recognized by its members. Usually, the officer attempts to receive assignments that are recognized as the more challenging within the department. For example, some officers strive for assignment to specialized investigative units such as homicide or to administrative activities such as planning so that their contributions to the growth of the department will be immediately recognized.

Self-Actualization Needs

Although the ego status needs are difficult to meet and their satisfaction is not often enduring, there are cases in which these needs have been adequately met and the individual moves to the highest level of the hierarchy. At this level, the officer is concerned about improving his self-concept. He needs assignments that are challenging and meaningful, allowing the officer to be as creative as possible. The officer must be able to achieve a sense of growth and satisfaction through the performance of these activities. Self-actualization focuses on the personal satisfaction the officer receives from work. At this stage he usually seeks out assignments that involve risk taking and experimentation. Behavior patterns on the self-actualization level generally foster innovative and creative projects and provide the officer with a higher degree of self-satisfaction. The behavior prompted by this need produces the mature and constructive contributions necessary for the accomplishment of the degree of professionalism sought by contemporary police departments.

In summary, the police manager's role is a complex one. The manager must first assess his or her own motivating needs and then those of his or her subordinates. Only through these assessments can the police manager truly motivate and most effectively utilize the personnel under his or her command.

It is the police manager's role to assist the staff through the hierarchy of needs. Generally, when a police chief examines his or her officers and finds them fixed at one of the lower levels, a careful analysis of the reason for this fixation may indicate that the constraints or barriers to reaching the next level are imposed by the structure of the organization and not by the quality of the personnel.

In testing police employees, a correlation has been found between Maslow's hierarchy of needs and the needs expressed by some of the officers. The highest need expressed was usually that of the ego, with the second being safety or security. Self-actualization was usually placed third. The expression of such needs, however, depended a great deal on the individual agencies tested. Where there were feelings of worth on the part of individual officers and managers, ego and self-actualization needs were higher. But where pay was higher than average, even though officers did not feel trusted or respected, the safety or security needs were rated highest.

Motivation-Hygiene Theory

The more mature the individuals become, the more important become their ego and self-actualization needs. During the 1950s, Frederick Herzberg conducted a series of studies emphasizing the difference between maintenance factors and motivation factors. His studies further dramatized Maslow's findings. As a result of Herzberg's studies, a theory of organizational behavior and motivation was developed.

Herzberg collected data on job attitudes from which assumptions concerning human behavior could be made. The motivation-hygiene theory was the result of his studies. More than 200 professional people were interviewed in an attempt to isolate the activities that gave job satisfaction from those that brought job dissatisfaction. From the information obtained by the studies, Herzberg defined two different categories of needs, independent of each other, that affect employee behavior in different ways. He found that if there was dissatisfaction, the employee emphasized the environment in which he or she worked. If, however, employees were satisfied with their jobs, they usually became more productive and had a stronger desire to help the organization grow. Herzberg titled the first category needs "Hygiene Factors" and the second category "Motivators," feeling that satisfaction of the second category of needs brought about superior performance.

Herzberg listed such issues as policies, procedures, administrative practices, techniques of supervision, working conditions, interpersonal relations, salaries, and security as hygiene factors. These may not be intrinsic parts of every police officer's job, but they are surely related to the conditions under which the officer must perform. Herzberg believed that hygiene factors do not produce growth in the individual or increase work output, but they do prevent losses in performance.

He defined as motivators the sense of achievement, challenge, professional growth, and recognition. Herzberg's use of the term *motivator* stresses that these factors have some positive effect on the employee, resulting in increased job satisfaction as well as total output capacity (see Figure 6.2).

There is a close relationship between Herzberg's theory of motivation and the hierarchy of needs developed by Maslow. Maslow refers to needs and motives; Herzberg deals with the goals and incentives that tend to satisfy these needs.

Wages would satisfy these needs at the basic level, and fringe benefits would satisfy them at the security or safety level. Interpersonal relations techniques are examples of hygiene factors that lead to satisfaction of social needs, whereas increasing employees' responsibility and authority, assigning them challenging work, and helping them to grow and develop are motivators that bring about organizational behavior and satisfy needs at the ego and self-actualization levels.

Figure 6.2 **Herzberg's Motivation-Hygiene Theory**

Hygiene Factors	*Motivators*
Salary	Challenging assignments
Fringe benefits	Increased responsibility
Security (civil service)	Recognition for work
Rules and regulations	Individual growth
Supervision	

The basic, safety, and social needs, as well as a part of the ego needs, are hygiene factors within an organization. The ego needs are divided because there is a difference between status and recognition for a job well done. Status may be defined as the position one occupies through seniority, by promotions, or as payment for a political debt. Therefore, the status position would not reflect the individual's personal achievements or provide recognition for what he or she has earned. Recognition, as opposed to status, is gained only through the competence and achievement of the individual. It is earned by the individual and granted by others. Recognition is classified as an ego need and, along with the self-actualization needs, is defined and classified by Herzberg as a motivator.

Hygiene factors relieve pain. They deal with the question, "How well do you treat the men and women of the police department?" Motivators, on the other hand, provide the opportunity to achieve and grow. They deal with the question, "How well do you use employees or police officers' skills?"

The relationship between Herzberg's and Maslow's theories are shown in Figure 6.3.

Figure 6.3 **Comparison of Maslow's and Herzberg's Theories**

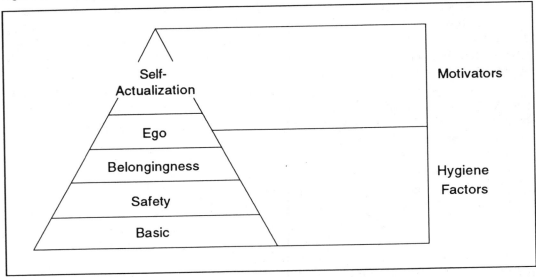

The dynamics of hygiene is that people strive for avoidance of pain. Another dynamic is that there are an infinite number of sources of hygiene, and as a result no police manager will ever satisfy every hygiene factor within the police department. Even when they are solved they have a short-term effect. For example, a pay raise does not satisfy people except for a specific period of time. Hygiene factors are cyclical in nature. They have a tendency to continually arise and have to be dealt with over the span of a specific time. The typical example is the purchasing of new vehicles. Within a few years the department may again have to face the purchasing of newer equipment to keep up the performance of the police officers.

Hygiene factors have what is called an *escalating zero point*. If last year they received a 5 percent pay raise, then they will strive heavily to achieve at least 5 percent, preferably higher, in the second year. This factor is demonstrated in the tactics that unions use in negotiating. In many instances police unions would like to negotiate last with the city so that they can use as a minimum base the same percentages given to others in city government. For example, if the fire department receives a 7 percent pay raise, the police union immediately begins with a minimum of 7 percent.

The police manager must recognize that a dynamic of the hygiene factors is that there is no final answer. There is no way that a police manager will ever know that he or she has satisfied every hygiene factor in the agency.

There are dynamics about motivation as well. Motivators bring growth. They allow individuals to personally grow in the agency as a result. Motivaton has a limited number of satisfiers, but this limited number has a long-term effect and is cumulative to the individual. That is, if the manager gives responsibility to a subordinate, for example, a captain or a sergeant, then gives additional responsibility six months later, that individual becomes motivated and the second added responsibility, assuming it is one that is desired, creates even stronger, lasting motivation.

Although there are answers for motivators, in many instances they become hampered by antiquated personnel and fiscal management rules.

Sometimes, however, the police manager finds it difficult to recognize the difference between hygiene and motivating factors.

As an example, let us examine the case of a police officer who is highly motivated and performing at 70 percent of his ability. He is satisfied with the existing police structure—the working conditions as well as the personal relationships with his supervisors. In fact, the officer has previously been involved in making important decisions affecting his job. Then the police manager transfers the officer's supervisor, and the new supervisor and the officer develop personality differences. In fact, the officer feels that he is better qualified to perform the supervisor's job, and he begins to resent the supervisor's larger salary—which actually covers a smaller workload. How, then, will this situation affect the police officer's behavior? The officer's performance and productivity depend on his ability, independence, and motivation. The unsatisfied hygiene needs for a supervisory position and the higher salary may restrict his output, resulting in a drop from a 70 percent capacity, for instance, to a 40 percent level. Even if the officer eventually finds a supervisor with whom he can work, and even if he receives a pay increase, his productivity will generally increase only to the original level of 70 percent. As a result, management has satisfied the hygiene factors for the officer but has succeeded only in restoring his productivity to its original level.

Conversely, if the same officer is still working at a 70 percent capacity, is satisfied with his working conditions, and is allowed to mature and to satisfy his motivational needs and his ego and self-actualization needs, a growth in productivity will take place. If the officer is allowed to exercise some initiative and creativity in handling his own problems, in accepting responsibility and authority, and in making as many decisions as possible, the result is that he matures and increases his ability. Although still working at a 70 percent capacity, his productivity has greatly increased.

Therefore, if the police manager is careful to see that the hygiene factors and the basic safety and social needs of the employees are satisfied, he or she can then take the time and effort to stress the motivating factors to satisfy the ego and self-actualization needs. Although the officer may still only perform at 70 percent capacity, his productivity will increase due to the encouragement and challenge offered by the manager.

Police managers will find that when hygiene needs are satisfied, dissatisfaction and work restriction will also be reduced but the individual will have little desire for achieving superior performance. If, however, the police manager emphasizes satisfaction of the motivating factors and allows the individual officer to grow and develop, then he or she will witness an improvement in the officer's productivity as well as in the quality of his or her work.

Prior to Herzberg, most behavioral scientists dealing with worker motivation emphasized what is termed *job enlargement.* The theory of job enlargement assumes that if the employees are given an increase in the number of tasks similar to or identical to those they are presently doing, they will gain more satisfaction from their jobs.

Herzberg disagreed with the job enlargement theory. He argued that to satisfy the worker's motivation factors, management must take the responsibility of enriching the job as well as expanding it. If the officer writes crime and traffic reports and then is allowed to write juvenile, property, and missing persons reports, the officer will be no more satisfied than if he or she had remained restricted to writing only one or two types of reports. Job enrichment, on the other hand, implies that the officer is given the challenge of added responsibilities in all of his or her activities.

The attempt to implement motivating factors to enrich the officer's job does not always succeed in completely satisfying ego and self-actualization needs. If the police department hires an officer whose ability exceeds the demands of the police job, then job enrichment would have no effect in satisfying ego or self-actualization needs. Therefore, job enrichment must be equal to the ability of the police officer. If, for example, an officer is selected, trained, and prepared to deal with problems on a day-to-day basis and then is assigned to push the button to open the jail for eight hours a day, even the further step of enriching the job by adding the responsibility of walking the floors once an hour will not serve as a motivating factor.

Herzberg's studies of motivation produced interesting observations, which in some ways support Maslow's position and in other ways suggest that the satisfaction of lower-level needs may have different results than will the satisfaction of higher-level needs.

Herzberg asked thousands of employees to describe situations that resulted in their feeling exceptionally good about their jobs. They were asked if the feelings of satisfaction in their work had affected their performance, their personal relationships, and their well-being. Finally, the nature of the sequence of events that served to return the workers' attitudes to normal were elicited. Following this sequence, the interview was repeated, asking respondents to describe events that made them feel exceptionally bad about their jobs.

Events were evaluated in terms of situations that led to feelings of dissatisfaction. They were defined in terms of whether the effect was long or short. "Long term" was defined as two weeks or longer.

They identified five major factors that helped produce satisfaction. These included achievement, recognition, the work itself, responsibility, and advancement. They identified the five major factors that led to dissatisfaction. These included policies, supervision, salary levels, interpersonal relationships, and working conditions. Salary, however, was generally considered to be both a satisfier and a dissatisfier, depending on the way the money itself was used. For example, a 10 percent pay raise that keeps officers more or less at their present level both in terms of their work and of living standards tends to be seen as not bringing about dissatisfaction. However, a large pay increase—as might result from taking another job—is sometimes viewed as a satisfier because it allows the recipient to use the money for some specific growth goals such as furthering a child's education.

In studies of police personnel at the supervisory, middle-management, and management levels, the following results were noticed. Personnel at the lower levels of the department have a tendency to rank the following five factors as strong motivators: (1) feeling of achievement from doing a challenging job, (2) the inner need to do a good job, (3) doing work that they felt was important, (4) having personal work-related goals, and (5) doing interesting work. Managers, on the other hand, ranked the following as the factors that they believed to be most motivating to subordinates: (1) doing work that they felt was important, (2) recognition and appreciation from supervisors and managers (the item ranked tenth by police officers), and (3) recognition from peers (ranked twelfth by subordinates). The possibility of promotion was ranked fourth by managers and sixth by officers. There is a slight difference, although recognition seems to play an important role in the eyes of both managers and police officers. The nature of the job itself is a motivating force for police officers, although such work-related motivation is not viewed as highly significant by police managers.

Theory X and Theory Y

Theory X and Theory Y were developed by Douglas McGregor during the 1950s. According to McGregor, the traditional organization is one that emphasizes centralized decisionmaking and reflects the pyramid structure typical of most law enforcement agencies. It was McGregor's belief that traditional managers share certain basic assumptions, which he labeled Theory X. He has defined these assumptions in the following way:

1. It is management's role to organize resources—money, equipment, personnel—in a structure that requires close supervision of all employees and brings about maximum control. (The recommendation of one police sergeant for every eight police officers, without any regard to the ability of the officers or the sergeant, is an example of the Theory X type of control.)

2. It is management's responsibility to direct the efforts of the personnel of the agency, keeping them motivated, controlling all their actions, and modifying their behavior to fit the needs of the organization.

3. If management's staff does not take an active part in controlling the behavior of the employees, the employees will be passive, even resistant, to the needs of the organization.

4. The average employee is, by nature, lazy and will work as little as possible, as work is inherently distasteful to him or her.

5. The average employee lacks ambition, dislikes responsibility and authority, and prefers taking orders to being independent.

6. The employee is basically self-centered, has no feeling for organizational needs, and must be closely controlled and even coerced in order to achieve organizational objectives.

7. By nature, the average employee resists change.

8. The average employee does not have the ability to solve problems creatively.

Most police departments use these assumptions as a basis for developing rules and regulations. Police departments occasionally develop organizational structures in which a superior closely supervises each subordinate. Furthermore, most of the police manager's time is spent checking and rechecking the daily activities of immediate subordinates. The widespread practice of allowing patrol officers to perform only menial duties and of assigning any tasks that require intelligence to the detectives or so-called specialized units is often viewed by personnel in the agencies as the practice of Theory X.

One of the first questions that police managers must ask themselves is whether the assumptions of Theory X are appropriate for use in running police agencies today. Educational and living standards in our country have risen immensely in the past decade. Among police officers today, the motivation for pay increases has greatly decreased.

Theory X assumptions about police officers are, for the most part, inaccurate. Many police agencies, in implementing such theories and assumptions, create serious management trouble, generally resulting in their failure to motivate personnel toward the achievement of departmental goals. Management by strong, centralized control will not usually succeed in our society. Theory X managers motivate people by attempting to satisfy basic and safety needs. Most people today, however, have reasonably satisfied these needs and seek motivation directed toward fulfilling belonging, ego, and self-actualization needs.

Douglas McGregor also developed a second theory of human behavior, called Theory Y, based on the assumption that it is management's role to unleash the potential of every member of the organization. If the individual can be properly motivated to obtain his or her own goals through the achievement of organizational goals, then the agency can be extremely effective.

McGregor's assumptions regarding Theory Y managers are:

1. It is management's role to organize resources—money, material, equipment, personnel—to reach organizational goals.

2. Work can be an enjoyable part of one's life if the conditions are favorable.

3. People are not by nature lazy, passive, or resistant to the needs of the organization but have become so as a result of their experience working within the organization.

4. Management does not place the potential for development within the employee. Motivation, capacity for accepting responsibility, and willingness to work toward organizational goals are present within the individual. It is then management's responsibility to recognize this potential and allow the individual the freedom to develop his or her abilities.

5. People possess creativity and can solve organizational problems if encouraged by management.

6. The essential task of management is to develop organizational conditions and operational procedures that will encourage individuals to attain their goals by directing their efforts toward organizational goals and objectives.

Police managers who accept Theory Y assumptions usually have (1) fewer levels in their departmental hierarchies, (2) controls with broad guidelines, and (3) minimal first-line supervision of police activities. The Theory Y police agency gives increased autonomy to middle management, first-line supervisors, and police officers. Allowing personnel to develop the projects and programs involves them in identifying and overcoming obstacles to their goals. Police officers under a Theory Y organization achieve satisfaction for their ego and self-actualization needs.

Some police departments allow individual police officers to become involved in activities such as planning and problem resolution on a daily basis. For example, the agencies implementing "management by objectives"—in which top management has clearly defined the major objectives of the department for the coming year and has advised middle management and first-line supervisors of these objectives—assign the individual projects to the squads for development. Departments implementing Theory Y involve officers in many management functions such as developing training programs, hiring personnel, and even assisting in the preparation of budgets. Some police agencies are finding that police officers are as satisfied by their jobs as they are by their hobbies and recreation. As a result, officers are spending off-duty hours preparing for the implementation of projects within their agencies. The police role begins to take on a different meaning to the officers and they, in turn, lighten the load of management.

Immaturity-Maturity Theory

As a result of the outdated management practices of many police departments and their emphasis on Theory X assumptions, the law enforcement profession still treats many police officers as immature.

During the 1950s, Chris Argyris conducted extensive studies of industrial organizations to determine the effect of management practices on the personal growth of the employees within the organization. Argyris listed seven changes that should occur in the employee's personality if he or she is to develop into a mature person and be an asset to the organization (see Figure 6.4).

First, individuals move from a passive state as infants to increased activity as adults. Second, as mature, thinking adults, they develop from a state of dependence on others to one of independence. Third, they increase their number of behavior patterns. Fourth, they move from erratic, casual, and shallow interests to deeper and stronger interests in specific directions. Fifth, the mature adult develops a time frame that includes the past, present, and future, as opposed to the child's frame, which emphasizes only the present.

Figure 6.4 **Seven Changes in Employees**

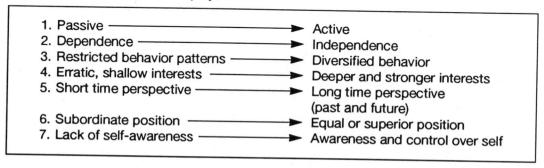

1. Passive ⟶ Active
2. Dependence ⟶ Independence
3. Restricted behavior patterns ⟶ Diversified behavior
4. Erratic, shallow interests ⟶ Deeper and stronger interests
5. Short time perspective ⟶ Long time perspective (past and future)
6. Subordinate position ⟶ Equal or superior position
7. Lack of self-awareness ⟶ Awareness and control over self

Sixth, as children they are subordinate to almost everyone, but as adults they assume equal or superior status to others. Finally, as children they lack self-awareness, but as adults they understand and are able to control themselves. Argyris postulated that these changes are normal and healthy, and they bring the individual from immaturity to maturity.

The major point is that although people rarely develop to the state of full maturity, as they grow older and learn from their experiences, they constantly move toward the maturity end of the continuum.

In many police departments, managers sometimes question the maturity of the personnel or even their desire to become mature. Apathy begins to spread through the department, and management immediately accuses the workers of being lazy and of having no interest in their jobs. Generally, when individuals come to work for an organization such as a government bureaucracy, the management practices utilized by the agency actually prohibit the employees from obtaining maturity. In many police departments, the individual police officers are given minimal control over their respective job assignments and, in fact, are encouraged to be dependent on and subordinate to the first-line supervisors and middle managers. As a result, these adults begin to behave immaturely, which, according to the assumptions of Theory X, is how many police agencies expect them to act.

The formal organizational structure of many police bureaucracies often forces the employee to remain immature. The emphasis of the organizational structure is toward fitting the individual to the job. The design for the organization always comes first, and this design is usually based on the concepts of scientific management-task specialization, chain of command, and span of control. Many police agencies attempt to increase the efficiency of the organization by using the police officers as interchangeable parts within the total structure.

Basic to these concepts is the fact that the authority and power to run the department rests in the hands of a very few individuals who are at the top of the organization and who make all major and most minor decisions. These decisions are usually made with little input from middle management and no input from the lower links in the chain of command. In fact, those at the bottom of the chain are strictly controlled by their superiors and by the rigidity of the system itself. Specialization of many police activities has resulted in the oversimplification of the duties, which soon become repetitive, routine, and unchallenging. This implies that in the task-oriented leadership of many police departments, supervisors and managers make frequent decisions about the work, and the police officers are responsible only for carrying out these decisions. As a result, the agencies have been overloaded with control measures such as strict budget practices, a performance evaluation system, and numerous other operating procedures that attempt to standardize operations so that initiative and creativity are carefully restricted.

This formal structure has led to certain assumptions about human nature that are directly opposed to promoting the maturation of the individual. In the Theory X type of police departments, the needs of the mature employees cannot be satisfied due to the inflexibility of the formal organizational structure within which they must work. New police officers soon recognize that Theory X assumptions prevail and that management has designated childlike roles for them, thus frustrating their natural development. The officers are forced to turn to outside activities for fulfillment, to leave the department, or to change their profession.

The present challenge to police managers is to provide a work climate in which every employee has the opportunity to mature, both as an individual and as a member of the department. However, the police manager must believe that individuals can be essentially self-directed and creative in their work environments if they are motivated by management. Implicit here is the manager's acceptance of Theory Y and the Argyris theory, which allow the individual to grow from immaturity to maturity.

Management Systems

As a result of behavioral research studies of numerous industrial organizational structures, Rensis Likert developed a definition of management styles on a continuum ranging from System 1 through System 4.

System 1

Under System 1, management is seen as having no confidence or trust in its personnel and seldom involving them in any part of the decision-making process. Top management makes a large majority of the decisions, sets the goals, and then issues rules, regulations, and orders through the chain of command. Subordinates are kept in line by the use of fear, threats, or occasionally by a reward, such as a letter of commendation. The emphasis within this system is on satisfying basic and safety needs. Usually any contact between the superior and the subordinate is brought about through the alleged mistakes or misconduct of the subordinate. The relationship between the first-line supervisor and the workers is usually one of fear and mistrust.

The trend in police departments today is to move away from System 1 and toward the other end of the continuum. However, some police organizations still place the control process in the hands of top management. This has affected the development of strong informal organizations within the agency, which, in many instances, oppose the goals of the formal structure. Most of the manager's time within System 1 police departments is spent in preventing conflict between the formal and informal structures.

System 2

The System 2 type of management places some confidence and trust in the lower-level police officers, but the structure still retains many qualities of a master–servant relationship. Most of the decision making and goal setting occurs at the top of the organization. However, management has a structure through which input can be received from the lower levels, and it even allows the lower levels to make some of the less important decisions. Rewards and actual or potential punishments are the tools used to motivate employees. Usually the manager's relationship to the police officer is viewed as distrustful. Police departments with System 2 characteristics will usually have some communication between the top, middle, and lower levels, but generally the upward communication is carefully screened to feed information to middle and upper management that the lower level thinks they want to hear. The superiors still inject a large amount of fear and caution in their subordinates. Under System 2, the police department's control process begins to be delegated to the middle and lower levels. The informal organization existing in System 1 police agencies is still present, but it is not usually in direct conflict with the formal organizational goals.

System 3

Police departments under System 3 demonstrate substantial but incomplete trust between management and subordinates. More decisions are made at the lower levels, but policies and high-level decisions still remain in the hands of those at the top. Communication flows both upward and downward, and rewards and occasional punishment are used to generate in the officer a greater interest in department goals. Because the amount of interaction between superior and subordinate broadens under System 3, confidence and trust begin to develop. Both the higher and lower levels feel responsible for controlling organizational activities. If informal organizations do develop within System 3 police agencies, they will either support them or give them only a partial resistance to their goals.

System 4

Under System 4, the management practices of the police department clearly indicate complete confidence and trust in the subordinates by top management and middle management personnel. Decisionmaking, although well integrated, is widely dispersed and made throughout the department. Communication flows not only up and down the structure but also horizontally among the peers. There is much participation and involvement in establishing goals; in improving techniques, methods, and operations; and in evaluating the success of the organization. There are friendly relations between supervisors and subordinates at all levels of the organization. The control process flows from the lower units to the top, and all levels are as fully involved as possible in decisionmaking. The informal structure, if one develops, usually supports the formal organizational structure. As a result, the social forces that develop within the department support the efforts to achieve its goals and objectives.

In summary, System 1 may be defined as a highly structured, autocratic type of management, whereas System 4 is based on more participation, teamwork, and mutual trust within the hierarchy. Systems 2 and 3 are the intermediate stages between the two extremes, which closely approximate the assumptions of Theory X and Theory Y.

Expectancy Theory

The expectancy theory states that performance is a function of the officer's ability multiplied by the motivation itself. Ability is a function of the officer's aptitude multiplied by training and experience.

Performance is a function of the individual's ability, plus desire and perception. The police manager recognizes that personnel of the department will reach high levels of performance if they first have the ability. That is, they have been trained and have the necessary skills. The second element is desire. This requires a will on the part of the individual to perform. And finally, there is perception. That is, the following question is answered: If I give effort can I meet my expectations?

Officers have expectancies about the likelihood that any effort they put forth will lead to intended behavior on the part of other people. They also have an expectancy about the likelihood that their outcomes will follow as a result of their behavior. An officer's motivation to perform in a particular way will be influenced by his or her expectancies about trying to perform at that level and the attractiveness of the goals involved. The police manager must consider that if the expectancy of an officer performing at a particular level is low, or the probability that the outcomes will be negative, then motivation to perform will be low and the goals of the agency may not be met.

Figure 6.5 **Expectancy Formula Theory**

Performance = Ability (Training) x Desire (Motivation) x Perception Expectation

My Performance [Your Performance—Your Outcome] My Outcome

The police manager also performs using the expectancy theory formula (see Figure 6.5). The police manager says, "If I perform in a certain way, will I achieve my outcome?" However, the performance of others depends on the goals that the others seek. Consider the police manager who desires an effective police department so that he or she can be considered a good leader and his or her officers who desire a decent standard of living. If, due to economic difficulties and political reality, the salary and benefits for the officers are low, they do not feel obligated to perform at a high level because their goals will not be achieved. Another example would be where the police manager wants to produce leaders for the future. The goal he or she strives for is a continuation of the values, beliefs, and principles presently exhibited by the leader. If he or she determines that the managers in the police department seek a higher skill level in dealing with other people, learning fiscal management responsibilities, and planning skills—and he or she provides them with these skills—they in turn will perform at a higher level, not just because of the training they have received, but because of the perception they have that if they do receive the training they can perform at a higher level, which is something that they personally desire.

The expectation theory is the basis for career development programs and can be implemented by employing five steps. First, the expectations of all parties should be made known. It is easy for each party to define two sets of expectations, the expectations that they have of the other and the expectations that the other has of them. For example, the captain can say to the lieutenant, "I expect you to always be on time and produce credible reports, and you can expect from me to support you and to give you immediate feedback." The lieutenant's expectations of the captain might be that he or she wants support, feedback, and a pay raise. And the expectations that the captain can have of the lieutenant is that he or she will complete reports on time and give his or her best effort. In comparing the expectations, some conflicts will arise. For example, not being able to guarantee a pay raise can be addressed. In addition, this list of expectations can be used as a way to evaluate performance, thereby raising the overall quality of management in the police department (see Figure 6.6).

The second step involves making the work itself valuable. As long as department organizational goals complement the personal goals of people in the agency, the sworn and nonsworn personnel will believe that working toward these goals will help them achieve their goals and as a result there will be a higher level of commitment.

Figure 6.6 **Expectation Agreement**

(Sgt) Expect of You (Deputy)	**You Can Expect of Me (Sgt)**
Be honest	Be straight with you
Be loyal	Be supportive
Complete timely reports	Keep you informed
Adhere to our policies	Compliment and correct you
Dress sharp	Encourage your growth
Be on time	
Live up to your word	
I (Deputy) Expect of You	**You Can Expect of Me (Deputy)**
Be honest with me	Be honest
Maintain open-door policy	Keep you informed
Give me new responsibilities	Know procedures
Support me	Be professional
Keep me informed	Study hard
Respond when I need you	
Involve me in budget preparation	

The third step involves making the work *doable*. Too often the police manager assigns a responsibility without really finding out how the subordinate feels about this added responsibility. Making realistic assignments and asking in advance about what can be achieved by the other person in any specific assignment helps to identify obstacles before they arise.

The fourth step is giving regular feedback. Feedback must be given as quickly as possible after the action taken. It should be specific and should address behaviors that the other person can change.

The last and probably the most important step for the police manager is to reward his or her subordinates when they do meet their agreed-upon expectations.

The factors that help determine a person's expectations and his or her perception of the likelihood of success include self-esteem, experience, the job situation itself, and the ability to share knowledge and receive input from others.

Some of the factors that help determine the likelihood of success include experience in a similar situation, self-esteem, the attractiveness of the goals, the belief in internal versus external control, the actual job situation, and the ability to communicate with others.

Conclusion

This chapter has attempted to examine organizational behavior and the theories of motivation prevalent in contemporary management. Examples have been cited to provide a framework against which police managers may analyze and understand their own organizational behavior. Analyzing and understanding organizational behavior is a necessary start; but only if managers implement decisions and develop their own style of leadership, utilizing the positive side of each theory, will they be able to advance the profession of law enforcement.

Bibliography

Maslow, Abraham H. *Motivation and Personality.* New York: Harper & Row, Publishers, 1954.

Herzberg, Frederick. *Work and the Nature of Man.* New York: World Publishing Company, 1966.

McGregor, Douglas. *The Human Side of Enterprise.* New York: McGraw-Hill Book Company, 1960.

Argyris, Chris. *Personality and Organization.* New York: Harper & Row, Publishers, 1957.

Likert, Rensis. *The Human Organization.* New York: McGraw-Hill Book Company, 1967.

Discussion Questions

1.   What characteristics of team policing enhance the fulfillment of the "need to belong"?

2.   According to Maslow's hierarchy of needs, there are five general steps of needs. Where are most students in this scale today? Where are most police officers? How about the police managers?

3.   How does Herzberg's motivational theory relate to the way cities, counties, and police departments are organized today?

4.   Are most police agencies oriented toward Theory X or Theory Y?

5.   Which is best—Theory X or Theory Y? Should one have a little bit of both? If it is best to accept a bit of both theories, what criteria would you use to decide when to use one approach or the other?

Transactional Analysis ‖ 7

Objectives

1. The student will be able to identify behavioral models and how they affect the overall change process.

2. The student will be able to identify how each of the ego states (parent, adult, and child) operates and to distinguish actions emanating from each ego state.

3. The student will be able to list and identify behaviors stemming from the parent and the child ego states.

4. The student will be able to identify the types of transactions—complementary, crossed, and ulterior.

5. The student will be able to identify the four basic life positions.

6. The student will understand the concept of "stroking" and how it affects police organizations.

7. The student will be able to identify the six ways in which people structure their time.

8. The student will be able to identify organizational games.

Behavioral Models and the Change Process

Throughout this book, there has been a strong emphasis on behavioral models regarding communication, leadership, motivation, and planning. Each of the models can assist the police manager in conceptualizing approaches to organizational problems. In addition, these models provide managers with a variety of approaches for making judgments as to needed changes in policy, procedure, personnel, and their own behavior. All models, however, are only approximations of reality. They are only useful when police

---

Chapter 7 is included with the permission of Dick McMahon.

managers can adapt the model to assist their understanding of the realities of the organizational environment.

Each of the models presented emphasizes the fact that the outcomes, in terms of results and side effects, show wide variance depending on the approach used in a given organizational situation. This emphasis on the dynamic character of organizational behavior highlights the complexity and importance of organizational development approaches to change. Thus, a change in leadership style may affect morale and relationships without having a major impact on production. Effective change comes only through the careful development of all aspects of the organization that influence the outcomes important to the manager. There are many excellent expositions of organizational development approaches. This chapter focuses on the police manager as an object of change and provides a model for conceptualizing this change process.

In most change approaches, the role of top management is singled out as the major force in the change process. Fortunately, most police managers are keenly aware of the importance of their leadership in change efforts. What is often absent, however, is the awareness of how their own personalities and established approaches to interaction with others interfere with their intentions. In many instances, the first change that must occur in the change effort is a change in the behavior of the police manager.

There are few people who believe that significant changes in personalities or behavior can be accomplished by simply "willing" this change. However, most individuals who reach police management positions are reasonably competent, mature individuals capable of effecting behavioral changes in the interest of becoming more effective as managers. Often such changes occur as managers become more observant of their own behavior and more sensitive to the impact of their behavior on others.

This chapter provides a brief overview of a model that offers significant assistance to police managers in understanding their personal reactions and the nature of their interactions with others. With a little effort and study, this approach can provide a conceptual or "thinking" approach to managing personal change. The approach is called *transactional analysis*.

Since the publication of his best-seller *Games People Play*, Eric Berne's psychological approach to human behavior has become more and more influential in a variety of settings in which behavioral change is deemed important.[1] Transactional analysis (TA), as it is presented in this chapter, is a conceptual tool that may assist police managers in developing considerable insight into their own behavior. As a general model, it can assist them in determining the extent to which their behavior and attitudes are consistent with their managerial intent. The terminology used is simple and easily learned. Its effect can be powerful. Most of what Eric Berne says is not new; what is new is that he has taken much of the mystery out of human behavior through a language system to which most people can relate.

Ego States

As a result of broad experiences with both individuals and groups in a variety of treatment settings, Berne became more and more convinced of the importance of analyzing the interactions of individuals in terms of the way they go about obtaining satisfaction of their needs. He was particularly impressed by the fact that individuals in their interactions with others exhibit behavior that is, at times, reminiscent of childlike behaviors, at other times like behaviors one might expect from one's parents, and at other times rational and mature behaviors. Berne saw all these behaviors as psychological realities representing different states of the *self* or *ego*. Basically, the ego states are thought to be much like the sound tracks on a tape and, depending on which track is activated by the situation, the police manager responds accordingly. Managers have learned to relate various behaviors to feelings and situations that they have previously experienced. When these "tapes" are turned on, they respond with the behaviors that they have used to deal with these feelings in the past.

As a result of a person's unique personal development, his or her feelings, reactions, attitudes, and experiences become organized into three major influence systems or *ego states*. These ego states are referred to as *parent, adult,* and *child* to call attention to the fact that the origins of their development come from different life experiences. If we know the nature of the experiences and feelings that make up each of these ego states, we can describe a given personality.

Transactional analysis is based on the belief that the ego states are consistent patterns of feelings and experiences faithfully recorded in the nervous system and evoked by stimulus situations we experience. It is the analysis of how the manager interacts with others in relation to these ego states that is important in the understanding of human behavior. Most managers have the capacity to identify many of the feelings and behaviors associated with each of the ego states. Through such analysis, police managers can develop the capacity to monitor these behaviors and work toward more effective performance. These ego states are shown in Figure 7.1.

Parent Ego State

The parent ego state contains all the attitudes, ideas, postures, gestures, habits, and reaction tendencies that were learned from parents, grandparents, older siblings, or other influential figures in the individual's life. Many of the assumptions, attitudes, ideas, and behaviors that are characteristic of the parent ego state were learned through modeling and were incorporated into behavior patterns without critical examination.

The characteristics of a police manager's parent ego state are entirely determined by the characteristics of his or her own parents and by those of other significant influential figures. Therefore, in acting out the parental ego state, the manager is interacting with behaviors observed in his or her own parents or other authority figures.

The parent ego state tends to be filled with opinions and prejudices about religion, politics, traditions, sexual roles, lifestyles, the role of authority, proper dress, the manner of speech, and so on. The critical or controlling aspect of the parent ego state is expressed in a domineering and judgmental fashion. What is right is right, and there is no room for compromise.

The parent ego state, however, includes the feelings and behaviors that make it possible for the police manager to give support, praise, encouragement, or compliments to subordinates. This nurturing side of the parent ego state is particularly important in working with peers or subordinates or in relating to individuals in difficulty. Some police managers have parent ego states that have very little capacity to nurture others; consequently, they have difficulty in relating to situations calling for this kind of behavior.

The parent ego state is particularly useful in helping to determine appropriate behavior when the manager has no other data available in providing support to subordinates. Managers who have had good "parental" guidance and nurturing behavior have many attitudes and actions that serve to make their interactions with others pleasant and effective. Other police managers have incorporated attitudes and behaviors that interfere with their effectiveness in dealing with conflict and change.

Figure 7.1 **Ego State Diagram**

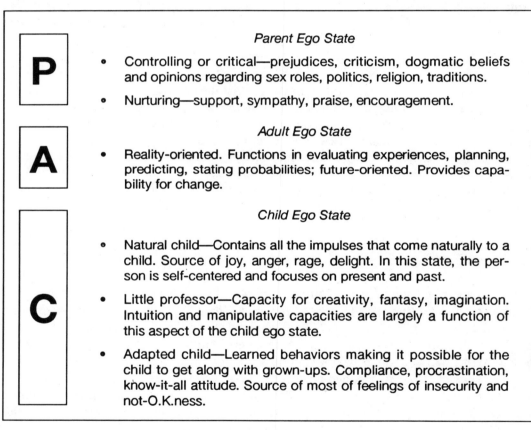

The content of each manager's parent ego state is unique. It is only through personal awareness of his or her own reaction tendencies that a manager can begin to change those behaviors that interfere with effective functioning. The nature of the parent ego state and the manner in which a manager expresses parent behavior can be modified through careful monitoring of gestures, feelings, and behavior. Thus, even though a manager cannot erase the parent "tapes," he or she can gain control through using his or her capacity to analyze situations objectively and test the effects of his or her interactions with others.

Adult Ego State

The adult ego state comprises the capacity to reason, evaluate situations, gather information, and store this information for future reference. It is not related to a person's age, even though the content of the adult ego state changes with age. A police manager who is operating in the adult state is oriented toward present reality and the objective gathering of information. This aspect of the personality is well organized, adaptable, and provides the manager with the capacity to monitor his or her thought processes. Consequently, the adult ego state is indispensable in changing personal behavior. In the adult ego state, the police manager is detached from his or her own emotional and other internal processes. While in the adult state, the manager may be unemotional but able to appraise child and parent feelings. In the adult ego state the manager considers past, present, and future. Thus, this ego state is essential for effective planning and overall management.

Child Ego State

The child ego state is essentially childhood preserved in its entirety. It contains the impulses that come naturally to the infant. It contains the recordings of early experiences, how one responded to them, and the positions taken about oneself and other people. A person who responds in an inquisitive, affectionate, selfish, mean, playful, whining, or manipulative manner is responding from the child ego state. There are three discernible parts of the child ego state.

The *natural child* is the part that is very young, impulsive, untrained, and expressive. When his or her needs are met, the manager responds out of the child state with affection. Angry rebellion at having his or her needs frustrated is also a reaction of the child state.

The *little professor* refers to the unschooled wisdom that we observe in children. It is the part of the child ego state that is able to influence the motivations and feelings of other people. It is through this aspect of the child ego state that the infant figures things out—when to cry, when to be quiet, and how to manipulate his or her parents. This aspect can be indicative of a highly creative mind, even though many of the child ego state creations might be impractical if not developed by the adult ego state. The police manager's capacity to create and fantasize is directly related to the degree to which he or she is able to permit the internal little professor to work.

The third aspect of the child ego state is the *adapted child*. This is the part of the child ego state that exhibits modifications of the natural child's inclinations. These adaptations of natural impulses occur in response to parental training and demands from significant authority figures. The manager who complies, procrastinates, acts like a bully, withdraws, or in other ways behaves as he or she did in response to the demands of his or her parents is acting from an adapted child state.

Each of the ego states is important to the manager's being effective in daily interactions with others. Effective decisionmaking requires that the police manager be able to process data through the adult state without undue influence from the child and parent ego states. However, to have fun, a manager must be able to indulge in his or her child ego state. To give support to others or to exercise control of situations, he or she must be able to rely on the parent ego state. Good adjustment comes when the police manager is able to use the ego state that is appropriate to the situation.

Police managers can diagnose ego states in themselves and others by observing people's visible and audible characteristics (see Figure 7.2). Certain words, gestures, postures, mannerisms, and facial expressions are typically associated with each of the three ego states. Managers can also use their own emotional reactions and thoughts to help interpret the ego state that they have observed in another person. A parental reaction in the manager may mean that a child ego state is being observed in the subordinate.

Feelings of inferiority or rebelliousness in the subordinate may mean that the ego state being observed in the manager is that of the parent. These clues assist in determining the effect of behavior on others and the appropriateness of interaction. Awareness of these clues can be of assistance to the manager in understanding differences in approaches to various situations and may provide a basis for determining changes that may be necessary in interacting with others.

Any one of the ego states discussed can serve as the determinant of the police manager's personality at any given time. For a manager to be well-adjusted, he or she must be able to move from one ego state to another, using the proper ego state for a given situation. People normally develop some form of control that helps them in their movement from one ego state to another. This control may be lax—that is, there may be very little control from the adult ego state and therefore the manager may move very rapidly from one ego state to another: from child to parent or from parent to child. The other extreme is a manager who has a very rigid ego state boundary. In this case, there is very little free movement between the ego states.

The manager who has a rigid or constant parent ego state tends to treat subordinates as if they are children, refusing to accept their abilities or ideas. As a police manager, he or she might constantly go about trying to help officers carry out their everyday responsibilities. The manager who is constantly using the adult ego state has developed little in his or her personal relationships with people. He or she is extremely logical and requires hard-core data before making any kind of decision. This type of manager, although quite effective in such fields as research, might be ineffective as a commander of personnel within a police department.

The constant child is one who refuses to accept responsibility and refuses to make decisions. This kind of an individual rarely climbs the ladder of promotions within the police department and is satisfied with staying at the entrance level for his or her entire career. This is not, however, to imply that all people who remain at the entrance level are doing so because of their reliance on their child ego state. The constant child uses devices such as seeking direction for minor tasks for which he or she has been trained or constantly asking for reassurance before making any decision.

Police managers must also be aware of problems of *contamination* and *isolation*. Contamination means that the adult ego state is contaminated by either the child or the parent ego state. A typical example might be that of the police manager who refuses to have women under his command. He uses strong rationalization and attempts to prove his point by citing the possibility of injuries and even finds data to help to reinforce his position. The action may appear to be adult; however, careful examination may reveal that this police manager is highly prejudiced in his attitudes toward women. It is this preju-

Figure 7.2 **Clues to Ego States**

	Parent Ego State	*Adult Ego State*	*Child Ego State*
Voice tones	Condescending, putting down, criticizing, or accusing	Matter-of-fact	Full of feeling; high-pitched, whining voice
Words used	Everyone knows that . . . You should never . . . You should always . . . I can't understand why in the world you would ever . . . I'll put a stop to that once and for all . . . If I were you . . . Stupid . . . naughty . . . ridiculous . . . shocking . . . poor thing . . . good girl . . . good boy	How . . . What . . . When . . . Where . . . Why . . . Who . . . Probable . . . In what way . . . I think . . . I seem . . . It is my opinion	I'm mad at you . . . Wow, terrific! (or any words that have a high feeling level) . . . I wish . . . I want . . . I dunno . . . I guess . . . Bigger . . . Better . . . Best
Postures	Puffed-up with pride, super-correct, very proper	Attentive, eye-to-eye contact, listening and looking for maximum data, continual action	Slouching, playful, beaten down, burdened, self-conscious
Facial expressions	Frowning, worried or dissaproving looks, chin jutted out, furrowed brow, pursed lips	Alert eyes, maximum attention given	Excited, surprised, downcast eyes, quivering lip or chin, moist eyes, rolling eyes
Body gestures	Hands on hips, pointing finger in accusation, arms folded across chest, patting on head, deep sigh	Leaning forward in chair toward other person, moving closer to hear and see better	Spontaneous activity, wringing hands, pacing, withdrawing into corner or moving away from laughter, raising hand for permission, shrugging shoulders

dice, rather than the facts he has gathered, that governs his behavior. This can be tested by providing counterexamples to determine whether the individual manager is able to deal with the new data from his adult ego state. If he refuses to accept its importance, totally rejects it, and makes a judgmental decision strictly from his parent ego state, there is contamination.

Isolation means the complete blocking out of an ego state. If the child ego state is blocked out, the manager is also blocking out the spontaneous, fun-loving side of his or her nature. Managers who are only fact-seeking and are never able to laugh at life or accept humor within the daily operations of their legal responsibilities might have blocked out their child ego state. If the parent ego state is blocked out, there is no conscience involved in the manager's decision. These managers show little remorse or shame. In many instances, they become criminal in their actions and may eventually be disciplined for dishonesty or unethical conduct. Managers who isolate the adult are usually in conflict with reality and may even have mental disorders severe enough to require hospitalization.

Of the three ego states, the adult state is usually the last to be effectively developed. Police managers who want to build a stronger adult ego state could follow some of the following principles from *I'm OK.—You're OK.*"[2]

1. Learn to recognize their child ego state, its vulnerabilities, its fears, its principal methods of expressing feelings.

2. Learn to recognize their parent ego state, its admonitions, injunctions, and positions.

3. Be sensitive to the parent, adult, and child ego states in themselves and in others.

4. Count to ten if necessary to give the adult ego state time to process the data coming into the brain and to sort out the parent ego and child ego realities.

5. Work out and develop a system of values.

Once this system of values has been established, decisions can be made within its ethical framework.

Transactions and Communication

Police managers must understand their own ego states if they are to make transactional analysis (TA) work for them. However, it is the application of this knowledge in their daily interactions that is most useful. In TA, an interaction with another person is called a *transaction*. In all transactions, the person's ego state will determine his or her response to others. Three major patterns of interaction can be identified: complementary transactions, crossed transactions, and ulterior transactions.

Complementary Transactions

In many transactions, the police manager will find communication going smoothly; he or she will feel comfortable in the relationships and find it easy to continue the conversation. These transactions are most frequently referred to as *complementary transactions*. In such transactions, both parties in the interaction are responding from ego states that are appropriate to maintaining the communication. In the example below, the manager tells a subordinate to have a report in on Friday, and the subordinate dutifully confirms that he will have the report in on that day.

> MANAGER: John, I want that report by Friday, and you had better not be late. (The parent ego state is dominant, and the expectation is compliance from the child ego state in the other person.)
>
> JOHN: Yes, Sir. No problem. (Child compliance back to the parent in the manager).

The manager's order is made in a demanding, uncompromising tone, indicating that he is coming out of his controlling parent ego state. The response of the subordinate indicates that he will comply without question. This response—from the child ego state—is the one the manager expected, and no apparent problem exists. Such transactions are referred to as complementary because the person who initiates the transaction communicates from a particular ego state and receives a response from the other person that meets his or her expectations. The following are examples of complementary transactions:

> 1st SGT.: These new recruits just don't have any guts. (parent to parent—judgmental)
>
> 2nd SGT.: You're right. I don't know how they expect us to do anything with these jerks. (parent back to parent)
>
> OFFICER: Let's knock off early and get in a few games of bowling. (child to child)
>
> 2nd SGT.: That's a good idea, where do you want to go? (child to child)
>
> 1st SGT.: How many officers do you think we will need during the 4-to-8 period this Saturday? (adult to adult)
>
> 2nd SGT.: From the data we have, I would say we need at least twelve additional officers. (adult to adult)
>
> OFFICER: Sgt. Brown, I really screwed up this report, can you help me? (child to parent)
>
> SGT.: Certainly, son, I used to have a little trouble with those reports myself. (nurturing parent to child)

In each of the transactions illustrated above, the person indicating the transaction received a response that was consistent with the stimulus message. Such transactions set the stage for continuing communication between the two persons.

Crossed Transactions

In some transactions with others, the manager may immediately be aware that something has happened to disrupt the relationship. For example, after an initial exchange, he or she and the subordinate may glare at each other, turn their backs on each other, change the topic abruptly, or show puzzlement at what has just occurred. The behaviors suggest that the transaction has resulted in a disruption of communication. In most instances, the manager initiating the transaction has received a response that was inconsistent with his or her expectations. Such transactions are referred to as *crossed transactions*. A crossed transaction occurs any time the person initiating the transaction receives a response that is perceived as inappropriate or unexpected. As an example:

CAPT.:   Have you spoken to the chief about the court schedule? (adult to adult)

LT.:   No, and I'm not about to. He can go jump in the lake. (child to parent)

In the example above, the captain is communicating from her adult ego state, expecting a reasonable, adult reply. The lieutenant, however, responds out of her child ego state in an angry, rebellious manner. The lieutenant's response is directed to the parent in the captain. The subsequent conversation will largely be determined by the captain's response. She may choose to stay in the adult ego state and try to find out why the lieutenant is annoyed with the chief. If she moves to her parent ego state, she may either berate the lieutenant for her poor attitude or be sympathetic. In either case, the crossed transaction results in a change in the level of communication between the two. Other examples of crossed transactions are illustrated below:

CAPT.:   George, you are changing shifts with Linda next week. (parent to child)

LT.:   You're crazy. How did you make captain anyway? (parent to child)

LT.:   Let's organize a card game this week. (child to child)

CAPT.:   If you would quit trying to figure out ways to avoid work, we might get something done around here. (parent to child)

In the first example, the captain changes the shifts of one of his lieutenants and directs that the change be made. George responds from his parent state by making derogatory remarks about the captain. This transaction will probably lead to disciplinary action, which could have been avoided by an adult-to-adult discussion about the change of shift.

In the second example, the lieutenant expresses her wish to organize a card game and the captain responds in a critical, judgmental fashion. The lieutenant may not mention cards again, but she will also carry around a lot of hard feelings toward the captain. The captain could have avoided this by crossing the transaction to her adult state and saying something like: "I wouldn't mind discussing that later, but right now I have a lot of work to do."

In both examples, the crossed transaction results in consequences that are not productive as far as the police department is concerned. By paying more attention to their communications, the commanders in each instance could have avoided costly reactions on the part of their subordinates.

However, crossed transactions are sometimes useful and necessary to gain control of situations or to bring about a change in behavior that is inappropriate to the situation. The general rule is that a crossover to the adult state is likely to be the most productive. For example:

LT.:   That stupid lieutenant couldn't supervise if he had a seeing-eye dog. (parent to parent)

CAPT.: What has he done to make you so angry? (adult to adult)

In this cross, the captain avoids getting into a parent-to-parent criticism of the lieutenant and begins to explore the problem between the two lieutenants. Although such a cross does not always lead to problem-solving behavior on the part of the responder, it provides a better chance than a parent-to-child or child-to-child interaction.

Crossed transactions leading to ill feelings, unproductive use of time, and organizational conflict can be avoided if police managers are aware of their tendencies and become more proficient in determining the appropriateness of the adult-to-adult pattern of communication.

Ulterior Transactions

The third type of transaction is referred to as an *ulterior transaction* and has two messages. One, the overt message, is communicated at the verbal level. At the same time, the second, or covert message, is communicated subliminally. This second message is intended to elicit a response different from that called for by the first message. Managers may use ulterior transactions in attempting to sell a project. For example, the following, which on the surface sounds like an adult-to-adult transaction, may take place between a chief and his command staff:

CHIEF: This is a really good project I have developed, and I would like you to see if there is anything wrong with it.

The verbal message appears to be a straightforward request for constructive criticism. However, the implication is that the chief thinks highly of the project and is already committed to it; he is therefore probably not really interested in seeing the staff come up with alternative plans. These implications stem from the manager's parent ego state and are addressed to the staff's child ego state. If the staff members accept the ulterior message, they will respond from their child ego state and say "Yes, chief, that project sounds good." If the staff members do not read the ulterior message and question the chief, they may get a parent-to-child response from the chief, such as "You don't really understand the problem."

When a subordinate, overworked and looking discouraged, comes in with a report, her verbal comment "Here is the report" is on its face an adult-to-adult transaction. However, her demeanor may provoke the manager to say: "You look down, what's wrong?" The subordinate's physical appearance communicates a message from her child state that she wants encouragement and support from the manager's parent state. The manager, in acknowledging the report in her adult state, may or may not respond to the child needs of the subordinate.

An ulterior message is often involved when a person announces, seemingly from his adult state, that he has done something wrong or is having difficulty. For example:

LT. TO CAPT.:   I've read this statute two or three times, but I just don't understand it.

On the surface, this is an adult-to-adult description of the lieutenant's state of mind. However, the child message asks for either a put-down for being stupid or for support from the captain.

Ulterior transactions are sometimes used to communicate feelings or ideas when the individual wants to avoid a direct statement, being uncertain of the response he or she might otherwise receive. However, ulterior transactions are a poor substitute for honest ones and are the basis for psychological games, which will be discussed later in the chapter.

The police manager, in dealing with ulterior transactions, must be aware of the following:

1.   In which ulterior transactions does he or she deliberately engage?

2.   Which of his honest transactions may be interpreted as ulterior messages?

3.   What ulterior transactions are others initiating?

Ulterior transactions can create major obstacles to effective communications in a police department; they prevent the agency from becoming as effective as it could be if honest transactions were more common.

Basic Life Positions and Organizational Sanctions

The police manager's ego states and the nature of the transactions that he or she customarily engages in are to a large extent determined by the manager's early life experiences. In all probability, one of the most important determinants of how we interact with others is how we view ourselves and other people. How we view our adult selves is very much a function of the view we held of ourselves as children. Likewise, the degree of trust we place in other people and our general beliefs about them are established on the basis of our early life experiences. In one way or another, at some time early in our life, we make decisions about ourselves and others that determine the nature of our future interactions. These decisions are referred to in transactional analysis as *basic life positions*.

There are four basic life positions, which are determined by whether one has made positive or negative decisions about oneself and others. People whose life experiences have been rewarding and who have had a sufficient amount of praise and encouragement will probably see themselves in a very positive light. That is, they are "O.K." If, on the other hand, they were constantly ridiculed, called dumb, or rejected by their peers, they will likely see themselves in a negative light, or as "not O.K." How other people behaved toward us determines whether we see others as "O.K." or "not O.K." All combinations of decisions are possible, which lead, in turn, to one of four basic positions.

First Position: "I'm O.K., You're O.K." If realistic, this is the position of managers who are psychologically healthy, mature, and able to develop open, trusting relationships with other people. They see others as having potential for development and assume responsibility for their own behavior. Although they may occasionally experience depression, they recognize that it is temporary and take steps to overcome their negative feelings.

Second Position: "I'm O.K., You're Not O.K." This is the position of managers who feel that others are out to degrade and persecute them. They blame others for their miseries and are unwilling to take responsibility for their shortcomings and mistakes. Their relationships are marked by a strong distrust of other people and a need to be in control of others and of all situations.

Third Position: "I'm Not O.K., You're O.K." Police managers in this position feel powerless. When they compare themselves to others, they come up short. Managers in this position are self-critical and overly concerned about their shortcomings and mistakes. They have a tendency to become easily depressed and are at times irrational in their decisions.

Fourth Position: "I'm Not O.K., You're Not O.K." Individuals in this position have given up on life. They see little good in themselves or in other people. They may be withdrawn, moody, and pessimistic, and it may be very difficult to develop any kind of effective working relationship with them. Usually they are not involved in steady employment at management positions in law enforcement due to the necessity of decisionmaking in police departments.

The concept of the basic life positions is useful in understanding individual differences in response to organizational sanctions and the differences in the use of sanctions by police managers. Most police departments have some form of positive and negative sanctions that reward good performance and punish poor performance. However, people differ in their reaction to advancement, awards, and praise as well as to negative sanctions such as suspensions, criticism, demotions, and transfers.

Managers who feel "O.K." about themselves and others seek and give as many forms as possible of positive recognition. Others who feel "not O.K." about themselves are more frequently in a position to receive negative sanctions than positive sanctions. Similarly, managers who take life positions that emphasize the "not O.K."ness of other people have a tendency to impose as many negative sanctions as possible. In all probability, the difference between police managers who constantly look for opportunities to criticize, suspend, or demote and police managers who are conscientious in their efforts to provide positive sanctions has a great deal to do with their life positions regarding other people.

Both positive and negative sanctions are acts that recognize the behavior of other people. In TA, such acts are referred to as *strokes*. Everybody needs a certain amount of stroking, or recognition, to survive. Infants need physical stroking if they are to develop properly. After infancy, the need for physical stroking diminishes, and a need for recognition from other people becomes essential to psychological development. Whether the manager praises or punishes a person, his or her acts recognize the other person, which is the basis of a stroke.

To be psychologically sound and to relate meaningfully to others, people need positive strokes such as praise, compliments, appreciation, and attention to their ideas and feelings. Positive strokes make subordinates feel stronger, more competent, and more effective. Negative strokes such as being criticized, being ignored, or having ideas and feelings discounted make subordinates feel weaker, less effective, and less competent. The police work situation can be a major source of strokes. Unfortunately, some police departments give many more negative than positive strokes, and their officers are angry, unhappy, and less effective on the job.

Positive strokes can take many forms. Simple acts of recognition such as a friendly "good morning" or a welcoming handshake are important in maintaining a sense of "O.K."ness. However, subordinates also need the more lasting strokes that come from having good work recognized, being given a chance to use their skills, and being rewarded for their service and hard work. At the deepest level, subordinates need the strokes that come from having an intimate, caring relationship with a manager they respect and trust.

Within police departments, managers and supervisors should be a major source of positive strokes. Many departmental change efforts result in different patterns of stroking. For example, placing decision-making responsibility in the hands of officers at lower levels in the hierarchy is a way of recognizing their competence and importance and becomes a powerful positive stroke. Likewise, moving to team decision making gives every officer a chance to be heard, which for most is an important stroke in their relationship with others.

As police managers become more aware of their own stroking tendencies, they often find that they too frequently fail to give positive strokes in appropriate situations. On the other hand, they may ignore the negative stroking situations that they find during the course of a day. Such stroking patterns often create cautious, unhappy subordinates who may begin to feel incapable of making sound decisions. In addition, the officers and supervisors working in police departments where there is a deficit of positive strokes will frequently do only that which is required of them and use their energies and skills to obtain strokes in their time off or through sabotaging the efforts of the police command structure.

It is essential to recognize that everyone needs a certain amount of stroking and that they will find some way to obtain the strokes they need. For the "I'm not O.K." individuals, negative strokes may be more important than positive strokes. However, most officers who make contributions to the police mission feel "O.K." about themselves and need positive strokes to maintain this "O.K." feeling.

Time Structuring

To obtain the strokes they need, subordinates structure their time in a variety of ways. The six ways that have been identified as providing opportunities for obtaining strokes are described below.

One way to structure time is to *withdraw*. The manager can withdraw through fantasy, by ignoring others and watching TV, or by going off by himself to a favorite thinking place. He may withdraw when he is uncomfortable, bored, or feeling "not O.K." In moderation, withdrawal is a healthy way to obtain vicarious strokes. The overuse of withdrawal may suggest that the manager is not getting enough strokes in his relationships with other people.

A second way to structure time is through *rituals*. Some rituals are social exchanges that we have learned from our parents, such as the proper ways to greet and introduce people, polite table manners, and so forth. Other rituals are unique to the culture or organizations to which we belong. There are many rituals in the typical police department. Some examples are the way subordinates address ranking officers, how seating is arranged at staff meetings, and how communication is formalized within the hierarchy. These are ritualistic in that they provide the structure for individuals in the various ranks to be recognized and respected by those below them in the rank structure. Observation suggests that the fewer opportunities for obtaining positive strokes in normal exchanges at work with the police department, the more important these ritual behaviors become. To be effective, a police manager must be aware of the importance of rituals within the department and within the community in which she works. She also needs to be wary when rituals become more important than results.

A third way to structure time is through *pastimes*. Pastimes include the general discussion between people of interests, values, and events. Pastimes are a rich source of strokes in the absence of other types of time structuring. Between casual friends, this is a major form of time structuring. An exchange of their latest "war stories" is a favorite pastime among officers. Managers can spend hours talking about the "new breed" of officer or "how it was in the good old days."

Being able to engage in pastimes is an important social skill in making new acquaintances, enjoying a luncheon, or relaxing with associates. Pastimes are also useful departmentally when there is informal discussion of issues relevant to the police organization. However, they can also be harmful, as when supervisors get together over coffee and "knock" the police department—an example of a parent-to-parent pastime. Too much use of pastimes during work hours suggests that there is a lack of sufficient stroking for good police work habits.

The fourth time structuring approach is *activity*. Activities comprise all manner of time usage related to recreation and work. Home improvement projects, golf, tennis, or any other occupation in which an individual spends time actively is an activity. Activities are a primary source of gaining strokes. When the police department fails to provide enough strokes for the activity of police work within the department, many officers find activities outside of police work to gain the strokes they are missing. For instance, they take on second jobs. The dramatic increase in recreational activities in our culture suggests that police employees are highly motivated to gain strokes and use their work not as a primary source of strokes but as a way of earning the necessary income to engage in those activities where they may obtain the strokes they need. The test of management is in the creation of a police department where police activities are a rich source of strokes.

Psychological *games* are the fifth way of structuring time. Psychological games are a devious way of obtaining or giving strokes. All have certain basic elements:

1. There is a series of complementary transactions that on the surface seem reasonable.
2. There is an ulterior transaction that is the hidden agenda or reason for the interaction.
3. There is a negative outcome or payoff that concludes the game and is the purpose for playing it.

Structuring time through games decreases the problem-solving capacities of the police department. Although games appear to have advantages, they are all to some degree destructive to effective work relationships. In departments in which officers are bored with their jobs or the work environment is devoid of positive strokes, the officers have more need to play games. The next section of this chapter will describe some typical police department games.

The sixth way to structure time is through *intimate relationships*. Intimate relationships are free of games and free of exploitation. The relationship is straightforward and honest, arousing feelings of tenderness, empathy, and affection. It involves a genuine caring for another person. Intimate relationships require a sense of "O.K."ness regarding oneself and others. The intimate relationship is a source of some of the most lasting and enriching strokes, but it is not the most typical form of structuring time in police departments.

Intimacy cannot be created or engineered by the manager. It must occur spontaneously. It occurs between people who may not even be expecting it, and it seldom occurs when the manager goes out in deliberate search of it. The experience of intimacy is the experience of feeling a massive dose of positive stroking. In an intimate relationship, people feel unconditionally stroked and accepted for who they are, not for what they can do, how they dress, how they look, or how important a position they hold.

The following conditions must exist for intimacy to occur:

1. All defenses must be down. This means the manager must give up some personal gains, ceasing to emphasize rituals and pastimes.

2. The manager must take the risk of being vulnerable. A manager who lets down his or her defenses may get hurt, and this is what the adapted child in him or her may fear.

3. The manager has to feel positively, not negatively, toward the other person. His or her nurturing parent and natural child must feel "O.K." about the other person. The manager has to be in a state in which he or she moves toward and not against the other person.

4. The manager must accept the other person unconditionally. If he or she places demands or sets up rules that control how close others can come, then he or she blocks intimacy.

The time-structuring characteristics of managers in a police department provide important clues as to the changes needed in the work environment. Where withdrawal, rituals, pastimes, and games make up the major stroke-acquiring transactions, the department's effectiveness will be seriously curtailed. Most change efforts focus on making the activities of police work more meaningful sources of strokes.

The police manager's own time-structuring characteristics are important determinants in the effectiveness of such change efforts.

Organizational Games

Psychological games are played by individuals who have a need to receive or give negative feelings, which are the payoff in the games. A fairly typical game played in police departments begins by a supervisor asking his or her subordinates for suggestions:

CHIEF: We're in a real pinch. Headquarters wants us to develop a better relationship with the community; any suggestions?

> 1st CAPT.: Why don't we approach all the business leaders on a personal basis and give them information about our department and have them submit their ideas and complaints?
>
> CHIEF: That's O.K., but it would take too much time.
>
> 2nd CAPT.: I think we should start with the schools and increase our contact with teachers, kids, and parents.
>
> CHIEF: That would be all right, but it doesn't relate to stopping crime.

Other commanders offer suggestions, only to be told that their ideas are "all right, but...." The chief finally leaves with the comment that "I guess you can't help me with this problem." This leaves the commanders feeling that they have wasted their time and couldn't help. The chief leaves feeling that "These guys can't help with anything." The bad feelings the commanders have and the bad feelings the chief has toward them is the payoff for the game of "Yes, but." The "Yes, but" player can be distinguished from one who genuinely requests help by the fact that the "Yes, but" player often asks for input but never accepts any ideas. The player will continue to play this game until his or her subordinates cease to offer suggestions.

Psychological games reinforce or confirm a person's basic life position about himself or herself and others. Thus, the police manager who is successful in playing "Yes, but" with his or her staff confirms his or her "O.K."ness and the "not O.K."ness of other members of the staff. Games played from the "I'm O.K., you're not O.K." position are attacks on subordinates and are designed to reinforce feelings that others are "not O.K." Other games are played from the "I'm not O.K., you're O.K." position and reinforce negative feelings the police manager has about himself or herself.

Some of the common games played by people in law enforcement are briefly described below.

If It Weren't for Him/Her (Them). This is a game designed to blame someone else for one's own poor performance or production. The "him/her" or "them" usually represents a person higher in the department. The chief may point to the city council. The payoff is that the player takes himself or herself off the hook and places responsibility on someone else for his or her failure to perform. Basically, this game allows an individual to maintain his or her own sense of "O.K."ness by placing others in a "not O.K." position.

Now I've Got You, You SOB (NIGYYSOB). This is a game in which the player attempts to catch another individual or group in a mistake, a lie, or a violation of rules and orders so that he or she can discipline the person in violation. This might be played by anyone in the police department. For example, a lieutenant, knowing of the tendency for officers under his or her command to sleep on the midnight shift, might make a surprise check to catch sleepers. He or she then imposes disciplinary measures on both the officers and their sergeant. The game permits the lieutenant to get rid of angry feelings toward others and puts the sergeant in his or her place. This person is also confirming in his or her own mind that he or she is "O.K." but that the others are "not O.K." This game tends to destroy the lieutenant's chances of developing trusting relationships with these officers in the future.

Blemish. In this game, the player may review a report or performance evaluation and pick out minor flaws in an otherwise good report. This person is the "nitpicker" who always has to find something wrong and seldom comments on the good parts of the report. The payoff for the blemish player is the bad feelings he or she gives to others.

Corner. The players of this game put others in impossible binds. The corner player may ask for a report with a tight deadline. When the report comes back with understandable omissions, the player returns the report with a reprimand. If the report writer turns the report in late to make sure it is complete and accurate, he or she is reprimanded for being late. The payoff is the reprimand the player gives to the report writer.

In addition to the games played for the purpose of punishing others or of proving their "not O.K."ness, there are a number of games that result in the player being put down or criticized or that are designed to provoke sympathy. Players of these games experience a keen sense of "not O.K."ness or inadequacy.

Poor Me. In this game, the players find themselves in a situation they do not like and spend hours griping to anyone who will listen. Usually the players get sympathy from the listeners. Players of "poor me" refuse to do anything constructive to remove themselves from the situation; if the conditions they gripe about were changed, they would find something else to make their lives miserable. "Poor me" players see themselves as "not O.K." and constantly find situations that confirm their dismal feelings.

Kick Me. Players of "kick me" constantly get into situations that provoke their managers or supervisors into taking some form of negative action against them. Some "kick me" players are chronically late for important assignments or turn in reports with errors. Even after close instruction as to what is required, they continue to make important mistakes. Hard-core players ultimately end up being "kicked out" of the police department by being fired. Others receive enough "kick" to prevent them from ever being considered for promotion and use this circumstance to play "poor me."

Stupid. This is a variation of the "kick me" game. In this instance, the players are constantly doing "stupid" things that provoke the supervisor or colleagues into commenting on their stupidity. "Stupid" players are usually bright enough to perform but constantly make mistakes or place themselves in jeopardy by their poor judgment. Stupid players may fail a sergeant's exam for years despite their intelligence. They usually comment that they are probably too dumb to pass the exam.

Wooden Leg. In "wooden leg," the player finds some excuse to avoid success or accomplishment. It is a cop-out game in which a person uses a physical or social handicap to avoid being successful. A long-term officer who has failed to advance may say that he or she would try something else but is too old. The middle-aged sergeant might use the excuse of age to not attend college classes even though they may be necessary for further advancement. Any number of excuses can be used as a "wooden leg," such as family background, lack of education, age, or lack of physical capabilities. By using excuses, people escape from the challenge to grow and get ahead; thus they are able to maintain their "not O.K." life position.

Although all the behaviors involved in these games can be exhibited by non-game-playing individuals, games can be recognized by the fact that they occur over and over again and that the outcomes are predictable for the individuals involved. The kind of games a person plays seldom change. The "kick me" player and the "Yes, but" player continue as long as there are people who allow them to get away with their games. The player of games from the "I'm O.K., you're not O.K." position needs individuals in the "I'm not O.K., you're O.K." position to make his or her games work. As in every game, certain players are necessary. The breaking up of games requires straight adult-to-adult transactions. By pointing out organizational games and being unwilling to support them, it is possible to discourage the players. The police manager's task is to recognize the time-wasting games played in the department and to begin developing an atmosphere that discourages games and encourages straight, honest, problem-solving behavior.

Conclusion

This chapter has attempted to summarize the basic concepts of transactional analysis and to provide a limited number of illustrations as to the implications of TA concepts in organizational and personal change efforts. The material presented does little more than introduce the basic concepts. For interested police managers, further study and training are essential for these concepts to be of value in their management practice.

There has developed a substantial body of literature that covers in detail the theory and implications of TA to management practice. In addition, there are many consulting firms ready and able to provide training and consultation to police managers interested in implementing these concepts in their police departments.

There may be many who criticize TA on theoretical and practical grounds. However, the model has wide applicability, its major concepts are easily understood, and it provides an excellent set of concepts for giving direction to personal change. These comments in no way suggest that personal or organizational change is easy or that TA will solve all the problems for a police manager. Like all other models, it is a tool that can prove effective in the hands of police managers who understand and believe in the approach.

Notes

1.   Eric Berne, *Games People Play* (New York: Grove Press, 1964).

2.   Thomas H. Harris, *I'm O.K.—You're O.K.* (New York: Avon Books, 1967).

Bibliography

Berne, Eric. *Games People Play*. New York: Grove Press, 1964.

_____. *Principles of Group Treatment*. New York: Grove Press, 1966.

_____. *The Structure and Dynamics of Organizations and Groups*. New York: Grove Press, 1963.

_____. *Transactional Analysis in Psychotherapy*. New York: Evergreen Original, 1961.

_____. *What Do You Say After You Say Hello?* New York: Bantam Books, 1972.

Understanding Personnel Through MBTI® || 8

Objectives

1. Students will understand themselves better.

2. The student will understand how others in law enforcement behave.

3. The student will understand functional behavior.

4. The student will understand different attitudes and behaviors.

Overview

How do the people in your police department get along? How do they feel about their superiors or their colleagues across the hall? Do they agree on how decisions are made and who should do what jobs? Probably not. Conflicts are inevitable in human organizations. These conflicts are believed to arise from personality differences, and they can be major obstacles to efficient operation. This chapter describes a method of helping police managers recognize these differences and use them to strengthen their agencies.

Personality, as used here, refers to the complex array of personal characteristics (needs, motivations, values, morals, etc.) that make people different. But these general terms do not describe the individual's basic attitude—or approach to life—that guides behavior and is reflected in personality (and sometimes conflicts with other approaches). As a result, psychologists have sought ways to identify what it is that makes up each person's preferred way of dealing with the world.

The Myers-Briggs Type Indicator® (MBTI)[1] does just that; it is an instrument that specifically reveals a person's personal traits and makes it possible to compare differences in fundamental approaches among individuals. The MBTI® frequently is used for management training and consultation. The police managers who have used it find that it helps them to recognize both compatible and incompatible styles. By understanding the differences in approach, managers can see how these differences affect relationships; thus they are better able to avert unproductive conflicts and improve the department's overall performance.

Functional Behavior

The MBTI® instrument identifies four basic preferences that relate to (1) the way people become aware of the outside world; (2) the way they come to conclusions about what they become aware of—that is, how they make decisions; (3) their degree of flexibility; and (4) their orientation toward the external world. The theoretical direction for the MBTI® came from Carl Jung's theory of types.[2]

Jung believed that when we become aware of the world around us and make decisions on the basis of that awareness, we use a combination of mental processes:

- Sensory (through the five senses), symbolized by the letter S
- Intuitive (indirectly—through the subconscious, what is learned through the senses, and by pursuing the possibilities of the situation), symbolized by N
- Thinking (rational), symbolized by T
- Feeling (on the basis of a value system), symbolized by F

Ideally, the individual develops a command of all these processes and uses them throughout life. But because of differences in life experiences, people vary in the degree of their development of these processes and have different preferences and approaches to the situations that life presents.

Let us begin with awareness. People get their fundamental view of the world through using the sensory process, the intuitive process, or a combination of the two. The degree to which a person prefers one over the other can be visualized on a continuum that places total reliance on the sensory process at one end of the scale and total reliance on intuition at the other.

| SENSORY | INTUITIVE |

Most of us fall somewhere between the two extremes. Those who find themselves on the sensory side of the scale prefer gathering the observable facts of a situation; they tend to be "realistic, practical, observant...and good at remembering a great number of facts and working with them."[3] Those who rest on the intuitive side tend to value imagination and inspiration, are good at producing new ideas and projects, and like to solve problems.

What about decisionmaking? When a person comes to settling, closing, or completing an issue, he or she primarily uses one of two processes: thinking or feeling. The person in whom the thinking (rational) process dominates tends to be logical, objective, and consistent, making decisions by analyzing and weighing the data. Those who rely mostly on the feeling process tend to make decisions on the basis of values, or "because it feels right." They also tend to be sympathetic, appreciative, and tactful in dealing with others. These processes can also be visualized on a continuum:

| THINKING | FEELING |

The processes of becoming aware and reaching conclusions develop independently. Thus the processes of becoming aware and the processes of making decisions can be joined in the following combinations:

ST (sensory plus thinking). People with this combination are mainly interested in facts; they make decisions by impersonal analysis. As individuals they tend to be practical and matter of fact.

SF (sensory plus feeling). People with this combination are interested in facts but are also in tune with feelings in themselves and others. They are sociable and friendly.

NF (intuitive plus feeling). People with this combination are interested not in facts but in possibilities for the future—they base their decisions on personal feelings. They are enthusiastic and insightful.

NT (intuitive plus thinking). People with this combination are interested in possibilities but approach them with impersonal analysis. In decisionmaking, they more or less ignore the human element.

Which combination of preferences an individual has developed makes a difference in the types of work he or she will enjoy. An ST (sensory-thinking) person would prefer a job that requires data gathering and the making of logical, calculated decisions based on the data (a good example would be patrol). An SF (sensory-feeling) person would probably prefer a project that requires extensive dealings with people (working with juveniles), whereas an NT (intuitive-thinking) person might prefer abstract concepts or ideas (homicide investigation). An NF (intuitive-feeling) person would enjoy a job that deals with people and requires creativity and originality (training, community relations).

Another aspect of personality type identified by the MBTI® is whether a person prefers closure and having things settled or prefers to keep options open. People who choose closure over keeping their options open are referred to as judgers (Js); those who prefer to keep things open and fluid are perceivers (Ps). Judgers like to decide matters quickly. They live in a planned, decided, orderly way, wanting to regulate life and control it. Perceivers, on the other hand, like to keep their options open; they are not dependent on order and stability. They are flexible and enjoy seeking alternatives, being spontaneously able to understand life and adapt to it.

The final trait measured by the MBTI® centers on relative interest in the outer or inner worlds—that is, on whether an individual is an introvert or an extrovert. Introverts concentrate on their inner world, more content in dealing with ideas and concepts. Extroverts enjoy focusing on the world around them and are more comfortable in action than in contemplation. Sometimes these words are given positive or negative connotations; in this context they merely describe individual preferences.

In terms of these four traits—preferred method of becoming aware, preferred method of reaching conclusions, preferred degree of closure, and preferred orientation toward the world—a person can be predominately:

1. S (sensing) or N (intuitive)
2. T (thinking) or F (feeling)
3. J (judging) or P (perceiving)
4. I (introverted) or E (extroverted)

Each preference contributes unique characteristics that help to shape the individual. People tend naturally to act and react in ways that are most comfortable for them. But one's preferred approach may not be the most appropriate for dealing with the situation at hand—or it may conflict with the approach preferred by a fellow officer. When this happens, knowing about and accepting the psychological preferences of both ourselves and those with whom we work can help to maintain healthy, productive relationships.

Generally, it is easier for police officers to develop the traits that are strongest in them. According to Jung, in becoming aware and in reaching decisions, most people rely on their dominant process instead of using their sensory, intuitive, thinking, and feeling capacities equally.[4] But people usually have at least some overlapping characteristics. For instance, the dominant preference in extroverts pertains to the outer world, but the extrovert also has an auxiliary quality that provides a reasonable balance. Without the inner life, extroverts would become extreme in their extroversion and thus appear to be superficial to better balanced officers.[5]

Introverts rely on their auxiliary as a connection with the outer world. If it is undeveloped, they will seem awkward and uncomfortable. Therefore, introverts who lack an adequate auxiliary tend to be at a greater disadvantage then extroverts who lack such a modifying quality.[6]

To extroverted officers, introverts may seem aloof, but the introverts' reserve may stem from the fact that their energies are fueled by ideas and not by social contact.[7] In ordinary dealings, introverts do not necessarily say how they really feel about an issue. Only when they feel strongly enough about something will they reveal their thoughts. Through understanding and a developed auxiliary, introverts can learn to deal effectively with the outside world without becoming full-fledged members of it.[8]

Data Experience

Through a variety of programs, the Myers-Briggs Type Indicator® has been given to 1,164 law enforcement personnel from the ranks of sergeant through chief. Although a majority of these participants came from North Carolina, about 500 came from other areas of the country. Of the 1,164 officers, 58 were women. An analysis of the MBTI® data (Figure 8.1) provides a realistic profile of types of people in law enforcement.

A slight majority (51 percent) of those tested were introverts. That figure seems to carry no significance until it is compared with MBTI® figures for the general population. Across the country, approximately 70 percent of those tested were extroverted and only 30 percent introverted. In other words, law enforcement seems to attract more basically introverted (that is, inner-directed) people than people who are basically outer-directed and prefer to interact with others. In regard to preferred method of becoming aware, through the senses or through intuition, ratios among police officers ran about the same as among people in general. Seventy-five percent of people tested, regardless of their occupation, prefer the sensory mode; 79 percent of law enforcement officers have this preference. The general population is about equally divided between those who reach decisions on a rational basis (thinkers) and those who decide on the basis of feelings (feelers). In this study, 83 percent of law enforcement personnel preferred thinking over feeling. About the same ratio existed in police preferences for judging (80 percent) over perceiving. The general population divides about 50:50.

The implication, then, is that the majority of law enforcement personnel are STJs—that is, they are logical in nature, designing their environment to close out issues as quickly as possible. They examine and direct issues on the basis of past and present experience, without much consideration of the future. Of the sixteen types, two styles are

Figure 8.1 **Data Analysis for 1,164 Police Managers**

Sensing Types		Intuitive Types	
With Thinking	With Feeling	With Feeling	With Thinking
I S T J N = 374 % = 32.13	I S F J N = 53 % = 4.55	I N F J N = 8 % = 0.68	I N T J N = 48 % = 4.12
I S T P N = 62 % = 5.32	I S F P N = 15 % = 1.28	I N F P N = 9 % = 0.77	I N T P N = 30 % = 2.57
E S T P N = 34 % = 2.92	E S F P N = 17 % = 1.46	E N F P N = 33 % = 2.83	E N T P N = 27 % = 2.31
E S T J N = 322 % = 27.66	E S F J N = 42 % = 3.60	E N F J N = 16 % = 1.37	E N T J N = 74 % = 6.35

Judging Introverts · Perceptives · Extroverts · Perceptive Extroverts · Judging Extroverts

	#	%		#	%		#	%
E	565	48.53	I	599	51.46	SJ	791	67.95
S	919	78.95	N	245	21.04	SP	128	10.99
T	971	83.41	F	193	16.58	NT	179	15.37
J	937	80.49	P	227	19.50	NF	66	5.67

common among police personnel: 32 percent of those tested are ISTJs and 28 percent are ESTJs; 60 percent of the total show a strong preference for one of these two related styles. Law enforcement managers must therefore consider how best to deal with these styles.

ESTJs are described as follows:

> Extroverted thinkers tend to use their thinking to run as much of the world as may be theirs to run . . . . Ordinarily they enjoy deciding what ought to be done and giving the appropriate orders to ensure that it will be done. They abhor confusion, inefficiency, half measures, anything that is aimless and ineffective. Often they are crisp disciplinarians, who know how to be tough when the situation calls for toughness . . . . They act forcefully upon the basis of their judgment, whether well-founded or not.[9]

On the other hand, ISTJs possess

> a complete, realistic, practical respect both for the facts and for whatever responsibilities these facts create . . . . The interaction of introversion, sensing and the judging attitude gives them extreme stability . . . . ISTJs emphasize logic, analysis, and decisiveness.[10]

Although these traits serve most decisionmakers very well, their high representation among police managers can account for some underlying problems in these officials' respective functions. Conflict can arise in working with citizens and fellow agency members who see the advisability of change. When dealing with a problem, ST commanders may not always be responsive to other points of view or sensitive to the emotional needs of others.

ESTJs are so in tune with the established, time-honored institutions that they may not understand those who might wish to abandon or radically change those institutions.[11]

ISTJs also rely on time-honored institutions and base their decisions on the facts before them. On a day-to-day basis, this approach probably proves very useful, but over the long run it can produce a police department that resists adapting to new law enforcement techniques.

Some police managers' impersonal analysis of situations and lack of feeling can make them less aware in reaching a decision on others' personal needs. Because they may rely on the past in decisionmaking, they may not be inclined to take risks or engage in creative or intuitive thinking. Consequently their organization may tend to resist change. The police chief who fits this description may find an obstacle in an intuitive city manager; he or she may look for stability whereas the city manager inclines toward being more experimental.

Temperament

Divergent types become departmental assets when the differences are recognized and put to use in problem solving. Even though there are some people who consistently fall in the middle of the continuum, nearly everyone has an enduring set of characteristics that give special quality to his or her behavior and relationships. This personal makeup is sometimes referred to as one's "temperament." It is this underlying quality that may determine one's leadership skills, teaching ability, and degree of successful participation in the departmental structure.

Specific temperaments have been associated with the four categories of Jung's typology.[12] The SPs (ISTP, ESTP, ISFP, ESFP), who share the first type of temperament, are called *negotiators*. For the most part, SPs do not like to be tied down or obligated. They feel a sense of joy, living for today and barely glancing at tomorrow. SPs are impulsive—they do things because they want to. Of all temperamental types, they are the most likely to "share and share alike." Resources are to be used; machinery is to be operated; people are to be enjoyed. SPs may have a flair for the dramatic and a disdain for detail. Frequently these people are described as exciting, optimistic, cheerful, and full of fun.

SJs (ISTJ, ESTJ, ISFJ, ESFJ) represent the second type of temperament. SJs are labeled as the *stabilizers*. They feel a sense of duty and a need to belong. But this belonging must be earned. SJs do what they are required to do, and they want to be useful. As a type, they feel obligated, responsible, and burdened. SJs are the ones who are most inclined to save for future emergencies because they believe firmly in "Murphy's law"—whatever *can* go wrong *will* go wrong. SJs and SPs make up over 70 percent of our population.

The third temperament group comprises all the NTs (INTP, ENTP, INTJ, ENTJ). They are referred to as *visionaries*. NTs have a sense of power and an urge to understand, control, predict, and explain realities. NTs want to be competent and make a fetish of intelligence. They are the most self-critical of all the types and are very sensitive to the credentials of their critics. To others, NTs may seem cold, remote, and sometimes arrogant. For the NT, work is work and play is work. NTs find SPs hard to understand.

The fourth type of temperament is represented by the NFs (INFJ, ENFJ, INFP, ENFP). NFs are called *catalysts*. They have a sense of spirit, being basically involved in the search for self. NFs hunger to become better people, and their purpose in life is to have a bigger purpose in life. NFs feel they must have integrity: there must be no facade, no mask, no playing of roles—only one's genuine self. NFs also bring meaning and a heightened sense of drama to their relationships, which often become intense. The other types have trouble understanding the NF, and the NF, in turn, cannot really grasp the others' commitment to what seem to him or her to be false goals.

If we can identify the respective personality types found within a police department and then determine the behavioral characteristics associated with each, we may learn something about the climate within that agency. For instance, NT commanders may direct an agency that runs like clockwork, but in doing so they may demand too much of themselves and others. NT officers may be insensitive to the needs of others—namely, their peers and the community's citizens. SJ officers, the dominant type in police departments, believe strongly in rules, and they obey their superiors. SJs feel that they must be prepared for every situation. SP officers, on the other hand, may be just the opposite. They are very restless and do not like routine. They are not particularly disciplined, yet they work best in emergencies because emergencies open up new possibilities. NF officers are so people-oriented that they see good in everyone and want to bring out the best in each person. They are inclined to let their hearts rule their minds.

Of the law enforcement personnel tested, 68 percent preferred SJ behavior, 16 percent preferred NT, 11 percent preferred SP, and 6 percent preferred NF. When we tested other people in government, we found that about 50 percent were SJs, and slightly more SPs were found among non-law enforcement government employees than among law enforcement personnel.

The question then arose whether law enforcement work itself tends to change one's preferences from the time of entry into the organization until the time of promotion. To explore this issue, we examined a single agency. Officers with five or fewer years of service were asked to complete the MBTI.® Forty-four agreed. That testing showed roughly the same kinds of preferences as our earlier tests—that is, a preference for introverted behavior and for sensing, thinking, and judging over intuition, feeling, and perceiving. Exactly one-half of the sample were either of only two temperament types—14 percent were ESTJs and 36 percent were ISTJs.

These data suggest some possible implications for the future. It appears that law enforcement as a profession may continue to recruit the same kind of people it now attracts and may lack members of other temperament types. Apparently the field attracts people who believe strongly in tradition, in accepting and fulfilling obligations, and in being well prepared for tasks; moreover, these people are willing to live in a hierarchical structure and are strong advocates of fundamentals. The kind of person who has these characteristics will accept amounts of responsibility that sometimes are beyond his or her individual ability and energy to fulfill. These people will reward others who act decisively and will try to preserve the morals and ethics of the organization and the community. They may, however, attempt to decide issues too quickly. Today's activities need to be planned and implemented in a timely order if the goals of the future, five or ten years ahead, are to be reached. The kind of person who is attracted to law enforcement may have difficulty in dealing with other types—for example, those who rely more heavily on feelings than on logic or are creative or intuitive in their approach to problems instead of drawing exclusively from the past and present.

But in this study, managers in law enforcement or those promoted to key managerial positions differ from line officers in that they more often have an NT temperament. It is possible that a department with NTs as commanders and SJs at other posts throughout the organization will benefit from the strengths of each. This will be true if the department is able to call on one group for preservation of the past and on the other for direction to the future. NT managers may have a tendency to be critical of subordinates, especially when viewed by SJs from their more relaxed point of view. NTs may make too many assumptions about their fellow officers, some of which may be accurate and others not. With NTs in managerial positions, law enforcement may find that the profession will be able both to conceptualize the future and to perform adequately in the present.

NFs apparently are not attracted to law enforcement, and that may be the profession's loss. The special quality of NFs is that they seek to help all other people reach their potential. Whereas NTs emphasize how to reach goals, NFs think about the possibilities in people. Therefore, NTs may help an organization achieve the maximum and NFs may help the individual people reach their goals. Without the NF's natural participation in task forces, group meetings are a little more difficult for the other three temperaments. NFs have a willingness to listen and are almost automatically empathetic and sincere in their relationships, and many people within law enforcement today must try hard to develop these qualities.

Uses for the MBTI®

The MBTI® may be used in a variety of ways to improve working relationships. For example, the police department may use the test simply to learn more about itself. As part of an in-service training program over a thirty-day period, all officers and supervisors might take the test. By participating in the inventory, members of the department can improve their understanding of themselves, each other, the department's managers, and the citizens they serve. Police managers can share the results of their tests with the supervisors and officers, giving their subordinates a better understanding of the managers' point of view.

Another example of the MBTI's® usefulness may come from the chief and subordinates seeking to improve their ability to communicate. Officers want a forum in which their views can be expressed and heard more readily. After taking the MBTI,® officers can discuss the results in relation to how their department operates. They may find that the chief is a sensory-feeling (SF) person, and the commanders below are predominantly sensory-thinking (ST) types. Therefore, most of the commanders' proposals may not address the issues of employee morale that the chief considers important. On the other hand, the commanders may become frustrated when their logical, precise proposals are consistently ignored.

A lack of feelers (Fs) in law enforcement may lead some officers to complain that they are not receiving enough praise or recognition for their work. Although the chief is an F, he or she may know little about these problems because the commanders (Ts) who report to him or her give little information about employee grievances. In addition, many of the commanders are also Js, who want to make quick decisions on the basis of given facts. Officers below them can become alienated because they are not allowed to participate in these decisions.

The Ss may disregard the intuitive Ns during decision-making sessions. They may dominate the discussions without really listening to the creative views of the Ns, who are thinking through the implications of the decisions and suggesting possible changes. After the MBTI® is discussed, the Ss realize the importance of including the Ns viewpoints in proposals.

In some police agencies communication issues may involve the preferences of the top commanders and the chief for extroversion (E) or introversion (I). Commanders who are introverts often assess situations in terms of their own reactions, often failing to pick up cues from others in the department. They may not seek contacts with their subordinates to determine sources of difficulty and therefore have little understanding of their subordinates' discontent. Inevitably, because it is the commanders who report to the chief, the chief also knows little about the complaints.

The three practical examples given above show five important uses for the analysis of personality differences through the MBTI:®

1. As a team-building tool. Those who take the inventory are able to recognize and accept the differences among them; improved communication can help them work together as a team rather than as a group of individuals.

2. As an aid in looking at issues from different perspectives. People with diverse styles can make different and valuable contributions to a decision-making

process. Groups often ignore ideas because the person who presents them has a preference type uncommon to the group—for example, when an intuitor presents ideas for change to a large group of sensory-thinking people (STs).

3. As a database. To help develop strategies for improving communication and coordination between people with different personalities.

4. As a tool to help police managers understand the ways in which program proposals come across to officers who have different preferences in regard to decision-making.

5. As an aid to officers in understanding why they may feel uncomfortable in certain job situations (for example, an ST would not feel comfortable in a job calling for creativity).

Another example of how the MBTI® can serve a police department involves the new chief who wants to build decision-making teams. The test can be used as a device to foster better understanding among team members, facilitate the decision-making process, and keep conflicts at a minimum.

Along with other instruments, the MBTI® has helped provide a composite of candidates vying for top management positions. City managers have used the inventory in choosing a police chief, but the results are not interpreted on a pass-fail scale. Instead, they help identify the kinds of interpersonal issues that can arise in a given environment. Then, once an applicant is accepted, any differences in style can be explained or ironed out. As an example, if the new chief is a heavy J (judger) and the manager is a P (perceiver), the two can (1) realize that they do not operate in the same time frame, (2) accept that fact, and (3) thereby work more cooperatively.

Overall, when interpreted properly, the MBTI® is a valuable means of describing people—keeping in mind that it merely identifies preferences and does not label these as being either "good" or "bad." Everyone has different gifts, and it is management's responsibility to appreciate the possible contributions of all these traits. Once people understand that individuals do vary, they can begin to understand that these variations are natural and that cooperation—rather than competition—can serve to maximize their potential usefulness.

Notes

1. *Myers-Briggs Type Indicator* (Palo Alto, CA: Consulting Psychologists Press, Inc., 1966).

2. C.G. Jung, *Psychological Types* (New York: Harcourt, Brace, 1923).

3. Mary H. McCaulley, "Introduction to the MBTI for Researchers," *Application of the Myers-Briggs Type Indicator to Medicine and Other Health Professions* (Gainesville, FL: Center for Applications of Psychological Type, Inc., 1977), p. 2.

4. Marilyn Bates and David Kiersey, *Please Understand Me* (Del Mar, CA: Prometheus Nemesis, 1978), p. 12.

5. Ibid., p. 13.

6. Ibid.

7. Ibid., p. 15.

8. Ibid., p. 54.

9. Isabel B. Myers and Peter B. Myers, *Gifts Differing* (Palo Alto, CA: Consulting Psychologists Press, Inc., 1980), pp. 85-86.

10. Ibid., pp. 105-106.

11. Bates and Kiersey, *Please Understand Me*, p. 189.

12. Ibid.

Discussion Questions

1. How can the MBTI® be used in a police department?

2. Are there any special types, as defined by MBTI,® that may make better police officers than other types?

3. Can the MBTI® be a useful tool in making promotions and assignments?

Functional Aspects of Police Management

Part Two

Once police managers understand the importance of the behavioral aspects of dealing with people within their agencies, they then must develop specific methods by which they can make effective decisions.

This section attempts to give police managers the tools they need to make the rational judgments necessary to maintain a stable organization.

This section opens with a discussion of the techniques of planning behavior. The police manager, in planning and implementing changes within a department, has responsibility for balancing the concern for risk and the concern for the system. This section discusses the alternatives and their positive and negative features.

The next chapter (Chapter 10) describes a method of decisionmaking that, if employed in the proposed step-by-step process, provides an effective tool for the police manager. This decision-making process is designed so that it can be implemented regardless of the police manager's style of management or communication process. The rational tool will help bring about effective staff work and give a clear-cut direction for all major decisions.

The management by objectives system discussed in Chapter 11 is a process by which a police manager can most effectively use the available resources. The process, which was designed for simplicity, has been tested and proven to be effective in both industry and government. Chapter 12 allows the student to begin the implementation of the early chapters of Part Two. Productivity is the overall goal of application of the functional aspects of police management.

Chapter 13 deals with the issues of fiscal management, fiscal control, and the budgeting process for a police department. This chapter destroys the myths that many police managers may believe about budgeting and explains the destructive role such misconceptions play in the development, execution, and implementation of a department budget. It is hoped that with this knowledge, police managers will face future budgetary processes with an open mind and a positive attitude as opposed to feeling defeated before even starting. One of the major obstacles to effective police management seems to be the lack of sufficient time for the average police manager to perform all the required tasks. Chapter 14 attempts to offer rational tools to help police managers control their time better.

By the use of a structured decision-making process, a specific management-by-objectives system, and wise utilization of time, the police manager can become more effective on a day-to-day basis.

Management Planning ‖ 9

Objectives

1. The student will become aware of the importance of individual activities in terms of the overall purposes and goals of the department.

2. The student should strive for stability within the department—to reduce randomness and chance in departmental operations.

3. The student will be concerned with the functioning of the police department as a whole—integrating the technical systems (e.g., departmental training, communications) with the human and social systems operating within the police department.

4. In decisions pertaining to the degree of risk to be taken, the student will consider:
   a. Available information
   b. Logical decisionmaking
   c. Assessments of the risk involved
   d. Estimates of the possibility of success

5. The student will become familiar with the four approaches of police management to planning.

6. The student will become aware of the four criteria to be considered before the most appropriate management planning approach is selected: (a) time, (b) severity, (c) frequency, (d) "ripple" effect.

Planning is the foundation on which much of police management is based. The effective police manager, if he or she intends to reach specific goals and objectives, begins to develop managerial planning strategies in order to eventually produce effective action. Planning involves the aspects of problem solving, problem identification, problem prevention, and, most importantly, decisionmaking. It is the police manager's responsibility to seek out and weigh alternative solutions and to anticipate their consequences.

Planning should occur both formally and informally at all levels of every police department. Whether developed by individuals or work teams, both short-term and long-term plans should be developed systematically. The quality of the final product depends in part on the ability of the people responsible for the planning and also on the influence that each has in solving problems and making decisions. The role of the police manager as a leader in developing planning strategies is important. Planning is strongly affected by the available facts and information and by the manner in which this information is used in identifying, evaluating, and solving problems.

The planning process can be approached in many ways, but we will discuss only the basic assumptions that can guide the police manager's thinking as he or she attempts to evaluate information, identify objectives, and use resources effectively.

Effective Planning and Use of Data

The quality and nature of police management planning revolves around two basic sets of concerns:

1.   The concern for system, which includes purpose, stability, and entirety.
2.   The concern for risk, which includes innovation and opportunity.

Concern for System

The three key ingredients within the concern for system are purpose, stability, and entirety.

Purpose. The first ingredient depends on how aware the police manager is of the importance of individual activities in relation to the overall purposes and goals of the police department. In the department, as goals or targets are established, there should be an attempt to establish a system of priorities, in the order of their importance, to the department's future.

Stability. The second ingredient within the concern for system is stability. The police manager should try to reduce randomness and chance in the operation of the department. It is a good policy to try to be in a position to anticipate and prepare for future problems. Standards, policies, rules, and regulations determine how the department should operate. The need for stability is reflected in the police manager's desire to establish some kind of order, sequence, and predictability in the police department as a whole and in the affairs of the individual officers.

Entirety. The third major factor that the police manager should be concerned with is the functioning of the police department as a whole. The department can be thought of as a complex system consisting of subsystems and units within the subsystems. In planning activities, it becomes the police manager's responsibility to link the information received from the uniformed operations with that from departmental records, communications, and training. In addition to the technical aspects, the police manager should be aware of the human and social systems within the agency.

The three ingredients—purpose, stability, and entirety—require careful coordination, for together they make up the concern for system, which the police manager should consider. The more aware the police manager is of the entire system, the better able he or she is to plan and work toward the department's stability and goals. On the other side of the coin, the manager who does not have an appreciation for the overall goals and purposes of the department may have difficulty carrying out his or her responsibilities effectively and making worthwhile contributions to the department as a whole.

The degree of the police manager's concern for the system can fall anywhere on a continuum, ranging from a high, or positive, concern to a low, or negative, concern.

The police manager should recognize, regardless of what level he or she has reached on the continuum, that a concern for the total system is necessary to maintain the direction and purpose that provides stability within the department. The manager may be at one end of the continuum, concerned only with the specific facts or elements within the total system and unaware of their interrelationship. Or he or she may be concerned with events or a combination of elements without perceiving that they are part of a system or subsystem that eventually affects the total operation of the department.

The effective police manager, in creating plans within any system or subsystem, should be aware of the effects that his or her decisions and planning activities will have on the entire department.

Figure 9.1 **Risk Continuum**

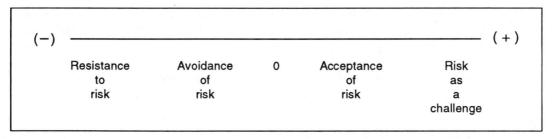

SOURCE: *Management Models—The Planning Process* (Westport, CT: Educational Systems and Designs, Inc., 1968). Reprinted with permission of Educational Systems and Designs, Inc.

Concern for Risk

The manager's concern for risk is demonstrated by his or her attitude toward innovation and opportunity. He or she should recognize that these factors are closely interrelated.

Almost every decision that the police manager makes involves some level of risk, opportunity, and innovation. The manager may take personal risks or those that affect the department. The police manager who attempts to be innovative by introducing something new into the department takes the risk of being rejected, laughed at, or, if the project fails, of receiving a reputation of incompetence. As far as the department is concerned, the risks of innovation include negative public reaction, higher costs, and a decrease in confidence among the personnel.

The decision pertaining to the degree of risk to be taken should be based on available information, logical decisionmaking, an assessment of the amount of risk involved, and an estimate of the possibility of success. An effective police manager is characterized by the willingness to take the risks appropriate to his or her level of authority and by a comprehension of the manner in which opportunity, innovation, and risk are interrelated.

The willingness to take risks is represented along the continuum shown in Figure 9.1. At the positive end of the scale, risk is viewed by the police manager as a challenge and an opportunity to utilize a given set of facts in the best interest of the entire police department. The negative end of the continuum represents resistance to risk. Thus, at one extreme, the police manager views risk as an opportunity rather than a threat, whereas the manager at the other end believes that the thrust of management practices should always be to avoid risk. From the middle, or the zero point, to the negative side there are various degrees of avoiding and resisting risk, and from the zero point to the positive side, there are various degrees of accepting and welcoming it.

Management Planning Model

Explanation

An understanding of the police manager's alternatives in planning behavior is assisted by a model based on the manager's concerns for system and risk. The management model reflects the following key management issues:

1. To what extent the police manager should be concerned with system.
2. To what extent the police manager should be concerned with risk.
3. How the police manager should interrelate these concerns in his or her everyday activities.

The model (Figure 9.2) shows the four possible relationships between risk and system. The manager may exhibit a high concern for system, purpose, stability, and entirety as well as for accepting risk as a challenge and an opportunity. The manager may be more negative and resistant to risk but still maintain a concern for system. The manager may have a negative concern for system and a resistance to risk taking. He or she may accept risk as a challenge but may have a negative inclination toward system, purpose, stability, and entirety in his or her planning activities.

Police managers should be aware that they may have to move from one approach to another, depending on the issues they face. In addition, there are varying degrees of system and risk within each approach. For example, although two managers may be concerned with system and accept risk as a challenge, one may view the challenge of risk more positively than the other.

The four segments of the model represent the different approaches of police management to planning: (1) purposeful approach, (2) traditional approach, (3) crisis approach, and (4) entrepreneurial approach.

Figure 9.2 **Management Planning Model**

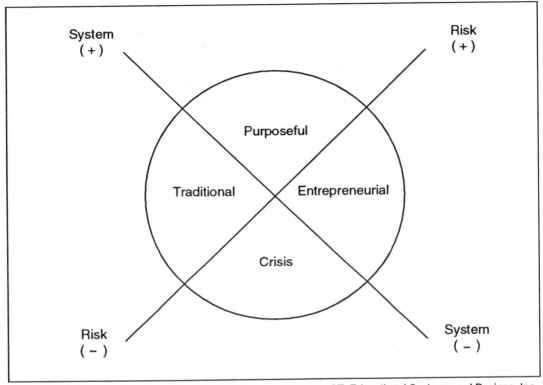

SOURCE: *Management Models—The Planning Process* (Westport, CT: Educational Systems and Designs, Inc., 1968). Reprinted with permission of Educational Systems and Designs, Inc.

Purposeful Approach. In this approach, the police manager is concerned with system, is willing to take risks, and wants to take advantage of opportunities. Under this approach, the police manager integrates purpose, direction, innovation, and creativity within the system to contribute to the growth of the department. The police manager who uses this approach does not view systems or stability within the department as ends in themselves or as means for minimizing risk but as ingredients important in maintaining a sense of direction and purpose. This manager will weigh the risk against the opportunity, taking into consideration the effect of the outcome on the entire police department.

Traditional Approach. The police manager who exercises this approach shows a high concern for system and stability and a desire to avoid risk, innovation, and creativity. This police manager wants to maintain the department in its present form, to support its traditions and precedents, and to minimize the risk situations. Tradition, precedent, and stability are highly regarded. The philosophy of this approach is best described by the statement, "We plan to stay on the same path, avoid rocking the boat, and eliminate any risk to our system."

Crisis Approach. This type of police manager demonstrates a minimal concern for system and a desire to avoid risk. He or she considers every problem, regardless of its importance to the functioning of the department, as a pressing issue that must be solved immediately. Each issue and incident is regarded as requiring quick and firm handling and is normally dealt with on the element or event level with little or no regard to the subsystem or system. Police managers using this planning approach attempt to minimize risk by maintaining a constant surveillance of subordinates and their activities, even if such surveillance stymies the department in its attempts to reach its goals.

Entrepreneurial Approach. This approach exhibits a low or negative concern for system and stability coupled with a strong willingness to accept risk and to take advantage of opportunities.

The members of police departments emphasizing this managerial approach are overly concerned with exploration and speculation. In many instances, they take inappropriate risks and may overtax themselves or the department with projects unrelated to specific purposes or goals. Police agencies involved in federal funding projects that distract them from their long-term direction and goals exhibit the entrepreneurial approach to management planning.

Responses Within Each Management Approach

The differences between the four approaches to police management planning can be further clarified by comparing the attitudes and actions of police managers supporting the different philosophies. The manner in which each management approach relates to the following activities will be described:

1. Planning in general
2. Long-range planning
3. The establishment of priorities
4. Structuring of the organization
5. The use of information
6. The achievement of control over activities

Purposeful Approach

1. Within the purposeful approach, the planning activity is designed to bring about sound direction and to help provide stability to the police department. If the opportunity for risk can contribute to the department's overall achievements and purposes, such opportunities are welcomed.

2. Long-range planning is both systematic and flexible to encourage innovation and creativity as new facts and opportunities come forth.

3. Priority is placed on building for the future while maintaining sound direction.

4. The department is organized so as to promote the flow of information among its members. Furthermore, the department's organization helps to handle short- and long-range problems and helps to balance risk taking with the concern for system.

5. The basis for future planning is contained in the information collected by the department. This information is used to provide control and direction for the department as it grows.

6. The department's goals are first examined, and then plans are implemented with systematic controls consistent with the overall purposes. These controls are sufficiently flexible to allow the individual members of the department to exercise initiative in making decisions that will further the department's goals.

Traditional Approach

1. Planning is designed to produce stable and sound direction. This requires specific procedures and steps as well as checks and balances so that the command level of the department can be assured that the action taken by subordinates is in strict conformity with the established plan.

2. Long-range planning is extremely systematic and is based on present practices and tradition. Whether these practices are beneficial to the department is not taken into consideration.

3. The highest priority of the traditional approach is to create a stable organization by developing rules and regulations to minimize risks.

4. The department is organized so that there is a clear-cut chain of command with a distinct delineation between staff and line operations. The staff functions are responsible for the creation and maintenance of the department's stability. The line operations are permitted to act only on opportunities approved by the command staff.

5. Much detailed information is collected on a systematic basis to reduce the risk of any chance occurrence within the department.

6. The established practices, procedures, and systems are designed to allow minimal deviation, thereby guaranteeing the close control of the staff over the entire department.

Crisis Approach

1. In the crisis approach, there really is no need to plan. Most situations that arise are emergencies, and they are dealt with on a day-to-day basis.

2. There is no long-range planning because in law enforcement, the future is totally unpredictable.

3. Priority is placed solely on current needs, problems, and issues.

4. The department is organized so that command-level people will be alerted when a problem arises in order to handle any emergency situation.

5. The information collected usually relates only to the problem at hand. It is designed to identify the cause of the problem, to provide solutions for it, and to prevent it from recurring.

6. Personal inspection by the manager is used as a control mechanism to guarantee that whatever mistakes do occur do not have any effect on the police operation.

Entrepreneurial Approach

1. In the entrepreneurial approach, action is the key to the department's success and plans restrict its freedom. Activities of the department are basically random and unconnected; therefore planning is impractical.

2. If the department is composed of sensitive and creative personnel who see opportunities and take appropriate actions, there is no need for long-range planning.

3. Priority is placed on discovering opportunities for improvement and growth.

4. Formal structures such as organizational charts and job descriptions are avoided because they tend to restrict the freedom and flexibility of the police personnel in responding to emergency situations.

5. Risk taking is promoted and trust is placed in the judgment of the department personnel. Therefore, only a limited amount of information is needed to assist them in solving problems and exploring opportunities.

6. Loose control is sufficient if the personnel possess the imagination and initiative to deal effectively with problems.

Selecting a Management Planning Approach

Before selecting a management planning approach, the police manager should evaluate its positive and negative features and its influence on the future of the department. The amount of energy expended in planning and problem solving should be in reasonable proportion to the potential gain to the department. If the energy expended is excessive, a quick solution to the problem may well be advisable. The manager should evaluate the potential gains in making a quality decision as well as the amount of effort necessary to obtain additional information. He or she should also be aware that the delays resulting from a long study sometimes slow the achievement of the overall goals of the department.

The potential gain or loss that the department may experience as a result of management planning is affected by specific criteria that the manager must weigh prior to selecting the most appropriate management planning approach. These criteria are time, severity, frequency, and "ripple effects."

Time is an important factor. Some problems that the police manager faces require an immediate solution. For example, a civil disturbance or the investigation of a serious crime must be dealt with as quickly as possible. In addition, long-range management planning is necessary to help identify the causes of problems, to develop plans and strategies for resolving future problems and, if possible, to prevent their occurrence.

The time demands in solving a specific problem often cause the police manager to consider different approaches to management planning. He or she may need one approach for short-term needs, another for those in the middle range, and still another approach for long-term needs.

Severity is the second criterion affecting the decision about the best approach to use. Usually, when the issue is pressing, such as an immediate threat, then the management approach that accomplishes the quickest results is the most effective. With a less severe problem, however, the manager may be willing to extend the amount of time in which to reach a decision, thus permitting the accumulation of additional information and an examination of alternatives.

Frequency is a third factor. If the issue arises only once, it often will affect only a few people. In this case, almost any of the approaches may be used. However, if the issue comes up with greater frequency, the purposeful approach may be more effective.

Ripple effects, that is, both positive and negative side effects, should be taken into consideration. The police manager should be aware of the possible results of using a specific approach to reach a decision. For example, if the department elects to implement a new field reporting system, then the manager should be sensitive to the effect of the system on the other members of the department as well as the operational personnel. In this case, the purposeful approach is the best management planning approach to use because it promotes the flow of information among the employees.

The police manager should realize that the selection of an approach should be based on whether it will promote or hinder the achievement of goals within the department. To select the proper management planning approach, the factors of time, severity, frequency, and ripple effects must be taken into account.

Conclusion

For many years, police management has defined planning as the development of a set of procedures and practices. The implication is that there is only one correct way to plan. This discussion has focused on the variety of approaches to management planning that are available to the police manager. The approach selected is determined by the manager's attitudes, assumptions, and concerns. The management planning model built around the two basic sets of concerns shows the responses elicited by each approach.

Although this discussion emphasizes that the purposeful approach is generally the most effective, the police manager should realize that only through an analysis of the situation and careful consideration of the criteria can he or she accurately decide which approach is best for the department.

Bibliography

Educational Systems and Designs. *Management Models—The Planning Process.* Westport, CT: Educational Systems and Designs, 1968.

Discussion Questions

1.   Discuss the level of expertise that, in your opinion, exists in the average police department today in relation to the manner in which commanders conduct planning.

2.   Do most police managers feel more inclined to accept risk as a challenge or are they strongly resistant to risk?

3.   According to the management planning model, which style is most prevalent in law enforcement agencies today? Which style should be used more, and how would you develop it? What technique should be developed for implementing the new style?

Problem Identification and Decisionmaking || 10

Objectives

1. The student will become aware of the differences between the management activities of problem analysis and decisionmaking.

2. The student will become aware of the distinctions between the types of management decisions: (a) routine, (b) resolving issues, (c) generating new ideas and techniques, and the most effective techniques by which they can be implemented.

3. The student will employ the four basic dimensions of a problem (identity, location, timing, and magnitude) as he or she searches for deviations within a problem.

4. The student will recognize the importance of and implement the management tool known as means-ends analysis.

5. The student will become familiar with and implement the eight steps of the decision-making process.

6. The student will become aware of the pitfalls common to the decision-making process in order to avoid them.

Problem analysis and decisionmaking are probably the most important issues that the police manager faces. On a day-to-day basis, the manager is continually thrust into situations that require logical, sound, and realistic decisions that, if successfully implemented, may lead to the resolution of problems and the achievement of specific objectives. Often, however, police managers are never quite prepared to adequately handle the rational aspects of problem analysis and decisionmaking.

Problem Analysis

Many police officers and police managers are not aware that there is a difference between the management activities of *problem analysis* and *decisionmaking.* They progress through their management careers using these terms interchangeably, and they attempt to apply identical approaches in dealing with each. Problem analysis is a careful examination of the facts to determine the cause of a problem so that positive action can be taken. The problem is defined as the difference between what *should be* happening and what *is* happening.

There are four basic steps to problem analysis: (1) recognizing problems, (2) separating and setting priorities, (3) specifying the priority problem to be analyzed, and (4) testing for cause.

Recognizing Problems

In the real world, things all too often are not the way we hope they will be. This is especially true in the day-to-day operations of the average police department. The behavior of police officers, supervisors, and civilian personnel often vary over a given period, as does equipment and the systems for effective use of equipment and personnel. Many times these variations are small and may go unnoticed. In fact, small variations in our daily activities are expected, and they do not arouse a strong concern for problem analysis or decisionmaking. Sometimes, however, small deviations, such as damage of a police vehicle or the excessive use of emergency equipment, may be a warning of a trend of deterioration. Such deviations then become significant factors, and their causes should be sought through systematic analysis. The key point in the first major step of problem analysis is to be aware of relevant problems.

To help identify the problem more clearly, the manager should ask the following questions:

1. Who or what is the cause or what is the identity of the problem that is being analyzed?
2. Where does the problem occur?
3. When does the problem occur?
4. How serious is the problem?

Separating and Setting Priorities

Of the many problems that the police manager notices, only a few demand immediate attention and action. For example, although Part I crimes may be rising at a slow rate, robbery may be rising at a rate twice that of any other crime. If the police department gives the same attention to the robbery problem as it does to the less demanding Part I crimes, the consequences could be disastrous. Problems with urgent and critical demands for attention should be given the highest priority. Other problems can be ranked by their relative importance. The criteria to use are different in each situation, and each police manager should establish his or her own priorities. Some criteria that can be used are (1) the growth rate of the problem, (2) the financial cost of the problem, (3) the effect the problem has on reaching stated objectives, and (4) the effects the problem has on such issues as condition of personnel, turnover rate, or morale. A small problem, when ignored, may rapidly grow to large proportions.

Specifying the Priority Problem to be Analyzed

Once a problem has been selected for analysis, the next step is to describe it accurately. Every problem has four basic dimensions: identity, location, timing, and magnitude. Any thorough description of a problem should include detailed information regarding these four dimensions. As the heart of problem analysis is the systematic search for deviations, it is essential that the basis for that search be carefully prepared. An accurate description of the four dimensions of the problem provides this basis.

The following six questions, when properly answered, can help analyze the problem and identify its priority:

Identity:	1.	What or whom does the problem concern?
	2.	What is the nature of the problem?
Location:	3.	Where, geographically, does the problem occur?
Timing:	4.	When does the problem occur?
Magnitude:	5.	What is the extent of the problem?
	6.	What is the trend—is the problem growing, stabilizing, or diminishing?

The matrix shown in Figure 10.1 is a tool the police manager can use in analyzing these important questions.

Testing for Cause

The cause of a problem can be determined from careful examination of all the possible causes. Each possible cause must be tested for a logical relationship with the facts. This is done by tentatively assuming a possible cause to be the actual cause, then testing it against the problem specification (six questions) and its four dimensions. If any of the facts of the specification discredit the possible cause that is being analyzed, that possible cause should be disregarded. This logical test is applied to each cause until one cause, or a combination of causes, is found to fit with the facts of the problem specifications.

To find the most likely cause, the police manager must ask, "If this possible cause is the most likely cause, how does it explain both the variations and the stable factors?"

Figure 10.1 **Problem Analysis Matrix**

Problem _____ _____ _____	Is	Is Not	(a) Differences	(b) Changes (Date & Time)	(c) Possible Causes	(d) Most Probable Cause
Identity 1. What or whom does the problem concern? 2. What is the nature of the problem?						
Location 3. Where, geographically, does the problem occur?						
Timing 4. When does the problem occur?						
Magnitude 5. What is the extent of the problem? 6. What is the trend—is the problem growing, stabilizing, or diminishing?						

(a) What is unique or distinct about the "is" of the problem as opposed to the "is not" of the problem?
(b) What circumstances were new, improved, modified, added to, or changed to bring about these differences?
(c) What was there in, around, or about these changes that could have triggered or created the problem?
(d) If this possible cause is the most probable, how does it explain both the "is" and "is not"?

The final test for cause is demonstrating that the cause actually triggered the problem in question. In the world of tangible objects, this testing or verifying is done through some sort of physical proof such as chemical analysis, measuring, or examining control areas. Less tangible problems centering around human behavior are often more difficult to verify. Reasons for problems in the department's morale must be found through more indirect means, such as in-depth interviews by a skilled counselor.

In verifying the cause, the police manager should answer the following questions: "What tangible, factual, scientific steps or research can I undertake to prove that this likely cause is the actual cause?"

Decisionmaking

General Principles

Three generally broad principles can be applied to the philosophy of decisionmaking. The first rule is *make the decision*. It is extremely important that decisions *be made:* an effective manager will soon be graded on his or her ability to *make* a decision rather than by the number of *correct* decisions that may be made. The second general principle is that once the decision has been made, *do not worry about it*. Implement it. The only times a manager should change the original decision is if it has been proved wrong or if a new and more effective approach has been established. The third rule deals with the question of consideration; the manager *should not try to satisfy everyone*. Managers are required to satisfy those people to whom they are responsible. A manager who attempts to satisfy everyone will not be able to make a sound decision or perhaps to make any decision at all.

Types of Decisions

Decisions of effective police managers are few in number but concentrate on solving important systemwide problems and deal with a high level of conceptual understanding. The police manager is not normally put in the position of making decisions quickly but instead is required to evaluate and manipulate many variables to arrive at an important decision which, when implemented, will strongly affect the day-to-day operations of the agency. The professional police manager wants to make sound rather than clever decisions.

Before analyzing how to make a decision, a conceptual framework must be established. In essence, before the police manager begins to make a serious decision, he or she must first place that decision in its proper perspective.

The first type of management decision is classified as *routine*. Routine decisionmaking is an important, daily activity of any police manager. Only through routine decisionmaking can a police department continue to function while allowing the manager the time he or she needs to solve major problems and make new innovations. Indeed, one criterion of an effective police manager is the ability to develop ways in which the routine and unimportant details of daily police activities can be handled. The police manager who is able to delegate as many decisions as possible to subordinates is the one who will not be spending a majority of time in routine decisionmaking.

The second type of decision directs itself to *resolving specific issues.* These issues result from actions taken by members of the police agency or from internal problems identified by external sources. An illustration might be the city manager who feels that the police department is not adequately and effectively using its present resources and who advises the chief to reduce crime as quickly as possible and to develop a new patrol allocation plan.

What happens under this type of decisionmaking is that the total police system is examined and isolated portions of the system are brought out for revising and revamping. An example of this occurs when the police chief recognizes that he or she does not have sufficient information with which to plan and make sound decisions. After careful examination of the total system, the chief realizes that the record-keeping function is outdated and neither collects nor analyzes the type of data that is needed to make decisions on a day-to-day basis. Pressure is then placed on the whole system; this pressure rebounds and directs itself to the records center. The result is the discovery of a serious problem in the records center, and finally some action is taken to develop a new system of record keeping so the necessary information can be collected, analyzed, and properly used.

The third type of decision is designed to *generate new ideas and innovative techniques.* Innovative decisionmaking in law enforcement is more difficult than routine decisionmaking or problem solving. In many cases the police manager lacks hard information to help reach adequate decisions. This type of decisionmaking requires the manager to take some risk, because all such innovations or new techniques and ideas will not be completely successful. This type of decisionmaking brings about progress in the profession and is extremely important for vibrant, growing police organizations.

Means-Ends Analysis

One of the key factors in decisionmaking is the development of a clear picture that shows the relationship between the objectives the department is trying to reach and the various alternatives the department must implement.

To build a chain that links the objectives or ends that have been set with the various methods available, a management tool called *means-ends analysis* is used. For example, assuming the problem involves poor performance on the part of records clerks and the records function in general, a specific objective—to improve the performance of records clerks—is set. The first question asked is, "Why improve their performance?" The answer is to help increase overall departmental efficiency, cut costs, avoid conflict that may exist between line and staff activities, and provide quality information for line operation. Through answering the question, specific broader goals or objectives have been identified at the level above the original objective.

Once the broader goals have been identified, we can proceed to the question of how they and the original objective can be achieved. The answer generated may be better or more supervision, an increase in the number of clerks, or retraining of the present clerks.

.The final means-ends analysis to meet the initial stated objective of increasing the production of records clerks is shown in Figure 10.2.

As shown in this illustration, the mechanics involved in developing a means-ends chain are not complicated. The first question involves the objective to be achieved. A move up the chain answers the question "why?" and a move down the chain answers "how?"

There is some value to the development of a means-ends chain before entering into decisionmaking. First, the means-ends analysis helps show the relationship of an objective at one level to the goal at a higher level, so that meaningful objectives can be set. Second, the means-ends analysis helps stimulate the development of a series of possible alternative solutions to a single problem. Third, it helps develop and translate rather broad objectives, such as increased efficiency, to some very sound actions at the bottom of the chain that can be specifically delegated to individuals; for example, the establishment of a forty-hour course for record clerks.

Fourth, the means-ends chain helps depict the numerous relationships and dependencies that the police manager must consider in the overall decision. Fifth, it helps to narrow the field of information and data that must be collected to make the decision final

Figure 10.2 **Means-Ends Analysis**

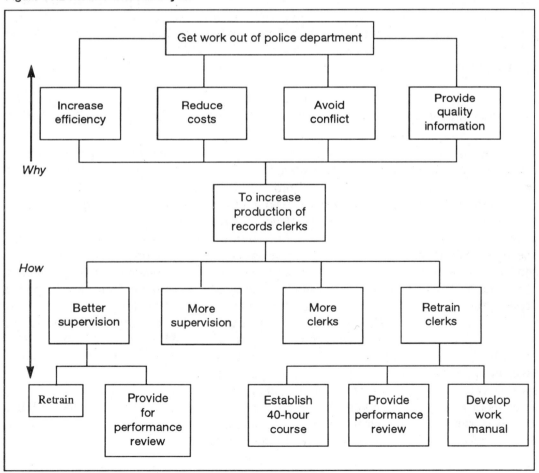

and to make the one that can be most effective for the police department. Finally, it helps highlight discrepancies between the objectives that have been set and the work that can be done at the bottom level of the work force.

Consider the overall goal or objective of trying to reduce costs for the department and the action of increasing the number of clerks at the bottom. They are inconsistent and would require either restating or eliminating the objective or eliminating the alternative solution of employing more records clerks.

The manager should realize that the means-ends analysis does not help select alternatives, nor will it dictate all the alternatives available. Means-ends analysis is nothing more than an organized method of brainstorming to help bring out objectives that should be achieved along with the methods that can be used to achieve them.

The Decision-Making Process

Once the means-ends analysis is completed, the following seven-step process can begin: (1) setting the objective, (2) identifying obstacles in the way of the objective, (3) collecting and analyzing data, (4) developing alternative solutions, (5) selecting alternatives to be implemented, (6) developing and implementing a plan, and (7) evaluating the results of implementation. This process can apply regardless of the type of decision being made. The importance of the decision, the time, and the information available for making the decision all affect the way the process is used.

Setting the Objective

Many management decisions become ineffectual because the process starts with a so-called problem that, when ultimately solved, does not contribute to the achievement of any objective. In this part of the overall process, the police manager determines the purpose and direction that the total decision-making process is to take by setting objectives.

Too many times, police departments devote the majority of their day-to-day activities to solving "problems." When the whole operation is carefully examined, an immediate question is raised: Why is so much time spent solving many little problems that constantly send you in numerous directions? The police command level should establish specific directions before becoming involved in the issue of decisionmaking. Consider the police department that revamps its records system without first establishing the purpose and necessity of the records. The money for sophisticated hardware is spent, consultants are hired, new personnel are employed and trained, physical space is revamped, problems generated by the change itself are solved, the new record system is implemented. After a short time, the police manager recognizes that the information received from the new record system is really not that different from the data generated prior to the expenditure of large amounts of money, time, and effort. The efficiency of the records has been improved, but the new system has not contributed to the overall purpose of the police department and in many instances may even be preventing it from reaching major goals.

The objective is a statement of reason or purpose, indicating that the police manager wants to solve problems and make decisions. These objectives should be tested for consistency against the department's overall goals.

Identifying Obstacles

The second step of the decision-making process is the definition and identification of conditions that obstruct and prohibit meeting the objectives. There are two parts to obstacle identification. The first is the ability to recognize deviations within the obstacles, and the second is to separate and set priorities to handle these deviations.

Sometimes it is appropriate at this point for the police manager to go back to the steps outlined for problem analysis. In many instances, however, the obstacles or stumbling blocks are fairly definitive and can be identified easily.

Collecting and Analyzing Data

When the objectives have been stated and the obstacles identified, the police manager should begin to determine the data relevant to the issue or the data necessary to make an effective decision. Facts and information should be obtained and organized. The police manager should determine which resources of time, money, and personnel are available and then determine the type and amount of information to be collected. It is possible to achieve an endless supply of information, but only if its limits have been defined can it be used effectively.

The police manager should determine how the information necessary for making a decision is to be obtained. How many times are police managers faced with the situation of examining reams of computer printouts when really only 2 or 3 percent of the data involved is necessary for making the decision? The police manager must determine in advance which criteria are eventually to be used in making a final selection of alternatives. The data that will be useful in examining each of these criteria should be collected.

Developing Alternatives

In this step, alternatives for reaching the objectives are determined and identified. If a thorough means-ends analysis has been prepared, alternative solutions will be delineated in the original means-end chart. The manager should be careful at this point not to restrict the number of alternatives or give consideration to whether they can be implemented. The major purpose of this step is to identify as many alternatives as possible, creating a clear picture of the total environment. The police manager can then select the most effective alternatives for resolving the issue.

Another way of stating this step is that the police manager is now in the process of searching for *all* possible solutions—*not* determining which is the best or most appropriate solution. The question being asked is, "What are the various solutions that can be considered?"

Most police managers recognize that if a solution is not included in the array of possible alternatives, then that solution cannot be chosen. Too often in practice, however, insufficient time is given in the development of a comprehensive list of possible alternatives or solutions. As a result, the effectiveness of the total decision-making process is hampered because only a few hastily identified alternatives are examined. Other solutions that may be even more appropriate for that police department are never examined.

Consider the police department that has stated a clear-cut objective of reducing the number of armed robberies by a specific percentage and carefully identified some of the obstacles to that objective. The next step might be to collect and analyze only information concerning successful projects or programs in other areas and not information available from the department itself. Too often the decision-making process comes to an abrupt end at this point. The police department decides that a program that was somewhat successful in another city will be highly successful in its city. In such a case, the number of alternative solutions has been greatly reduced by the narrow approach taken by the police manager.

Selecting Alternatives

When alternatives have been identified, the advantages and disadvantages of each should be carefully examined and weighed before selecting which alternative or series of alternatives is to be implemented.

The key factor in this step is establishing criteria for selecting the best alternative or alternatives.

A decision-making criteria chart, shown in Figure 10.3, can be an asset to the manager in the analysis of alternative solutions. Four major criteria normally considered in most decisions are included in the chart. First, does the alternative really contribute to the objectives? Second, how much will be spent if the alternative is implemented? Third, is it feasible—are the people available, does the manager have the authority, and is this alternative within the control of the manager? And last, how does the alternative affect the total system, considering the positive and negative side effects?

In completing the decision criteria chart, the police manager weights each of the alternatives as they are compared with each of the criteria. The weights can either be in a simple designation of high, medium, or low or can even be given a numerical value of 1 to 10.

Developing and Implementing a Plan

This step requires the programming of the decision. Before beginning the implementation of the decision, the resources of the department, especially the personnel, should be taken into consideration. A plan for the orderly process of implementing the selected alternatives should be established. This plan should provide for standards and controls, along with some feedback system. The controls, measurements, standards, specific objectives, time limits, and feedback system are necessary to allow the decisions to be carefully evaluated.

Figure 10.3 **Decision Criteria Chart**

Statement of Objectives: _____

Alternative	Contributing to Objectives (Output)	Cost (Input)	Feasibility	Side Effects	
				Positive	Negative

The plan should contain the data to be collected and analyzed in order to evaluate the total process. Ideas become great through their implementation. The police manager should continually strive to implement his or her carefully analyzed decision. This implementation process is the heart of the decision-making process. It is at this point that the decision or ideas generated earlier become realities in the day-to-day operations of the police department.

Evaluating the Results

The decision-making process and its divisions should be evaluated in terms of predetermined objectives and criteria. Evaluation begins the recycling process at the end of any of the steps developed earlier. For example, the collection of data as defined in Step 3 may result in the need to establish new objectives (Step 1). There is no straight line from the stated objective to the evaluation of the decision that was made. Constant examination and evaluation must occur at each step.

The evaluation process includes specifying measurable objectives, formulating a practical evaluation design, specifying data collection procedures, and specifying the data analysis methods.

Pitfalls of the Decision-Making Process

There are pitfalls that police managers will encounter if they are not careful in the overall decision-making process. It is possible to establish objectives that do not provide some framework within which decisionmaking can take place. Objectives using superlative terminology, such as "best," do not create a clear picture of what the department seeks; as a result, no real guidelines are developed.

There could be an inappropriate statement, or no statement at all, of what can be expected in the way of obstacles to be overcome. The police manager could define the obstacle in such a way as to limit the possibility of alternative solutions. Consider the police manager who decides that the only obstacle to reducing robberies is the judge who hears such cases. In essence, this manager has listed only one or two possible solutions, none of which may be under his or her control. The result will probably be no action at all.

Another pitfall common to the decision-making process is the failure on the part of the police manager to reexamine the previous steps as each succeeding step is developed. As data are organized, gathered, and analyzed, new obstacles may be discovered and perhaps a new objective established. There may be times that the data the police manager collects in the decision-making process are irrelevant. Consider the police manager who constantly examines pages of computer printouts to design a project to reduce robberies when a careful examination of just a few of the elements—time of day, location, day of week—may be sufficient to bring about programs that can be effectively implemented to reduce robberies.

There is also a tendency to begin to select alternatives before all the possibilities have been presented, thus limiting the solutions. As personnel work around and near such managers, it quickly becomes obvious that the alternatives that they both develop and select are the alternatives that the *manager* wants to implement.

The police manager should be aware of the need to establish specific criteria on which to base the numerous alternatives from which those to be implemented will finally be selected. If, for example, cost, time, and side effects are disregarded in the decision-making process, the resulting program will be doomed to failure long before its implementation begins.

Another and final pitfall that should be avoided is failing to follow up on decisions to guarantee that they have been implemented. This means developing checkpoints within the implementation process to guarantee that projects are implemented, evaluated, and adjusted when necessary.

Discussion Questions

1.   What models are available for decisionmaking?

2.   Should all managerial decisions be made using the special format?

3.   What makes an effective decisionmaker?

4.   Should there be a special format for decisions reached by all top managers of a police department?

5.   Is the decision-making process in a police department similar to that within industry or other phases of government?

6.   What are examples of some of the most difficult decisions a police manager has to make?

Management by Objectives ‖ 11

Objectives

1. The student will become familiar with the management by objectives (MBO) principle as an important tool in the decision-making process.

2. The student will become familiar with the specific guidelines for setting objectives within the context of the MBO system.

3. The student will be able to establish an evaluation system to determine the effectiveness of the individual program level, the goal level, and the objective level within the department.

4. The student will be able to implement the MBO system on the basis of the assumptions of McGregor's Theory Y.

5. The student will become familiar with the drawbacks of the MBO system.

Introduction

Management by objectives is a functional process that has been discussed by many authors. Each author has provided similar, but not identical, definitions.

A complete volume on this subject, called *Policing by Objective*, has been prepared by Social Development Corporation, Hartford, Connecticut, under the direction of Val Lubans. It now appears as a prescriptive package distributed by the National Institute of Law Enforcement and Criminal Justice of the Law Enforcement Assistance Administration.

The system described in this chapter has been implemented effectively in various police departments. It is by no means the only management tool and can and should be adjusted to meet the needs of the individual police agency.

Management by objectives, or MBO, as it is more commonly known, may be viewed as a management tool that aids in the decision-making process. The numerous principles developed under decisionmaking also apply to MBO. MBO is designed as a method by which police managers and their subordinates can identify areas of growth, set standards to be reached, and measure the results against the standards that have been set. MBO relates directly to what is expected of the department and is usually expressed in terms of objectives. It relates to the development of teamwork within all levels of the department by establishing common goals and projects.

The concept of management by objectives is based on a number of behavioral science assumptions. The police manager who emphasizes MBO assumes that all officers want to know what is expected of them and whether they are performing satisfactorily. The manager further assumes that the officers want to participate in and influence decisions that affect the overall purpose and goals of the police department.

MBO may also be viewed as a method of changing the present system of making decisions. It is an important tool in the decision-making process and provides a control component for monitoring success toward the specific goals of the department. MBO can also be used as a training and development tool. It is a method of maximizing the utilization of all personnel within the police department. MBO has also been used as a method of enhancing the communication process within police departments.

An examination of a police department includes three broad areas of analysis. The first, the input process, consists of the elements that must be present before the department can begin to achieve any goals or objectives. The inputs include personnel, money, time, and equipment. The second consists of the activities of the people within the department. If something can be described as "doable," it must be included as an activity. Examples include typing, driving, developing plans, patrolling, and investigating. The third area involves output, which is the result achieved by the input.

MBO addresses itself to all three areas. It starts with the result, or output, area. The MBO process requires police managers to carefully define what results they are attempting to achieve in a specific period, usually of three to five years. This careful analysis of goal and objective setting before agreement on projects is an effective way of increasing the efficiency of the activities within the agency.

Under the MBO process, not every activity of the department should be included. The MBO process is designed to help bring about the changes necessary to upgrade departmental performance. MBO may be viewed as a tool of change and should be directed toward approximately 20 percent of the activities within a police department.

MBO can best be implemented in line operational functions, as opposed to staff or administrative functions. This is because it is easier to set objectives to define the results. This does not, however, imply that MBO cannot be used in staff functions, but it is generally better implemented first in line operations with the assistance of staff personnel. The disadvantage of this implementation process is that it generally has a tendency toward forcing line personnel to possibly downgrade the role that staff plays in the overall operation of the police department.

Some police managers attempt to implement MBO as a "system of management," claiming that it fulfills all the broad managerial purposes of planning, organizing, controlling, communicating, and staffing. This is not necessarily true. In fact, when MBO is viewed as a system of management, it tends to downgrade the routine activities of the police department.

In viewing MBO, police managers must constantly keep in mind its role as a rational tool to aid and assist them in making the broad managerial functions of planning, organizing, staffing, and implementation easier. It does *not*, however, take the place of these broad functions. Furthermore, by ceasing to place emphasis on other activities of the police department and by spending too much time in attempting to implement MBO, managers may fail to achieve the real purposes of the department. This has been one of the major downfalls of MBO in some government agencies in which police chiefs have attempted to implement MBO as a strong control tool instead of using it as a rational tool to assist them in long-term, short-term, and everyday planning.

There is a distinct difference between MBO and program budgeting. A description of what constitutes a program budget will help to clarify the MBO philosophy and system.

Plan-program budgeting is essentially a method of controlling budgetary expenses, with an emphasis on programs such as suppression of crime or investigation of criminal activities. The program budget attaches a dollar amount to every activity within the police department. Under this budget, activities are grouped together in broad categories such as investigation, patrol, management services, and technical services.

The major differences between MBO and program budgeting are as follows: (1) program budgeting does not have specific objectives attached to the programs and (2) program budgeting refers to all departmental expenditures, whereas the MBO portion may amount of only 20 percent of activities within the department.

The cost of implementing an MBO project does not necessarily correspond to the total amount given to the department. For example, if a police department that is operating under a program budget is given $500,000 for control and reduction of crime, that amount must cover the cost of prevention, suppression, investigation, apprehension, prosecution, and recovery of property. In this same department, an MBO program would direct this broad budgeting toward specific objectives, such as a 10 percent reduction of robberies. An evaluation of this reveals that the objective under the MBO program would cost the department only a small portion of the total amount allowed under program budgeting for control and reduction of crime. The manager is able to evaluate the total cost of the broad activity as well as the smaller cost of reaching a specific objective.

MBO is a tool to be used for bringing about the desired growth of the organization; it is not a control mechanism for expenditures.

Police managers who accept MBO must also respect the personnel in the department and have faith in them. Their philosophy must be consistent with the means structure as defined by Maslow and with the assumptions of Theory Y as defined by McGregor. They should be able to recognize the potential for contribution by the people in their command.

The MBO System

MBO can best be described as a seven-part process. These parts (shown in Figure 11.1) are:

1. Recognition of community values and departmental beliefs
2. Statement of departmental mission
3. Establishment of long-term goals
4. Establishment of short-term objectives
5. Development of projects
6. Development and implementation of action plans
7. Evaluation of the system

Figure 11.1 **Management by Objectives System**

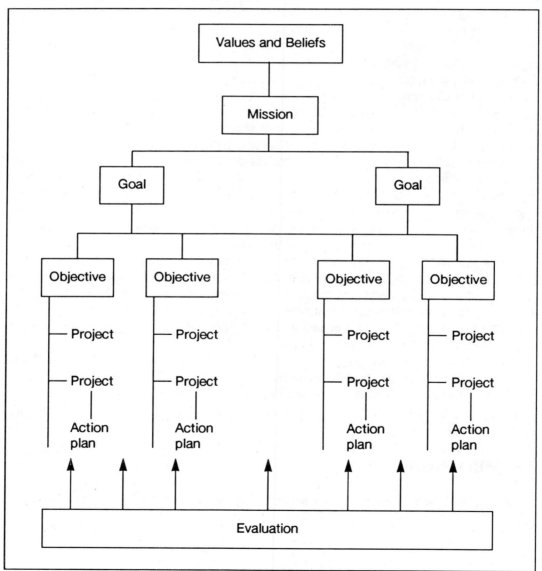

Values and Beliefs

Values are defined as the social principles that have been accepted by the community. These include attitudes about honesty, community ethics, level of service, crime, vice conditions, and traffic problems. The values of the community are usually exhibited through the policy statements issued by the city council. The police chief should help to establish and interpret these policies as they apply directly to the police department. These policy statements are often issued in the form of departmental beliefs.

Examples of belief statements dealing with the issue of crime might read as follows:

> Criminality resulting from poverty, unemployment, and slum conditions is a community problem, not a problem for the police alone. The police have a responsibility to prevent and suppress crime and to solve crimes once they have occurred, but the police cannot prevent or solve every crime that occurs. The police must have the active cooperation, assistance, and moral support of the community that they serve.

> For a crime to occur, two factors must be present: opportunity and desire. It is the function of the police department to minimize the opportunities for crime by such means as open, conspicuous, and aggressive patrol. Desire, however, is a factor controlled by potential offenders and those who influence their thinking. It is a factor over which the police exert little control. Each police officer is chief of police within the area to which he or she is assigned. Officers are accountable for the crime and vice that exist on their beats, and they have a responsibility to prevent crimes whenever possible.

Mission

The mission statement is the broadest, most comprehensive statement that can be made about the overall purpose of the police department. Another way of viewing the mission statement is that it spells out the primary responsibility of the police department, which justifies its continuing support by society and provides initial direction for the management of the police organization. The main purpose of a mission statement is to provide a focus for the resources of the police department and for the development of goals, objectives, and projects.

A simple mission statement for a police agency might be the following:

> Our mission is to ensure the safety and protection of both the property and person of all of the inhabitants of our community and to regulate and control the flow of traffic in order to facilitate the movement of persons and goods within our city and to reduce the impact of crime on the inhabitants of our city through investigation, apprehension, and adjudication of persons involved in criminal offenses.

Goals

Under an MBO system, goals may be viewed in two different ways. The first is that goals should be idealistic—perhaps impossible to achieve. An example of this view would be a goal to eliminate crime. The second and more popular view is that goals should be measurable and within reach, even though they may require a long period for implementation.

Goals, although broad in nature, may be specific in terms of the major accomplishments desired by management over two years' time. Examples of such goals might be: "the reduction of Part I offenses by 10 percent within the next two years," or "the reduction of the average monthly traffic accident rate by 5 percent within the next three years."

Objectives

Objectives are considered short-term achievements. They must be attainable within a given period. The maximum period for accomplishment of objectives within the MBO system is one year. The objectives themselves must be tied to specific measurements. An example of an objective is: "to reduce the number of robberies in the eastern sector of the city by 5 percent within the next six months."

In establishing objectives, it is mandatory that the manager stay away from superlative phrases such as "finest" or "best." Within the MBO system, there should be a minimum of one and a maximum of six objectives for each established goal. Objectives should be used as guides in the planning and implementation of specific projects. They should be seen as tools for measuring the progress that is being made toward the achievement of goals. Objectives should define the results that are to be achieved, not activities that are to be performed.

In addition to being measurable, objectives must satisfy two other conditions—they should be both feasible and cost-effective. The levels of accomplishment within each project must be practical in the sense that they are attainable. The goals and the objectives must also be cost-effective; that is, the expected contribution to the individual project objectives, as well as the overall objectives of the MBO system, must justify the cost of the individual projects.

The following guidelines for setting objectives will help the police manager achieve the most from the MBO system.

1. *Define results to be achieved, not activities.* In stating objectives, the result should be described, not the activity necessary to meet this result. For example, an objective of "putting the stakeout squad in high crime areas," is really an activity that should be designed to meet some stated objective, such as "reduce robberies by 10 percent within the next six months."

2. *Relate the objective to goals at the next higher level.* As objectives are established, it is important that the police manager focus on the overall good to be achieved and that the goals be balanced with the major purpose of the police department, which is the protection of life and property. There is a natural tendency for police managers to set objectives that they feel will be interesting, and they may ignore objectives that are necessary. The police manager, especially if at the middle level of the department, should view his or her role as it fits into the total MBO system and then assist in establishing objectives that can best contribute to the stated overall goals of the department. He or she must be careful to avoid establishing objectives that are based on what he or she can or would like to obtain.

3. *Set objectives at a reasonable level.* The objectives should be challenging and should call on the police managers to do better in the future than they did in the past. There is sometimes a tendency for police managers to establish objectives at such a high level that they may be impossible to achieve. In writing objectives, managers should be careful to balance the need to challenge with the need to achieve. Police managers should not set impossible objectives for themselves or their subordinates.

4. *Use language that everyone will understand.* Objectives should be written clearly and simply in language that both subordinates and supervisors can understand.

5. *Emphasize realism.* Objectives are valuable as guides for action only when they are prepared in a realistic manner. The police manager at the middle level should not try to impress superiors by establishing objectives that are unrealistic.

Projects

Once objectives have been determined, it is time to begin to put into action the projects that have been designed to meet these objectives. Projects involve the establishment of the step-by-step process that will be used to reach each of the objectives. A single project may have an effect on more than one objective. For example, if the objectives to reduce robbery by 5 percent and burglary by 10 percent have been established, a project using a tactical unit in certain areas of the city may have an effect on both objectives.

Every project that is implemented under an MBO system must be specifically designed to attain one of the already established objectives. Within the individual projects themselves, objectives can be set that define the period needed for implementation of the project and the results that are to be achieved by that project. For example, how long will it take to assign personnel to the tactical unit, to have the unit analyze present crime trends, and then to begin to take positive action toward reaching the objectives of reducing robbery and burglary?

Projects should also be designed for the short term. If the objective is to reduce robbery by 10 percent within a twelve-month period, then there may be three or four projects during this twelve-month period that are part of the attempt to reach the stated objective. Each project may require only two or three months. They may overlap, or some may begin immediately and continue throughout the entire twelve-month period.

Even though a long-range goal and a series of specific objectives have already been determined, it is important that individual accomplishments also be included with each project. These steps for accomplishment are the objectives within the individual projects. It is really these project objectives that are carefully evaluated at the beginning of the process and later analyzed to determine the success or failure of the objectives of the overall MBO system.

Action Plans

Action plans are the detailed steps of activities necessary for the completion of the individual projects. They dictate the responsibility that has been assigned to particular people, define the mutually acceptable target date, and determine how the task itself will be verified once it has been completed. All action plans relate directly to the projects to which they are assigned.

A simplified form can be used for the development of action plans, such as that shown in Figure 11.2.

Figure 11.2 **Example of an Action Plan Form**

	ACTION PLAN		
Project Manager			
Task	Responsibility	Date	Verification

Evaluation[1]

Evaluation in the MBO system is considered one of the most important steps. Evaluation is the process of determining the amount of success in achieving the predetermined objectives. Evaluation may be interim, to determine the amount of progress that has been made, or final, to determine the ultimate level of accomplishment.

Evaluation information is required for three different types of measurement: (1) external measures that determine the amount of success or failure in achieving the predetermined objectives and goals; (2) internal measures that determine (a) the efficiency and effectiveness of the individual and (b) the difficulties or stumbling blocks that were encountered and describe how they were overcome or why they could not be overcome; and (3) research measures that yield insight into cause-effect and other relationships that are useful as an empirical and theoretical base for future program planning.

The police manager should realize that the best evaluators of the projects that are implemented by police personnel are the individuals who conduct the implementation and manage the organization itself. As individual projects are developed, evaluation criteria can be established for each. Consider the attempt to evaluate a special stakeout unit designed to reduce armed robberies. The criteria for determining the success or failure of this project would be how many robberies actually occurred; how much time, money, and effort was placed into the project; and how long it took to reach the success level that was finally attained.

Police managers can help evaluate this project. First, the area of the city in which the special stakeout unit is to be employed should be examined for its present robbery rate. Then, at the end of the project, the number of robberies must be determined. The manager should also use another area of the city as a "control" area to be evaluated in terms of any reduction or increase in robberies. The police manager should determine whether other crimes in the stakeout area have increased or decreased. The rates of apprehension should also be examined, both in the control area and the experimental area.

Many criteria can be used to determine the success or failure of a project, but the most effective approach is to decide on only a small number of criteria as a measure.

The police manager can establish an evaluation criteria chart similar to that for the decision criteria discussed earlier. The numerous projects can be listed on one side, and the criteria—such as implementation gained from each and feasibility—can be listed across the other. Information gained from each project can be evaluated against the stated criteria. The police manager then has a simplified evaluation system to use in determining the effectiveness of the individual program.

In addition to the careful evaluation of individual projects at the project level of the MBO system, evaluation must be conducted at the objective and at the goal levels. Evaluation at the objective level can be based on analyzing the effect of complementary and duplicating projects designed for achieving the same objectives. Whenever possible, the police manager should establish both evaluation and control groups to isolate the effectiveness of the individual project from any external effects. In addition, projects that are directed toward the same objective should be separated, either in time or space, so as to avoid a subjective decision concerning which project had the greater effect on the stated objectives.

Evaluation of groups of projects is also necessary to determine which strategies proved to be most effective in achieving the objectives and goals. In larger cities, projects can be grouped by geographic areas, concentration of target population, or type of area, such as residential or commercial.

Evaluation includes a series of activities: (1) specifying measurable objectives, (2) formulating a practical evaluation design, (3) specifying data collection procedures, and (4) specifying data reduction and analysis methods.[2]

This overall process is shown in Figure 11.3 and applies whether the evaluation is being conducted at the goal, objective, or individual program level.

Specify Measurable Objectives

To have proper output from this first step in the evaluation process, the objectives should be "measurable." Therefore, the output should clearly identify the individual data elements that must be used to determine the amount of success.

In Step 1, the objectives must be converted to numerical terms. For example, if the objective was the reduction of robbery by 10 percent within a six-month period, then the 10 percent must be translated into numerical figures—from 60 robberies per month to 54 robberies per month.

In addition to translation to numerical figures, there should be an identification of the performance measures that will be examined in the individual projects being directed toward the objective. Using the 10 percent robbery reduction as an example, the basic performance measures may include such broad factors as location, time, and whether the robbery is classified as commercial, residential, or open-space. Once these performance measures have been identified, data elements can be collected and analyzed for each of the performance measures. Data elements for location may be the specific address, reporting area, census tract, patrol beat, or any combination of these. The data elements for time may include the month, day of the week, and hour of the day designated in groups of four hours, eight hours, or individual hours. The data elements for commercial

Figure 11.3 **A Schematic Flow Model of the Evaluation Process**

SOURCE: Norman Baker, Edward Unger, Terry Sprott, Thomas Buskirk, and Gordon Miller. Developed for the Atlanta Impact Program (LEAA).

robbery might include banks, gas stations, food markets, and liquor stores. For residential robbery the data elements might include house, apartment, hotel, or motel; and for open space, they could include street, alley, parking lot, or park.

If evaluation is to be conducted, the objectives should be measurable, feasible, and cost-effective.

Step 1 is described in Figure 11.4. As this figure indicates, the output of Step 1 is a measurable objective that is feasible and cost-effective and internally consistent with criteria, performance measures, and basic data elements.

Figure 11.4 **A Schematic Flow Model of Step 1: Specify Measurable Objectives**

SOURCE: Norman Baker, Edward Unger, Terry Sprott, Thomas Buskirk, and Gordon Miller. Developed for the Atlanta Impact Program (LEAA).

Formulate a Practical Evaluation Design

The important words in this step are "practical" and "design." The purpose of the evaluation design is to assure the police manager that it is possible to distinguish between changes caused by the projects and other changes that may have occurred within the department. Therefore, the evaluation design must distinguish the impact of other projects from the effectiveness of the projects being evaluated.

The manager has two types of designs from which to choose in evaluating individual projects. The first is referred to as "before-after" design and the second as the "control-group" design.

Use of the before-after design is the more common method of evaluating projects in terms of success or failure. This approach involves only one step—comparing the level of activity prior to the implementation of the projects to the level of activity after the projects have been implemented. A simple example is the comparison of robbery rates in a certain area of the city during the first six months of Year I (prior to the implementation of the MBO system) and the robbery rates of the same area of the city during the first six months of Year II (after the projects have been implemented). The difference in the robbery rates during these two time periods is an indication of the success or failure of the MBO system.

The control-group design is based on the assumption that it is possible to identify two environments, two geographical population areas, that have similar characteristics. One area is designated as the experimental group, and the other as the control group. The basic data elements are collected for both groups, with the further assumptions that the factors influencing one group (except for the projects being implemented in the experimental group) also influence the other. The assumption is that the only difference between these two groups during the period of program implementation is the project activity. Therefore, it is safe to assume that the difference between the performance measures found in the experimental group and those in the control group can be attributed directly to the projects that are being implemented in the experimental group.

At least one of the approaches should be used to guarantee some valid evaluation; however, in many instances it is impossible to use both the control-group and the before-after approaches.

The evaluation design must also be practical. It should be possible for the police manager to collect and manage the required data elements so that careful evaluation can be made. In this instance, the manager should consider such questions as: (1) Are the data we need currently being collected for some other reason? (2) If the answer is no, then can these data be collected only by implementing minor modifications of the present data collection system? (3) Would it be necessary to develop a completely new data collection system?

The manager must also examine the cost of obtaining this information and whether it will be reliable and valid.

Step 2 is shown in graphic form in Figure 11.5. The results of this step are (a) a practical evaluation design, (b) the identification of required basic data elements, (c) the specification of interim goals and objectives, and (d) the timetable for the accomplishment of these interim measurements.

Figure 11.5 **A Schematic Model of Step 2: Formulate a Practical Evaluation Design**

```
                              Basic data
                         elements from Step 1
  INPUT
  ----------------------------------------------------------------
  PROCESS
                         Determine the type of design
                            that will be utilized

            Control group                        Before-After

     Identify potential experimental        Check to confirm that no
        and control "groups"                critical exogenous conditions
                                            are expected to change

       Check such aspects as                  Specify prior data
     crime rates, trends, offender         necessary to forecast trends
         population, police
      operations, and exogenous
             factors
                                              Identify agency
      If satisfactory "groups"            personnel who can provide
    exist, designate experimental         subjective inputs regarding
        and control groups                    exogenous factors

                      Check if the design is
                       practical: existence
                    availability, cost, validity,
                       reliability, necessity
  PROCESS
  ----------------------------------------------------------------
  OUTPUT
                      Practical evaluation design
                    Required basic data elements
                       Interim goals, objectives
                  and timetable for accomplishment
```

SOURCE: Norman Baker, Edward Unger, Terry Sprott, Thomas Buskirk, and Gordon Miller. Developed for the Atlanta Impact Program (LEAA).

Specify Data Collection Procedures

Within this step, the police manager should perform the following activities: (1) determine how the data will be collected, (2) specify by whom the information will be collected, (3) decide on the frequency with which the information will be collected, and (4) design forms that will be used to collect the information.

These activities should be formulated for all of the required data elements that will be collected and analyzed.

The information system presently in use should be examined in considerable detail, and it should be used as much as possible. In some instances, the police manager may determine that the information necessary for evaluation *is* being collected but is not being used for output purposes. Therefore, minor adjustments should be made that will produce this information in the output process. For example, if the manager wants to know whether robberies have been directed toward gas stations, liquor stores, or banks, he or she may find this information in the field reports. The manager would then only have to take this information from the field reports and have it analyzed on a monthly basis. If,

Figure 11.6 **A Schematic Model of Step 3: Specify Data Collection Procedures**

SOURCE: Norman Baker, Edward Unger, Terry Sprott, Thomas Buskirk, and Gordon Miller. Developed for the Atlanta Impact Program (LEAA).

however, the information is not currently available, then the manager must take the necessary steps to guarantee that the information will be collected and analyzed.

The process of Step 3 is shown in Figure 11.6, with the output being the specification of the information collection procedures.

Specify Data Reduction and Analysis Methods

This step is necessary to enable the police manager to measure the success of projects in reaching the goals and objectives. This step also helps to describe relationships between projects, and it provides knowledge that may be useful in future planning and project activities.

The success of each project must be measured so that the police manager will have a way of monitoring, controlling, and directing the activities within each project from its inception to its conclusion. By assessing the program's failure or success and that success's contribution to the overall objectives and goals of the MBO system, the police manager can make recommendations as to whether the individual project should be continued, modified, or eliminated. In addition, the description and explanation of the data produced from the projects can be used to analyze the reasons for the degree of success or failure of the total MBO system. The manager can use this analysis to improve management practices and upgrade the operation of the entire department.

With regard to the measures of success, the police manager should attempt to determine the degree to which the projects have achieved their individual goals and objectives as well as the objectives of the MBO system. This data analysis can also help to formulate a value judgment as to whether the projects should be continued or expanded to other units within the department.

The data reduction and analysis methods include such activities as weekly reports, monthly reports, before and after comparisons, comparisons of the control group to the experimental group, and the use of maps, charts, and graphs. In the larger police agencies, this data reduction and analysis would include the use of computerized information systems and highly technical procedures for summary evaluation of the information.

In addition to specifying the data reduction analysis methods to be used, the police manager should identify the individual responsible for the evaluation analysis. In many instances this can be personnel who have already been assigned to activities such as operations analysis, research and development, or crime prevention. The manager should also determine when interim evaluations will be conducted. The number of interim evaluations depends on the length of the project, its cost, and its complexity. Within this step, the police manager should also specify how the evaluation results will be used, especially with regard to the overall management practices and procedures of the department.

Step 4 is described in Figure 11.7, with the output being the full specifications of the evaluation process.

Figure 11.7 **A Schematic Model of Step 4: Specify Data Reduction and Analysis Methods**

SOURCE: Norman Baker, Edward Unger, Terry Sprott, Thomas Buskirk, and Gordon Miller. Developed for the Atlanta Impact Program (LEAA).

Implementation

Once the manager has some understanding of the MBO system, he or she must develop such a system and begin to implement it within the department. The MBO system is most effectively put into practice through the use of 9, 9 team management. It must also be based on the assumptions of Theory Y.

Establishment of Goals by Top Managers

It is the responsibility of top-level managers to determine long-range goals and to give direction and set parameters for the managers at the middle level. It is the middle managers who are responsible for the development and implementation of the objectives and projects.

Establishment of Objectives for Each Goal by Middle Managers

Once top management has determined the goals for the agency, middle management must submit a series of objectives for each stated goal. In this step, the managers at both levels must have an opportunity to clarify the stated goals and proposed objectives through effective communication.

Selection of Objectives by Top Managers

In this step, top management reviews the objectives with middle management. Depending on the ability of middle management to implement the management by objectives system, top management selects from one to six objectives for each stated goal. The selection of objectives by top management should follow as closely as possible the priority listing of objectives by middle management. It is top management's role to carefully evaluate each of the objectives submitted for inconsistencies and to adjust the measure of achievement in each objective if they feel it is either too low or too high.

Finalization of Objectives by Middle Managers

In this step, middle management is given the responsibility of finalizing all stated objectives, even though top management can place certain guidelines on how each objective is to be stated. For example, they may require the objective to state, first, what it will accomplish (reduction of robbery by 10 percent); next, the cost of the objective (not to exceed limits already established within the budget); and third, its completion date (within the next six months).

Overview of Projects for Each Objective Submitted by Middle Managers

In this step, middle management is required to submit for approval by top management a list of projects to be implemented in order to reach each objective. This step requires close coordination between top and middle management as well as horizontal coordination between the middle managers. The projects should be carefully screened to avoid duplication and to evaluate all possible consequences and side effects. Consider a project to implement a special tactical unit in one control area, a special stakeout squad in another high-crime area. If both projects are implemented at the same time, even though both have merits and will have some effect on the overall objective of robbery reduction, the effect of transferring personnel within the patrol force to handle both projects may seriously hamper the overall operation of the uniformed forces. The negative side effects may cause more harm and prevent the department from reaching its overall goal of reducing robbery.

Development of Detailed Projects by Middle Management

After the projects have been approved by top management, the middle managers must develop specific formats for the implementation of each project. The middle manager should refer to the seven-step process developed under decisionmaking and use it to develop the individual projects. Each project has its own objectives, it defines the obstacles to completion of the project, and it determines the data that is to be collected and analyzed. In this case, it would not be necessary to develop alternative solutions because the project has already been selected. But the manner in which the project is to be implemented can be developed according to how it will be evaluated.

A simple one-page information sheet can be developed to give all necessary data concerning each project. This information sheet should include such items as (1) who will be responsible for the project; (2) the stated objectives of the project; (3) which overall objectives the project might affect, as well as its effect on the objectives of the MBO system; (4) what results are expected; (5) what steps are to be taken and who is responsible for each step; and (6) the beginning date, the interim evaluation dates, and the ending date.

This form should also include such items as (a) *staffing*—the personnel who will be involved with the project in each of its steps; (b) *coordination* of the individuals from within the department, as well as those outside the department whose services will be necessary for the successful completion of the project; (c) *training*—what additional training of individuals is necessary; and (d) *evaluation*—the determination of the overall success or failure of the project.

Evaluation

Steps within each project should be carefully evaluated on review dates for success as well as failure and for determination of changes that may be required. This evaluation should be flexible enough to allow project directors to initiate changes they deem necessary or to recommend that the project be cancelled due to lack of success.

This step-by-step implementation process forces the police agency and the manager to plan systematically.

Additional Use of the MBO System

As a police department evaluates its direction, it views numerous issues to help define where it is, and it examines its values, beliefs, problems, environmental factors, and the elements contained in the evaluation process. To define direction, it establishes a mission statement, goals, and objectives. To analyze and describe how it is going to achieve the mission, goals, and objectives, projects and action plans are developed.

Environmental factors may also affect the MBO system. Environmental factors are defined as those over which the police department has no direct control. Typical examples might be the appointment of a new city manager, who emphasizes values and beliefs different from those already established by the police department, or a new governing board that has different priorities—or it could be a new law that requires a different course of action or that changes present procedures in the police department. Such environmental factors can easily be integrated into the MBO system.

Specific problems that require immediate action might also arise during the implementation of the MBO program. These can easily be integrated into the total MBO system. The police manager must recognize that if serious problems do arise—for example, a high turnover rate, a reduction or freeze in spending, or a type of crime that drastically increases—he or she will be able to use the MBO system at any level to take positive action to overcome the problem.

Assume that armed robberies suddenly increase at an alarming rate. Within the MBO system, there might be an objective dealing with armed robberies. However, the objective might be too low-priority or the projects themselves might not really deal with the areas of the community in which the problem exists. With new information developed through the evaluation process, a new objective can be established, an old objective can be changed, new projects can be implemented, or old projects can be upgraded to help meet the newly established objective that is designed to overcome the problem.

When MBO is viewed as an ongoing system of assisting in day-to-day operations, it takes on a new meaning. The total picture of how the MBO system operates is shown in Figure 11.8.

Drawbacks of Management by Objectives

Management by objectives is not a panacea for all management ills. The police manager must constantly realize that he or she is responsible not only for the implementation of projects designed to meet specific objectives and goals but also for day-to-day implementation of the many functions and activities necessary to bring about a successful police

Figure 11.8 **Management by Objectives System**

operation. The police manager cannot seriously deplete organizational units such as the patrol force in order to emphasize the implementation or meeting of a specific objective.

The manager cannot allow MBO to override the responsibilities of caring for day-to-day activities. The police manager's job is to decide which objectives are to be sought, at what point in the organization they are to be implemented and by whom, and to what degree the total effort of the organization should be devoted to reaching stated objectives.

Another pitfall in the implementation of MBO is *the attempt to involve every member of the agency in some way in attempting to obtain the objectives.* This may upset the stability that has already been created and may do more harm than good. Consider the police department that has an adequate records and information system. To force them to revamp their present practices and procedures for the sole purpose of doing a "better job," may be expensive, frustrating, and, in the long run, bring about more negative than positive side effects.

In summary, then, the police manager, in the implementation of an MBO system, should determine the time and effort that can be devoted to bringing about change in the department, who can devote this time, and who can determine what effect the implementation of change will have on the stability already created within the organization.

Notes

1. Developed for the Atlanta Impact Program (LEAA) by Norman Baker, Edward Unger, Terry Sprott, Thomas Buskirk, and Gordon Miller.

2. Ibid.

Bibliography

French, Wendell and Hollman, Robert. "Management by Objectives: The Team Approach." *California Management Review 17* (Spring 1975):13-22.

Gazell, James A. "MBO in the Public Sector." *Business Review 27* (July 1974):29-35.

Humble, John. *How to Manage by Objectives*. New York: AMACOM, 1972-1973.

Kirchoff, Bruce A. "A Diagnostic Tool for MBO." *Personnel Psychology 23* (Autumn 1975).

McConkey, D.D. *How to Manage by Results*. New York. American Management Association, 1965.

Morrisey, George L. *Management by Objectives and Results*. Reading, MA: Addison-Wesley, 1970.

Discussion Questions

1. Is MBO an effective tool?

2. Should MBO be part of every police department?

3. When should MBO be implemented and when should it be eliminated from the managerial process?

4. How can MBO be a detriment to the police department?

5. What are some methods of implementing MBO?

6. What are other MBO models?

7. Should the police department be the strong driving force for the implementation of the MBO system citywide?

Productivity || 12

Objectives

1. The student will be able to present basic productivity improvement principles.

2. The student will be able to identify influences that can impede productivity improvements.

3. The student will be able to stimulate nontraditional ideas concerning the delivery of police services.

Productivity Revisited

Those appointed to the Law Enforcement Advisory Group of the National Commission on Productivity (1972) were filled with enthusiasm as they began the task of publishing a report that would help law enforcement agencies improve the delivery of police services. Representing a cross section of the country's more progressive agencies and supported by a professional research staff, they knew their efforts would be fruitful.

One of the trademarks of the group was the ability to simplify the subject matter. First, they identified two basic ways to improve productivity: accomplish more with current resources or accomplish the same with less resources. Next, they reduced the measurement of productivity to a simple formula:

$$\text{Inputs} \longrightarrow \text{Thruputs} \longrightarrow \text{Outputs}$$
$$\text{(Resources)} \quad\quad \text{(Policies, Procedures, etc.)} \quad\quad \text{(Results)}$$

Thus, if a four-person team of officers (Inputs) operating under traditional procedures (Thruputs) averaging eight arrests (Outputs) per week were encouraged to try a sting operation that resulted in an average of 12 arrests per week, their productivity would have increased 50 percent. They learned to watch for external variables that affected outputs. For example, it was realized that conviction rates as outputs did not give a true picture of the productivity of an officer or group of officers because the ability of district attorneys, and in some cases the judicial hearing officials, could alter such an output.

Chapter 12 is included with the permission of James P. Morgan.

One of the more significant "distancing" suggested by the group was to release police departments from the burden of crime rates. They were adamant that Uniform Crime Reports (UCR) should not be used as an indicator of police productivity. The causes of crime were not and still are not controllable by the police. The decay of moral values should not be laid at the feet of the police. Although police find themselves intervening at earlier stages than called for in their traditional job description, in most cases they are addressing the symptoms of family, school, and even church failures. Arrest is society's solution for their failures and that "cure" is the responsibility of the police. Even when the police are effective in this area, the criminal justice system as a whole cannot handle the solution. Early release and recidivism negate the effectiveness of the police in carrying out society's perceived cure.

As they searched the country for procedures, policies, and innovative technological advancements, their list of examples grew. These were presented in the final report. Some were not new but they were reduced to basic productivity improvement techniques that could be understood and used by a variety of law enforcement agencies. Civilianization of police departments had been discussed for years, but when they were able to focus on the cost effectiveness of this concept it made more sense. If an $18,000 civilian property clerk could do the same work previously accomplished by a $27,000 sworn officer who was actually trained to do patrol work, there would be a 50 percent reduction in the cost of resources to accomplish the same result. That also meant a 50 percent increase in productivity.

They gave examples of programs that saved money and those that were costly but had tremendous returns. Early case closure was an example of the former because detectives did not waste their time on property cases that had little chance of being solved because of lack of clues or passage of time. Computer-Aided Dispatch (CAD) was and still is a program that has the potential to increase police effectiveness as a result of the expenditure of large sums of money. Depending on the degree of sophistication, altering patrol patterns in anticipation of where crimes might occur based on historical data was a productivity program that could cost large sums if computerized and updated hourly. It could also be accomplished through the use of pin maps that cost much less but was less sophisticated.

After their report was completed and distributed to all law enforcement agencies in localities of 50,000 or more population, workshops were held throughout the country by various training agencies and organizations. The word was out on how to figure productivity improvements and what types of programs could be implemented to help achieve desired percentage goals.

Post-Report Reflections

After producing its report, the Law Enforcement Advisory Group of the National Commission on Productivity disbanded. The Commission, however, remained active. Their full-time staff was augmented by consultants for particular areas. It soon became clear that although the report was technically correct and had many excellent ideas, there were peripheral areas that affected productivity more than ever could have been imagined. Before addressing such areas, acknowledgment must be made that the desire for productivity improvements caused some agencies to spin their wheels needlessly. They were concerned with doing something correctly. They never stopped to see if they were doing the right thing—investigating and building a case that was not prosecutable; creating computerized reports that no one used; and conducting an excellent surveillance on the wrong person are some examples of inefficient use of resources.

Productivity and News Media

Although during productivity training programs the reality of political considerations thwarting improvement efforts was usually mentioned, it was not until post-report field visits that the extent of this fact became clear.

The word *political* is used in a very generic sense to describe the wide range of outside influences that dictate the use of police resources, which is a key factor in the productivity formula. For example, whether consciously or unconsciously, the media often play a role in many decisions made by and involving police agencies. Think about the visit of a candidate for the position of chief of police. The first day consists of the traditional tour of the city and an introduction to key in-house players. The next day might be critical because if "they" (owners and editors of local newspapers) approved, as far as he or she was concerned, the job was the candidate's. This group may have to give its approval of a candidate before he or she could be hired. It may also approve an eventual firing and may agree not to publish any letters to the editor critical of the termination. During the new chief's administration various programs and innovations are cleared by the paper. If the paper approved, which it does in almost every instance, the police agency will receive a favorable editorial and a good chance for success because public opinion will be orchestrated. This type of external power is, of course, a double-edged sword. When it helps get things done effectively it is a good productivity tool. The media can, however, divert resources to less productive ventures by highlighting newsworthy events that then must become the object of increased police attention. The annual publication of the crime rates is a good example of this. Much time and effort is spent by police officials defending their record in relation to reported crime in other areas. A police department that has developed open communications with the community might have more people report crime because they trust that the police will take action. A neighboring location might be just the opposite and as such have fewer crimes reported. The media's attention to an increase in crime in the first area, although legitimate, could cause an adjustment in philosophy or resource allocation that might unintentionally hurt police-community relations.

Sometimes the timeliness of media reporting can also cause resource allocation problems for the police. Any time that resources are deployed on emotional or dated material, overall productivity will suffer because the quantity and quality of outputs will normally not be cost-effective, but rather will only address a publicized problem.

Recently, in a southern city with a population of over 500,000, national attention was focused on attacks against motorists on an interstate highway within the city. This situation was brought to the attention of the public by the media in late October. Actually the problem had peaked in July and August, and police resources had been focused on the problem. With the notoriety months later, however, the police had to take extreme measures to demonstrate they were on top of the situation, productivity notwithstanding. It is always possible for the media to generate interest in an event. Four months after a woman had been shot on this highway, she appeared on a television talk show. Once again the police had to demonstrate that they were still focused on this problem.

Productivity and Elected Officials

Sometimes productivity concerns are circumvented for goodwill. For example, police resources often will be redirected when an elected official, or a close friend of an elected official, becomes the victim of a crime. Although not always efficient it is wise to do so to maintain a positive public image. It is the erosion of effective resource allocation by continuous outside pressures, rather than occasional patronage, that can cause a decline in productivity and morale. When you really think about it, however, people of influence and wealth in a community probably receive the least routine patrol protection because they choose and can afford to live in areas where crime is at a minimum. People who live in such communities also pay the most in taxes. Their ability to live in nice communities and pay high taxes in turn gets them minimum police protection in localities that practice productivity through incident-based resource allocation.

Productivity and Social Concerns

During the years after the productivity report there was a gradual move toward social concerns. The technical aspects of productivity began to give way to sensitivity. The fact that motorized patrol was more efficient than foot patrol because one person in a car could patrol six streets faster than an officer on foot became less important than having personal contacts with the citizens of those six blocks. Communities chose to fund an extra officer so that he or she could patrol three blocks on foot, and the motorized officer got out of the car and covered the other three.

Community-based policing, if done properly, combines social sensitivity and productive resource allocation. It allows the street officer working with and for the citizens of his or her area of responsibility to identify needs and help implement resolutions, whether police connected or not. It is doubtful that we will ever return to the ideal beat officer of the 1940s and 1950s. He managed to know everyone on his beat in spite of the fact that his race did not always reflect the ethnic makeup of the community that he patrolled. This knowledge of the beat enabled him to act as arbitrator in all types of incidents up to and including criminal activities. The criminal justice system was the last resort for an effective officer. This propensity not to arrest for the good of all parties concerned was abused by some officers and eventually destroyed the beat cop system.

As law enforcement agencies expanded their recruitment base, they were able to attract representatives of all races and sexes. (Most did so voluntarily, but some were complying with court orders.) Although most departments now have the capability of placing members of a community in their neighborhoods as officers, at least two problems have arisen that have prevented this potentially effective resource allocation from being universally adopted.

Having experienced the evolutionary corruption of beat cops through growing familiarity with the community, questions have been raised concerning the potential acceleration and ease of the process by placing officers in the neighborhood where they were raised.

The other problem has occurred in several urban police departments. Following resource allocation models developed to produce more effective policing, many departments have sought to place ethnic officers in neighborhoods of similar ethnic composition. This has been successfully opposed by black officer groups who feel that it is not fair that their members are consistently deployed in black neighborhoods that also happen to be high-crime areas. Their complaint follows the equal pay for equal work argument. Because all officers are paid basically the same, why should some always work in the nonviolent areas that have low calls for service, whereas others must face the dangers and workload of a crime-ridden neighborhood? Once again, productivity must take a back seat to other influences.

After two decades of experience with impediments to productivity improvements, what might we expect as we move toward the year 2000 in an environment of social sensitivity?

Productivity and the Future

There is no doubt that research, education, and training will continue to open the doors of opportunity for interested police departments, especially in a socially sensitive setting. At the absolute least, these forces will stimulate dialogue on important topics such as racial and ethnic issues. From such discussions we can expect suggestions on ways to recruit, retain, and promote minorities along with the development of model cultural differences training programs. The greatest and most costly input the police have is their employees. Until replaced by robots, this resource will continue to function with human feelings and make mistakes. This will in turn affect their output. Thus, it is the role of thruputs such as training, policies, and procedures to maximize the potential for productivity improvements without ignoring community social norms.

For progress to continue there must also be communication between organizations that represent different levels and types of law enforcement. Because there can be no single organization that speaks for all law enforcement [although a Law Enforcement Steering Committee (LESC) has tried to provide a forum for such an effort] it is important that all avenues be kept open and critical issues be identified and discussed.

Another area that has come to the forefront in this atmosphere of social sensitivity is the use of deadly force by the police. How does this affect productivity?

From a purely material viewpoint, there is the cost in dollars to pay off claims in wrongful shootings. Nationwide it runs into the millions. That is money (resources/inputs) for which the police get zero outputs. Paying judgments could be considered the most counterproductive use of resources that law enforcement agencies can experience.

There are some less tangible but nevertheless significant problems arising out of the use of deadly force. Obviously there is the potential for the disruption of police-community relations. Additionally, officers involved in fatal shootings often leave police work due to emotional strain and lack of department support. Even those not involved in a shooting sometimes leave over the lack-of-support issue. When experienced, trained officers leave, they are replaced by rookies who cannot be expected to immediately be as productive as the officers that they replace.

Until recently there has been no logical fallback alternative to deadly force when officers are faced with the possibility of someone, including themselves, being seriously injured or killed when confronted with a dangerous situation. Oleoresin Capsicum (OC)—a nonlethal, inflammatory agent—is rapidly emerging as one alternative weapon for law enforcement. OC is a powerful inflammatory, rather than an irritant (such as CS and CN gases), that causes swelling of the eyes and airways. These reactions, coupled with a burning sensation on skin exposed to OC, leaves an adversary severely impaired. All of this can be accomplished in a distance of 10 to 20 feet or more, depending on the brand and delivery system used. Not only could the use of a nonlethal weapon reduce or possibly eliminate the financial and time drains associated with lawsuits, it could also reduce sick leave used by officers to recuperate from injuries received when trying to subdue a dangerous, combative subject without the use of lethal force. Unfortunately, carrying a firearm no longer deters violent behavior on the part of suspects because many people are aware of the restrictions placed on its use. A usable nonlethal weapon might restore some sense of deterrent to the hostile environment often present in police-suspect encounters. The potential to prevent violence and still subdue a disorderly or violent person will always result in a better and more humanistic use of law enforcement resources. The perceived inability of police to control the criminal element has diminished their image and has resulted in a movement from public to private police.

The use of private security by corporations, communities, and individuals represents the ultimate in productivity. Unlike public police, who must address multiple needs and interest groups, private police are normally hired for a specific mission and answer directly to the individual or group that identified the need.

Sometimes local police do get into the business of "renting" officers. When there is a special function, usually a private one, that requires extra directed policing, some departments assign off-duty officers to work such events and charge the host group for such service. Campus police often charge the university athletic department for officers assigned to sporting events that generate income. This type of focused patrol with reimbursement to the police department represents user fees, which is a form of productivity gaining popularity with public administrators.

Although some uniformed private security employees are paid minimum wages and their producivity is suspect, there are some, such as those assigned to sensitive industries, that are paid more than public police. This is especially true in the investigative field. Take away the myths created by films and television and the private investigation industry has the potential to provide more productivity than regular detectives. Not long ago a governor hired the investigative arm of a security firm to handle certain types of cases he felt would not receive sufficient attention from the public resources at his command. Although his critics strongly opposed this "private army" concept, the results achieved by this approach were not subject to nearly as much criticism. Thus, although the overall quality and quantity of local police services can at least match that provided by the private sector, on any given day or in any given case, private security could probably direct more attention and resources to a client's needs. Tradition and the lack of financial incentive will always seriously restrain the public sector from competing with private industry. The police field is no exception. An example of this follows.

After anywhere from two to six months of basic recruit training, individuals take on the responsibility of a patrol officer. Every call they answer contains one or more unknowns. So they must be careful, but not show fear; sensitive, but not permissive; in command of the situation, but not overbearing; thorough, but not slow. If and when they become good at this very complex job, they might be promoted to detective or investigator. At this point, usually making more money than a patrol officer, they are sent to a crime scene after everything has happened, many times accompanied by a partner, and then perform their specialty, say investigation of burglary, homicide, and so forth. To a casual observer it would appear that these two positions should be reversed insofar as the pay is concerned. But the hardest, most complex job comes first in police work and pays the lowest salary. Then the best at doing that job are rewarded by being promoted to a position that in some ways is perceived as less rigorous. Should this process be changed? For example, the Federal Bureau of Investigation (FBI) trains civilians to be investigators in less time than it takes most urban police departments to train their recruits.

If police departments would begin thinking about nontraditional placement and promotion methods, then the door will be open to types of nontraditional processes and procedures that could result in significant productivity improvements.

For instance, why not evaluate highway/traffic police on the basis of reducing fatal and nonfatal accidents rather than the number of speeders that they catch? Allow officers assigned to a particular area to decide what type of enforcement procedures to use based on accident data. Although speed can be a key contributing factor in some crashes, often it is emphasized mainly because of the ease with which it can be proved. It would be more productive to identify the true causes of crashes in a particular area and devise enforcement efforts to reduce the chances of such incidents happening. In some communities, however, the results desired from selective enforcement are fines, not accident prevention. In these cases productivity could still be claimed and measured easily. From a professional point of view this would be an example of doing something right, but not doing the "right" thing.

Earlier in this chapter a sting operation was mentioned briefly. These operations can prove to be quite productive. Using little people power, with minimum risk, large quantities of stolen goods can be recovered and those involved in the thefts arrested. Could this be carried a step farther in the future? What if insurance companies were to fund a clearinghouse in conjunction with the police? Those in possession of stolen goods would appear at a given location and turn in such merchandise for a percentage of what it is worth. If the property could be matched with reported stolen property, they would get their money and the police could close a case with a minimum of time and expenditures. Because this would only work if immunity was granted to the person turning in the property, a case could be made that this type of program would encourage criminal activity. Perhaps this drawback could be eliminated, but the important thing to remember is that many times the actual cost of investigating a larceny is more than the value of the property stolen. That is why early case closure is often used in minor thefts in which no suspect is developed at the outset. The problem envisioned with this presently used productivity program was that people would be upset over the lack of attention to their theft. This was addressed and the process is now used by most major departments. Perhaps the negative aspects of a police fence program could also be resolved.

Another time-consuming activity is the time police officers spend taking reports and conducting preliminary investigations that are filed primarily for insurance purposes. There is little chance of solving these cases, so resources are wasted. The only winner is the insurance company, which uses the police report as their data for making a decision on a claim. Why not reverse the process and require the insurance company to make the report and file a copy of it for the police?

What about money as a productivity motivator in police work? If the ability of traffic officers to reduce crashes and injuries using their own cause-and-effect analysis results in additional highway funds for a locality, why could there not be a bonus for individual efforts? Years ago in New York City the old "safe and loft" squad was relentless in its efforts to locate stolen property in major theft cases. These detectives had an extremely high recovery rate. When it was reported that they were receiving percentages of the dollar amounts recovered, the practice changed, as did part of their motivation. During the same period, New York City narcotics detectives could receive up to $99 cash "expense" money each month based on the quality and quantity of arrests made. Because their regular gross pay averaged around $700 per month, this was quite an incentive.

Thus, money has been used in police work as a motivator for officers as well as informers. If, however, money was the key stimulator for productive police work, it could lead to many professional problems, up to and including possible corruptive influences.

These ideas are raised not to identify them as bona fide productivity programs but to stimulate brainstorming on a variety of police processes. If any police department is following a procedure just because "it's always been done that way," that area is a potential target for productivity improvement. The future effectiveness and efficiency of police agencies depends on using the brain power that has been and continues to be attracted to police work.

Discussion Questions

1. Why should crime rates not be used as an indicator of police productivity?

2. What outside, nonpolice influences might be able to dictate the use of police resources?

3. What are some events that might have stimulated the general move to social sensitivity that affects police productivity?

4. What traditional police operations might be done better by others, need not be done at all, or could be improved without additional funding?

Fiscal Management | | 13

Objectives

1. The student will be able to define what a budget is and to distinguish budgeting from other functional areas of police management.

2. The student will be able to discuss the purposes of fiscal management.

3. The student will understand and be able to explain the stages of the budgeting process.

4. The student will know the differences between the three basic types of budgets, their formats and their purposes.

The police department's annual budget is one of the most important policy statements made by the department. It reflects the predominant values and thinking of the managers of the police department, the city or county administrator, and local political leaders.

Budgeting

The most common definition states that a budget is a plan, expressed in dollar terms, by which a set of programs is authorized for a future period, usually one year. This definition is often questioned. One of the first issues raised is whether the budget really is a plan, or whether it is just an agreement or contract between the governing board and the department heads on how much money they may spend in the upcoming year. Although the budget is expressed in dollar terms, it is seldom viewed strictly as a fiscal device. In some instances, it is a device used to indicate priorities and to indicate the role that department heads may play in conjunction with other department heads, the city manager, and the governing board. Under a strict economic definition, a budget is an allocation of resources among competing demands from different departments, including the police department.

A more acceptable definition is that a budget is a comprehensive plan, expressed in financial terms, by which an operating program is effective for a given period. It includes estimates of services, activities, and projects included in the program; the resultant expenditure requirements; and the resources available for their support.

Purposes of Budgeting

The budget is significant from several standpoints. First, it encompasses comprehensive reviews of police department activities, usually on an annual basis. Second, it specifies limits as to what the police department can do; in this sense, it serves as a legal document. Third, it is used to accomplish managerial ends such as designating who is responsible for what activities, setting a pattern for centralization or delegation of authority within the police department, and mandating economies that must be brought forth in the future. It sets out what the police department will accomplish or attempt to accomplish. In this sense, it is a workload plan. It is used to enact new programs or significantly change existing programs within the police agency. It helps bring information to the proper level for decisionmaking and, when implemented correctly, provides upward and downward information, so that these decisions may be properly carried out at all levels within the police department.

There are two overall approaches to the establishment of a budget as far as the chief of police is concerned. At one end of the spectrum is *incremental budgeting* and at the other end is *zero-base budgeting*.

Under incremental budgeting, there is an assumption that activities that have occurred within the past fiscal year are presently effective and will become the foundation for the future. This budget focuses on revenue growth. A typical example might be the police chief who is obligated to submit the budget in a format that discloses how much was spent last year on a certain item (such as new vehicles), how much will be needed this year, and the difference between these two figures. For example, if the chief requires an additional $3,000, a justification is needed for the additional expense. The assumption is that the amount of money spent for purchasing during the last year was spent in an efficient and effective manner.

Zero-base budgeting, on the other hand, implies a review of the entire budgeting process. It requires setting priorities; communication to the police department of the relationship between these priorities and their costs; and the establishment of goals, somewhere in the department, not only for the upcoming year but also for at least three to five years into the future. In essence, the police department must know where it is headed and how it will get there; it will then be able to measure its effectiveness. This budget explains, on an annual basis, why the police department exists.

In practice, no budgeting system is 100 percent either incremental or zero-base. Usually, budgets are built on a few aspects of each system.

Stages in the Budgeting Process

There are four broad stages in the budget process. The first is the *preparation stage*, which is the responsibility of the executive branch of the government, including the police department. The budget calendar is usually established by the city manager, who works backward from the legal data required for the enactment of a budget. For example, if a budget must be enacted by July 1, the city manager may demand that the police department's budget be submitted at least 45 days in advance. It then becomes the police department's responsibility, under the direction of the police chief, to establish its requests. The police chief must first know the date required for submission of the initial budget requests to the city or county manager, the budget director, or whoever may be responsible for first reviewing the police department's budget. Depending on the size of the police department and the amount of involvement required by members within the department, the commanders of the police agency can establish a budget schedule designed to meet the required date for initial budget requests.

The second stage in the budget process is *adoption*. This is a legislative function that requires some legal action, such as a special ordinance passed each year or a resolution by the governing board. Each police chief should carefully review the state's statutes governing the budgetary adoption process for his or her individual community so that he or she will be aware of the legal requirements and the formal process that must be followed.

The third stage is *execution*. This is an executive function and is a fairly detailed process of the establishment of a fiscal control system, usually at the direction of the city or county manager. The police chief, therefore, need not be concerned with the development of an execution process. His or her primary concerns should be to have a clear understanding of how the budget forms are to be used, what forms are to be submitted for what types of requests, how the summary information can best be used for the upgrading of the police department, and how well the department is proceeding in implementing the programs and expenditures of its approved funding.

The execution process includes the development of purchase orders, pre-ordering, receipts to be received for merchandise purchased, and the disbursement of funds. Each of these procedures is generally citywide or countywide in nature; the individual police department is usually not responsible for developing special procedures for the police agency.

The fourth major stage in the budget process is the *postaudit stage*, which is a legislative function by which, on an annual basis at the close of each budget year, an audit is taken to show that the funds have been properly expended, that the police chief has not overexpended the department's budget, and that the budgeting has proceeded in a proper manner. This also has the effect of protecting the city and the department from potential accusations of misappropriation of funds.

These four stages and their relationship are shown in Figure 13.1.

Types of Budgets

There are three basic types of budgets. The first is the *line-item* or *object budget*, the second is the *performance budget*, and the third is the *program budget*.

The *line-item* or *object budget* groups expenditures by classes or objects. It concentrates primarily on efficiency, focusing the dollar amounts on inputs (what the police department intends to purchase), not on outputs (what the department intends to achieve). Normally, only the increase in any specific amount is questioned by the budget director, city or county manager, or governing board. This type of budget forces the police chief to concentrate on the incremental philosophy of budgeting. The line-item or object budget was created to resolve problems of corruption that existed at local levels many years ago. Today it is used as a strong control tool by fiscal managers; it really does not assist in the development of departmental programs or explain the purpose of the individual police department.

Figure 13.1 **Stages in the Budget Cycle**

The police manager must recognize that a line-item or object budget will always be present someplace within the budgetary process. It may be the sole budgetary style, or it could be part of a different type of budget, such as the performance or program type. It may be used as a planning tool or as a means of auditing expenditures. A line-item or object budget, therefore, is important for all police managers to understand. Although this type of budget may on the whole be more negative than positive in nature, it is one of the more common types of budgets in law enforcement today. In addition, a clear understanding of its value can assist the police chief in the overall fiscal management of the police department.

Line-item budgets are usually divided into the following four major categories: (1) *personal services*, which includes salaries, fringe benefits, and other costs relating directly to people; (2) *operating and maintenance*, which includes supplies such as gas, oil, forms, pencils, and even paper clips; (3) *charges and services*, which covers special contracts, rentals, travel funds, and training; and (4) *capital outlay*, which is the money expended for the purchase of equipment such as cars, desks, and weapons.

An example of the format of a line-item or object budget is shown in Figure 13.2.

Figure 13.2 **Line-Item or Object Budget**

Item	Amount
Personal services	$25,000
Contractual services	5,000
Supplies/materials	5,000
Miscellaneous items	500
Capital outlay	10,000
Total	$45,500

Sample—Object Budget with Divisional Breakdown

Item		Amount	Total
I.	Personal Services		
	A. Salaries		
	Headquarters	$5,000	
	Patrol	5,000	
	Detective	5,000	
	Services	5,000	
			$20,000
	B. Fringe		
	Headquarters	$1,250	
	Patrol	1,250	
	Detective	1,250	
	Services	1,250	
			$ 5,000
		Total personal services	$25,000

Note: Contractual services, supplies/materials, miscellaneous items, and capital outlay categories would all have similar breakdowns.

A *performance budget* specifies activities of the police department, the performance data being the information by which the police chief determines the necessity for incremental increases or decreases. The format is much like that of the line-item or object budget. It normally measures activities such as number of tickets written, crimes solved, property recovered, and calls for service handled. It is divided into these types of services by organizational unity. For example, it compares the number of calls for services handled by the Uniformed Operation Division to those handled by the Criminal Investigation Division. An example of a performance budget format is shown in Figure 13.3.

Program budgeting, developed by the RAND Corporation for the U.S. Department of Defense, demands an analysis between cost-benefits and cost-effectiveness. This first requires a statement of the goals of the police department, such as what effect they will have on crime and calls for service. It then focuses on what programs and activities will be used to achieve these goals. Finally, it emphasizes output measures. Budgeting becomes a planning tool in the everyday operation of the police department. It demands a justification for expenditures for new programs or for deleting old programs that have not met their objectives and are no longer effective because of changing conditions within the police department. Program budgeting requires that the decisions for implementation be left with the police department and not controlled by some outside agency.

Figure 13.3 **Performance Budget**

Accident Investigation		*Amount*
Personal services		$85,000
Contractual services		5,000
Supplies/materials		1,250
	Total	$91,250
Performance Statistics		
Investigate (initial)		
Property damage		$ 2,000
Personal injury		500
Fatal		10
Arrest and follow-up		$ 2,400
Cost per accident		
Property		$ 25
Personal injury		75
Fatality		375
Issue summonses		
Hazardous violations		$20,000
Nonhazardous violations		15,000

The program budget is also a means of planning future costs on the basis of past experience and predicted events and conditions.

There are numerous programs in which law enforcement can become involved. Some of these include prevention of crimes, investigation of crimes, apprehension of violators, presentation of criminals for judicature, services to the public, and career development of personnel. An example of a program budget is presented in Figure 13.4.

The police department shares the broad responsibilities of its overall program with such other agencies as public works, traffic engineering, and the fire department. Each agency contributes to the program objectives and needs to show those expenditures in its respective budget.

Regardless of whether the budget is designed as a performance or a program budget, a line-item budget must be prepared to support the theories behind the overall budget process. The line-item document may be developed and kept at the police department level, or it may be a separate document helping to support the performance or program budget request.

Figure 13.4 **Program Budget**

```
                        Program—Community Safety
Subprogram—Crime Prevention and Suppression                    $100,000
    Program Elements   (a)   High school education                10,000
                       (b)   Preventive patrol                    50,000
                       (c)   Crime prevention, security-oriented  25,000
                       (d)   Crime prevention, treatment-oriented 15,000

Subprogram—Investigation and Apprehension                      $ 25,000
    Program Elements   (a)   Crimes against persons                7,000
                       (b)   Crimes against property              15,000
                       (c)   Community security                     3,000

Subprogram—Movement and Control of Traffic                     $ 30,000
    Program Elements   (a)   Traffic patrol                       15,000
                       (b)   Accident investigation                7,000
                       (c)   Traffic regulation                    3,000
                       (d)   Traffic safety education              5,000

Subprogram—Maintenance of Public Order                         $ 10,000
    Program Elements   (a)   Civil disturbance prevention         $3,000
                       (b)   Noncriminal investigation             7,000
                                                   Total         $165,000


                 Program—General Management and Support

Subprogram—Staff Support                                       $ 80,000
    Program Elements   (a)   Information services                 20,000
                       (b)   Technical services                   10,000
                       (c)   Discretion and supervision           40,000
                       (d)   Planning and evaluation              10,000

Subprogram—Employee Development                                $ 20,000
    Program Elements   (a)   Employee training and education      12,000
                       (b)   Employee recruitment                  8,000
                                                   Total         $100,000
                                             Grand Total         $265,000
```

Note: Each program element contains the "objective" and cost summary by object—personal services, operating and maintenance supplies, charges and services, capital outlay.

The Budgeting Process

The budgetary process is by no means completely under the control of the police department. Numerous parties are involved, each playing a separate role and each affecting the decisions of the others.

The first important person in the budgetary process is the chief of police. Working with other members of the police department, his or her budget reflects the professional or expert approach to resolving problems that face the police department. The police chief is oriented primarily toward successful completion of his or her mission. His or her responsibility is to initiate most of the policies that are eventually accepted into the budget.

The second key person is the budget or finance officer. He or she is usually an administrative generalist and is oriented to financial and managerial norms. The budget or finance officer tends to be more restrictive in budgetary recommendations and carefully considers the progress of the police department, the goals it has established and whether they are being met, and how well guidelines established within the present budget have been met.

Conclusion

This chapter was designed to give the police manager an overview of the budget process, the types of budgets available, and the roles that different people play in the budget process. This has a strong effect on how the police department obtains its funds and how much flexibility is given for day-to-day operations.

Police managers should not be overwhelmed by the budgetary process. It can and should be carefully studied, analyzed, and understood by all commanders in a department so that they will be able to assist the chief of police in preparing the police department's budget, negotiating its approval, and executing its mandates.

Discussion Questions

1.   How do most police managers feel about the development of the department budget?

2.   Should the city manager or budget director be allowed to develop the police department's budget?

3.   Why should a police department request more funds than it actually needs to accomplish its mission?

4.   Assuming the city government has a tradition of asking for more funds than are necessary, should the police department adhere to this practice or should it attempt to break from tradition?

5.   Who should receive copies of the police department's budget and why?

6.   How much authority and flexibility should a team commander using team policing have over the development and implementation of the group's budget?

Time Management | 14

Objectives

1. The student will be able to establish his or her work week assigning specific and designated periods within each day as to how time will be allocated during the normal work week.

2. The student will recognize the importance of delegating tasks, redefining activities, and giving these responsibilities to subordinates.

3. The student will become familiar with rules used to achieve effective delegation.

Police managers must recognize that the delegation of tasks is one of their most important functions. By distributing work, they are able to use their time effectively.

The police manager should realize that time is one commodity available to all people. Time cannot be stockpiled, nor can it be recycled. And unlike money, materials, and ideas, it does not increase with added responsibility.

There are two types of time that the police manager faces. The first is defined as *management time*: time spent planning, organizing, leading, and controlling. The second, *vocational time*, is time spent performing activities that only the police manager can perform. Examples include attending special staff meetings, meeting with the city manager or members of the city council, and honoring specific invitations to attend meetings of civic organizations and professional associations.

What often happens is that as police managers are promoted within the organization, they maintain the same amount—if not more—of vocational time that they had previously. As a result, management time is rarely available. The manager may attempt to find this extra management time by staying extra hours, starting with an eight-hour day and constantly adding to it until he or she is spending twelve to fourteen hours a day performing the police management role. If it is impossible to continue to find this time at the police building, the manager may take the work home. The result is that both the professional activities of the department and the manager's personal life suffer.

The solution is to delegate tasks as much as possible, redefining activities and functions, and passing these responsibilities on to subordinates. The police manager can make more effective use of management time by having a system for using the rational tools of management.

Demands on the Manager's Time

The first demand on the manager's time is made by associates. If the police manager is an assistant chief, time must be allocated for conferences with the chief of police. The chief of police must spend time with the city manager, the mayor, or the city council. Usually there is an immediate priority on this part of the manager's time. In this situation police managers are playing the role of employees and are acting in compliance with the requests of superiors. They are performing work, and the rewards and the risks are usually extremely low. The police managers and their superiors, the city manager and mayor, for example, must agree to meet at definite times during each work week. The professional manager will do all that is possible to help assistant managers use their time more effectively. It is the police manager's responsibility, however, to bring this issue before the relevant superiors and arrive at a consensus as to how they can best work together to conserve the time that is needed for each to perform adequately.

The second demand on the police manager's time is created by the system or organizational structure itself. The demand of the system is the time the police manager must spend inspecting, evaluating, and attempting to bring about conformity within the department. Depending on the nature of the required activity, the manager could be supervising or possibly even doing the work of subordinates. The police manager carefully should evaluate each task and be certain that he or she is not doing something that should be done by subordinates.

Consider the police captain who constantly establishes daily work schedules and daily assignments because six months earlier a new subordinate asked him to perform the task once. The captain continues to perform the activity. The result is that the subordinate finally accepts as fact that the captain intends to devote management time to performing the activity that is really the responsibility of the subordinate. The police captain, as a police manager, should redelegate that task to the subordinate, where it rightfully belongs, thereby giving the captain more time to operate as a manager rather than performing as a first-line supervisor.

The third major demand on the manager's time is categorized as *self time.* This is when the police manager thinks, plans, and evaluates information to assist in future decisionmaking. The police manager should set aside time each week to be creative, innovative, and carefully think out and plan for the future. If used well, the time spent in this category can bring about change and progress.

The effective police manager, recognizing that there are three demands on his or her time, could establish a work week in half-day blocks as shown in Figure 14.1, assigning specific and designated periods within each day as to how he or she will allocate time during the normal work week. For example, the manager may allot only two blocks of activities that require time away from running the police department. At least one or two blocks may be set aside for developing ideas, for planning, and for making the best use of his or her ability to help the department grow. Each police manager should carefully evaluate the amount of time spent with the organization and the amount necessary to be spent with the city manager or superiors. He or she should assess the present ability of subordinates to handle the delegated authority and the amount of time that must be spent helping them develop the ability to accept added responsibilities. The pressures placed on the police manager by the community, the law enforcement profession itself, and any other priorities must be taken into consideration. The final judgment, of course, belongs to each individual police manager.

Only through a careful evaluation of how a manager spends his or her time on a day-to-day basis and a recognition of the necessary high-priority activities can he or she learn to use time during the work week most effectively.

Figure 14.1 **Manager's Work Week**

	_AM_	_PM_
Monday	Review and inspection	Self-development
Tuesday	Inspection	Public contacts
Wednesday	Personnel conferences	Self-development
Thursday	Department staff	Division staff
Friday	Public contacts	Weekly evaluation

Delegation of Responsibility

Delegation is the art of gradually giving increased responsibility to one's subordinates. This means defining the functions and responsibilities for which the subordinate is responsible. When these functions and responsibilities have been defined, the level of authority to accomplish each of these tasks is established between the police manager and the subordinate.

There are three levels of authority. At the initial level, the subordinate is obligated to report first and is allowed to act on approval. The subordinate must come to the police manager to explain each decision and how he or she intends to implement that decision; the subordinate then receives permission from the police manager. Needless to say, it is a time-consuming method and requires close contact between the police manager and the subordinate. The next level is defined as authority to act first and then report. Within this category, the subordinate has the right to implement decisions but is responsible for advising the police manager of his or her activities and their results. The third level is defined as complete authority. It assumes that trust has been developed between the police manager and the subordinate and that the police manager is confident that the task will be accomplished effectively.

Consider, for example, the simple task of establishing a monthly work schedule. The police manager can initially request that a subordinate complete the schedule, bring it to the police manager, and—upon approval of the police manager—begin to implement the decision. After two or three such schedules have been developed by the subordinate, the manager begins to gain confidence in the subordinate's ability and can then raise the level of authority by advising the subordinate that there will be no further need to bring the schedule to the manager before implementation but that the subordinate is to advise the manager of the schedule. The reporting can actually occur after the schedule has been implemented. Once a high degree of trust has been established between the manager and the subordinate, the manager can advise the subordinate that he or she is fully, totally, and completely responsible for the development and implementation of the schedule. The manager will only inspect periodically to determine that the quality of scheduling still meets the level agreed on prior to the granting of the complete authority.

When the function and responsibilities as well as the level of authority have been defined, the goals can be established for each task. In this way the subordinate can be evaluated and held accountable for the success or failure of the task. For example, in the issue of scheduling of police officers, once the manager has agreed on the minimum number of police officers to be available for specific days and periods, the subordinate knows what results are expected and is responsible for achieving them.

Delegation is the transfer of responsibilities and involves a four-step process. First, the police manager must transfer responsibility to the subordinate. Second, the subordinate must accept this responsibility. Third, a mutual trust must develop between the police manager and subordinate, and fourth, there must be some system of follow-up of the responsibility that has been transferred and accepted.

What can delegation accomplish for the police manager? Delegation will help ease the manager's job pressure; it will provide more time for planning, organizing, leading, and all other management functions and activities that bring about growth of a police organization. It will also give the police manager the opportunity to improve the quality and quantity of his or her own personal operation. And last, it may actually leave time for the manager to be absent from the department while still feeling confident that the agency is functioning in the most effective manner possible.

Delegation, by the same token, has effects on the subordinate who accepts the responsibility. First, it tends to make the responsibilities of the subordinate more satisfying because he or she is making a large number of the decisions not only in implementation but also in evaluation. Second, it encourages and helps the subordinate grow and develop within the department. Third, it brings about increased motivation on the part of the subordinate and those who work for him or her. In essence, it begins a chain reaction from the top of the department all the way to the bottom. For the person accepting the responsibility, the recipient of the delegation, it fosters initiative and competence to the point at which someday he or she, too, can effectively perform the art of delegation.

Effective Rules of Delegation

To make delegation an effective tool, the manager should follow certain general principles. First, the police manager must be willing to delegate part of his or her clarified responsibilities and authority so that he or she is sharing overall responsibility with subordinates. Next, the police manager must carefully describe the responsibility delegated to the subordinate so that there is a clear understanding of exactly what is being delegated. Third, the manager should exercise patience and allow subordinates the opportunity to assess possible difficulties that may arise in accepting added responsibility. Fourth, there has to be some agreed-upon follow-up so the manager is guaranteed that the authority is used in the manner intended. This is best accomplished through agreed-upon, stated objectives. Fifth, and probably most important, the manager must have faith and trust in the subordinate. If trust does not exist, the delegation process is doomed to failure from the beginning.

There are certain cardinal "don'ts" that the manager must remember. First, the police manager should not wait until he or she is overwhelmed with work before exercising the art of delegation. Next, the manager should not expect subordinates with this new authority and responsibility to perform perfectly right away. In every organization, there must be both the freedom to succeed and the freedom to make mistakes. Third, the manager must not become a "backseat driver" but should allow his or her subordinates to experiment with their new responsibility until they become as confident as the manager. Finally, the manager should not wait for things to deteriorate before stepping in and offering help. Through a fairly controlled system, the manager can prevent the project from becoming bogged down by helping to overcome obstacles and moving the project toward its stated objectives.

Once the subordinate has accepted more and more responsibility, the police manager will find it easier to delegate more projects, activities, and responsibilities. The manager who helps subordinates develop is gaining more time for his or her own management activities.

Rules of Monkeys

Consider the average police chief when first assigned to his or her new position. In a few weeks the police chief has moved from sitting at an empty desk, going home at a reasonable hour, and having spare time for some planning to the life of a harried individual, always late getting home, taking a great deal of work home, and spending many hours each day performing tasks that could and should be performed by subordinates. How does the average police chief get into this situation?

In the beginning, the police chief will probably be extremely cautious in delegating authority and responsibility. After a quick examination of her subordinates, she realizes that it is their activities that have caused her to be in this predicament.

An examination of the situation may reveal that the chief's first key assistant is an average individual named Charlie, who is assigned to research functions and activities of the department. Charlie considers it his job to submit to the chief of police numerous memoranda that call for decisions. He submits one memorandum, request, or decision at a time, and the chief has to consider each of these separately.

Jane is responsible for the service functions of the department. She normally sends the chief, for her approval, weekly status reports that include a statement of problems and recommended solutions. The police chief has very little time to act on these reports. Jane is the type of individual who would act only after the chief has sent her a memorandum approving specific recommendations.

Next is Sam, who holds a staff position responsible for administrative activities such as budgeting and purchasing. Sam is uncertain of his responsibilities and authority. Daily, he brings every single question that is asked of him to the chief and refuses to make a single decision on his own. In fact, if forced into making any kind of a decision, he always prefaces it with "the chief wants . . . ."

The fourth individual is Louise, the chief's administrative assistant. An energetic extrovert, she is responsible for public relations, establishing the chief's schedule, and writing speeches for her when needed.

The police chief finds herself working from seven o'clock in the morning until six o'clock in the evening at the office, taking large quantities of work home, and spending at least one or two more hours away from her family each night attempting to solve numerous problems which she feels only she, as the chief, is capable of resolving.

The work week eventually expands to include at least a half a day each Saturday. One Saturday, while en route to the office, the chief sees Charlie, Jane, Sam, and Louise getting ready to tee off at the local golf course. On her arrival at the police department, the chief carefully analyzes the piles of paper on her desk and reexamines her conversations during the past week with these four key subordinates. She quickly realizes that they constantly say to her: "How's it going?" It becomes obvious that the four subordinates do not report to her but that the chief is working for the four subordinates. In fact, the chief has been afraid to visit with them, to have a cup of coffee with them, or even to go to lunch with them—afraid that she could not answer their favorite question: "How's it going?"

How does the average chief of police get out of this situation? The answer is by implementing the following five "rules of monkeys." A "monkey" is defined as a task or an assignment of work, a function or activity that must be performed. The five rules of monkeys that bring about effective delegation are the following:

1. *Feed it or shoot it, but never let it starve to death.* Either the manager must be willing to stipulate that the monkey, or task, is not to be performed at this time within the department for whatever reason there may be or, if he or she feels that the task is one that must be performed, he or she must be able to "feed it." Feeding of monkeys means that the manager takes the time and the effort, after delegating the task to a subordinate, to converse with the subordinate at designated times so as to keep track of progress. This can be accomplished by the use of a tickler file system.

2. *Only have those monkeys out that you can afford to feed.* The manager must not delegate so many tasks or activities that he or she loses control of the operation under his or her command. The manager need delegate only the activities or monkeys he or she has time to follow up and only those monkeys that subordinates are qualified to work. The number of monkeys the manager can have running about the agency depends on his or her time commitments, the ability of personnel to accept the responsibility of working the monkeys, and examination of activities within the agency.

3. *Never conclude a feeding without scheduling the next feeding session.* The manager should never accept statements from subordinates such as "as soon as possible." Every time a discussion is completed concerning where the monkey is, then a new time must be scheduled and specific results agreed on before the next monkey feeding date.

4. *Subordinates will find the time to work the monkeys if you have time to feed them.* What this means is that the manager who takes the time to delegate responsibili-

ties—to give the monkeys to the subordinates instead of working the monkeys himself or herself—will have time to act as a manager and play the role of advisor, inspector, and monkey feeder.

5. *Keep the monkey off your back.* This rule means literally what it states. It is not the manager's role to become involved in constantly making sound decisions, but it *is* his or her role to see that the sound decisions are reached. The best way this can be accomplished is by consistently delegating to subordinates the authority and responsibility to feed and handle the monkeys, thereby allowing the manager to be a monkey supervisor and not a monkey keeper.

In the previous example, how does our chief go about implementing these five rules and bringing about successful delegation? For illustration purposes, the necessary action is explained in two steps.

Step 1. In this step, the police chief comes to work at 9:15 A.M. on Monday morning instead of the usual 7:30 or 8:00 A.M. She then interviews Charlie. Prior to this interview, all of Charlie's memoranda are placed in a neat pile. As Charlie enters, these memos are returned to him with the following instructions: "Charlie, I want you to divide these memos into three separate stacks by Wednesday at 10:00 A.M. The first stack should contain those recommendations that you feel qualified to handle; the second pile will deal with matters on which you feel you need more information but that you believe you can eventually handle; and the third pile will deal with matters that only I can resolve."

Next, the chief asks Jane to examine the status reports carefully and to do the following: redline all the problems already solved, greenline all the problems that need immediate attention, and blueline the problems that need more study. Jane is then told to return by Wednesday at 11:00 A.M.

Sam is then interviewed. He is asked to carefully write out his job activities in the following format: "I do such-and-such for so-and-so in order for this to be accomplished." Sam is asked to return by Wednesday afternoon at 2:00 P.M.

Next, the chief asks Louise to examine the weekly calendar carefully and underline those commitments that only the police chief can handle, setting aside all other commitments and reviewing the information at each of those meetings so that she, Louise, can represent the police chief.

Step 2. The first act of Step 2 that the police chief should take is to begin to relax and unwind. Then, when Charlie returns on Wednesday at his designated time, the manager can examine the memoranda that Charlie brings with him. Charlie can be congratulated for handling those tasks that he has felt able to perform. At this time, the manager can restate his confidence in Charlie and redefine Charlie's authority. On completion of this, Charlie is asked to review the memoranda on which he feels the chief must act. Charlie is then asked to return at a specific date and time.

As Jane enters for her second visit, she also is congratulated for having accepted responsibility and having already solved the redlined problems. As for those that have been underlined in green, Jane's new authority is established by the chief. Based on this new definition, Jane can accept as many of the greenlined problems as possible. In addition, Jane is asked to reexamine the bluelined problems (those that only the chief can handle or that need more study) and is asked to redefine these problems. Prior to Jane's leaving, another meeting date is established.

As for Sam, authority is carefully delegated to him. The authority delegated to each of the key subordinates need not be equal. In fact, the amount of authority and responsibility that each subordinate receives depends on the task to be performed, the amount of time that the manager intends to spend with the subordinate, and the subordinate's individual abilities. The amount of authority delegated to Sam may be less than that given to Jane or Charlie. Sam is asked at this time to redefine the tasks that he can delegate to someone else, to redefine tasks that other units in the agency should be handling, and to outline the steps whereby he intends to accomplish the remaining tasks. Again, another meeting date is set.

As for Louise, she is congratulated on the amount of information she has gathered and on her ability to comprehend organizational problems. She is given the responsibility of making as many appearances during the week as possible to free the chief to handle the more important functions and activities. A meeting date is set, possibly at the end of the week, in which the manager reviews the results and establishes new tasks and activities for Louise.

The results of implementing the monkey-feeding system as shown in steps 1 and 2 are to force the subordinate to make decisions. The specific time frames that have been established allow the police chief to plan her work schedule and actually have productive management time during each week. As for the individuals themselves, Charlie will be spending more time doing the job for which he is being paid; Jane will realize that she has been writing memoranda to herself and will begin to take action on problems as they arise. Sam will be defining his own authority and job ability; and Louise will begin to become involved in the whole scope of department activities and will serve her true purpose, lifting the responsibility of administrative tasks from the police chief.

Furthermore, decisions are now being forced down the ladder and will eventually be made at the lowest possible levels. Controls have been established through the use of the monkey-feeding system, and tasks are being returned to the subordinates.

Now, when the police chief travels to all her divisions and meets with subordinates, she asks the question, "How's it going?"

Staff Meetings

There are three types of staff meetings: (1) general staff meetings, (2) problem-identification meetings, and (3) brainstorming meetings.

The first type, the general staff meeting, can be used to pass information from the top to the bottom of the organizational structure. In such instances, it is usually a good idea to use an agenda to organize the meeting. These meetings are designed to advise agency personnel of decisions that have already been reached. Information concerning the stages of implementation for certain projects is usually passed back and forth. Staff meetings do not usually resolve problems, nor do they develop creativity or resolve conflicts that may exist.

The second type of staff meeting is designed specifically for problem identification. This is actually a series of meetings, the first having been designed to establish or name problems that are serious obstacles to the achievement of departmental objectives. Once all the problems have been listed a second staff meeting is conducted, with the primary purpose of listing problems, in priority, as they are to be dealt with. Three to five major problems are chosen; the remainder are usually given a secondary status by the command level of the agency.

In this role, the police manager focuses on the major problems or obstacles in the department. After the priority list has been established, a third meeting is held to set specific objectives and develop a schedule for resolution of these major issues.

The third type of staff meeting is for brainstorming. To initiate the process of brainstorming to assist in problem solving and problem identification, simply gather the members of the decision-making team, state the problem, and invite each participant to call out ideas that he or she might have concerning the issue involved. There are some guidelines that should be followed. First, no criticism or evaluation should be allowed during brainstorming. Comments such as "That's not a good idea" will only tend to cut off the communicative process and will lead some team members to defend rather than generate ideas. Second, team members should be encouraged to come up with as many ideas as possible. It is much easier to reduce the number of ideas at a later time than it is to bring up new ideas. Third, at this point, the emphasis should be placed on quantity, not quality. The more ideas and solutions that are developed, the more likely it is that good ideas or solutions will be brought up. Fourth, team members should be encouraged to build on each other's ideas. In a police department, a brainstorming session is usually most productive after the police manager has developed a high degree of trust with the other members of the decision-making team.

Discussion Questions

1.   Can police managers be more effective in the use of their time?

2.   Should a police manager have a fairly structured timetable, so that he or she can adequately perform all assigned duties?

3.   Should all top commanders of a department have the same amount of time available for the same functions—such as staff meetings, interviewing, and working with subordinates?

4.   What tasks occupy most of a police manager's time in the average police department?

5.   What would be some broad categories into which you might place a police manager's time and what percentage of his or her time is spent in each category?

6.   Should police managers spend most of their time dealing with internal issues of the department, external issues with other government agencies, or with the public?

Modern Police Management: Major Issues

Part Three

Once police managers understand the psychological and functional aspects of their role as chiefs of police or commanders, they are ready to begin making changes. This section attempts to show police managers how such changes may be instituted.

In Chapter 15 the manager is made aware of the issue of *power*—power being defined as the ability to influence others so that the goals of the police department may be met. In this chapter, the police manager is given information concerning the types of power, techniques for using power, and the reasons for seeking power or influence.

A major issue facing police managers today is civil liability. Chapter 16 attempts to assist police chiefs in a broad manner so that they will be able to deal with their roles as managers within the framework of law. This chapter is not meant to be a complete text on legal responsibilities but only an overview, giving police managers some understanding of the issues that must be dealt with in the broad context of civil liability.

Chapter 17 discusses the issue of labor management. Again, it is not an in-depth study of the problem but presents, in outline form, the steps that police managers can take to deal with unions and possibly prevent their development while also preserving the police managers' rights to develop new programs within their police departments.

Chapter 18 is designed to excite the student's inward values and beliefs. It discusses a historical background of ethics and, more importantly, shows the effects of an ethical system on a police agency.

One of the most thorny issues, and one that can have serious repercussions, is that of promotion. Chapter 19 deals with the latest techniques for designing an effective promotion process. It discusses the role of assessment centers and how they can help police managers to run their departments more effectively.

Use of Power || 15

Objectives

1. The student will be able to identify the two types of power.

2. The student will understand the approaches of power.

3. The student will understand the reasons why people want power.

Police organizations use the terms *authority* and *power* interchangeably. Authority is defined as the formal power that goes with a given position in the department. For example, the chief has more authority than the captain. The fact that such authority exists does not mean that the chief will be more influential than the captain in the running of the police department.

Power is defined as the ability to influence others toward stated goals and purposes. In this chapter, we will attempt to deal with three major issues with regard to power: (1) types of power—formal and informal, (2) approaches to the use of power, and (3) reasons for seeking power.

Types of Power

Formal Power

There are two basic types of power—formal and informal. Formal power is that which is granted to police managers by the nature of their position in the organization. Formal power has certain distinguishing characteristics.

Formal power comes in an instant. Police managers can point to the date, time, and place when they received this power as dictated and the position that goes with it. However, they are generally aware that this power can also be lost in an instant—when they are demoted, dismissed from the police department, or retire. Such people no longer have the formal power associated with their positions in the department. Police managers recognize that formal power comes from outside. It is therefore entirely controlled by the manager's actions or behavior.

Police managers who rely heavily on formal power may be caught in the trap of believing that they are more important than they really are. The result is that subordinates tend to play organizational games, making the formal power of the police manager less effective.

Informal Power

The second type of power, informal power, is power that one earns over a long period. Whereas formal power can be granted in a moment, informal power can only be earned through long-term relationships and the kind of reputation necessary to demonstrate to the world that one is capable of dealing with the issue of power.

Informal power is internal in nature and is long-term both in development and in use. It does not relate directly to one's position within the police department.

Police managers who may hold the rank of lieutenant or captain and who teach in the police academy may have greater degrees of informal power than others of higher rank within the same agency. It often happens that people with informal power are able to help reduce conflicts and bring about changes in a police department even though they are not directly related or involved in the conflict or change. The police captain who, in training, is able through informal power to influence the actions of other captains and commanders by bringing them together to resolve a conflict may have a greater effect on the outcome of patrol operations than individuals who are directly involved in the patrol division.

Effective informal power gets things done through other people. It does not depend on wealth or status and it cannot be bought—it must be earned. Informal power might require sitting at a large desk in a large office, but it is not directly related to the size of the desk, the number of phones, or even to the office's position in the building or the number of people being managed. Instead, people with strong informal power have the ability to use such power for good purposes. Police leaders with informal power clearly show that they know what they are doing, how they are doing it, why they are doing it, and what other people are doing about it.

Informal power helps bring out creativity within the individual and his or her co-workers. It also tends to foster a high degree of self-confidence.

When police managers are able to mix both formal and informal power in day-to-day operations, their level of influence on both subordinates and superiors seems boundless.

Police managers who receive formal power should feel confident in accepting such power, but they should not take the acceptance or maintenance of formal power alone as a great and serious matter. If, instead, they see it as something they could easily put aside, they will never become slaves to it. The growth of formal power is fostered by adherence to sound values and the use of this power to help others grow.

To keep developing informal power, police managers must first learn to establish priorities and be willing to learn about the various approaches to this end. There are three major steps in developing informal power:

1. *Being visible.* That is, making themselves available so that subordinates can get to know them as human beings. In short, being visible means being available.
    When something must be done, the leader with informal power is available and usually knows how to do it.

2. *Maintaining integrity.* Integrity is the willingness to be open and maintain one's values and principles.

   Leaders who strive to develop informal power have a clear idea of their strengths, limitations, and goals. They also have a clearly defined system of values. They do not appear lazy or dependent on others. When they value a principle, they have chosen it carefully, cherish it, and pursue it on a day-to-day basis. Police leaders with informal power know how to trust themselves as well as others.

3. *Maintaining performance.* Performance is the ability to listen, to be open and honest, and to live up to one's word. This, the production side of management, is especially important in the development of informal power.

   Police leaders with power are capable of doing a job and doing it well. They are dependable and willing to take on a variety of tasks within their police departments. For example, the effective police leader who attempts to build an informal power base is not reluctant to take assignments in almost any unit within a department.

A technique common to many informal police leaders is to carry a small notebook or set of blank cards with them at all times. When discussing issues in the hallway or in someone else's office, they make note of dates and commitments so that they can follow up on this information later on, making sure that they keep their word and perform. Police managers who have a high degree of integrity and can be counted on to perform develop an informal power base that is almost impossible to destroy.

With regard to relationships within a police department, the formal power of police leaders is not of primary importance. Power or influence is the capacity to get things done, and police leaders clearly recognize that such power is unevenly distributed among their personnel.

Police managers who take over new sections or departments have to consider the methods that were in use before their arrival. For example, if someone takes over as chief of police and finds that the agency has previously responded to the formal power structure, the new chief will have relatively more formal power and may be able to initiate rapid changes. In instances in which departments have been more responsive to informal power, the new police chief does best to work closely with the most influential (informally powerful) people so that they will help to initiate needed change. Normally, a new police chief can transfer and possibly even dismiss or force into retirement people who have depended on formal power in the past. But to try to use the same techniques on those with informal power tends to undermine the implementation of change, creating conflicts between the new chief and informal leaders.

Approaches to the Use of Power

There are six basic approaches to the use of power: (1) control, (2) manipulation, (3) threat, (4) referent, (5) needling, and (6) coordination.

Control

Control is formal use of power. It emphasizes rank and organizational position and involves the use of authority in controlling other people's behavior.

At first glance this approach may seem negative; however, like all approaches, it has advantages and disadvantages.

The advantages to the use of control include the ability to control a situation quickly, to coordinate activities in the manager's department, and to coordinate activities with those of another department. It also allows the police manager, when necessary, to conceal the motives for the use of such power. This approach brings about conformity and can affect many people simultaneously. It is effective in short-term projects or emergency situations.

When a police department is ordered to perform in a certain way, such as by court decisions, then the use of formal authority as an approach to power is an effective method.

There are negative features as well. Sometimes accuracy is lost in relying on control. It tends to create moral issues, especially when the decisions reached under this approach affect the lives of individuals and groups within the department. It sometimes brings about frustration and, when relied on exclusively, tends to generate organizational game playing. Also, if this approach is uncompromisingly and rigidly implemented, it becomes difficult to reverse or modify.

Manipulation

The second approach is manipulation—which depends largely on more or less indirect methods of ensuring cooperation and getting things done. Manipulation may be either positive or negative, depending on how it is viewed by those who are being manipulated. It has five main aspects:

1. The withholding of full information as to the reasons behind certain actions. For example, an officer may be asked to undertake advanced training without being told that this step is connected with plans for his or her future promotion.

2. Dependence on long-term personal relationships. For example, a police lieutenant may be able to persuade a police sergeant to observe departmental principles or rules on the basis of their earlier effective implementation in which they both cooperated.

3. Reliance on hierarchy. For example, it is difficult for a lieutenant to manipulate a captain or major; downward manipulation is generally easier.

4. Ability to exploit others' needs for approval or participation. For example, a police commander may announce that meetings will begin at a certain hour and that people who are late will be excluded. By closing the door once, the commander will have threatened the latecomers' sense of participation. This tactic can be very effective in preventing subsequent tardiness.

5. Dependence on cumulative effects. The use of power through manipulation is built on one example after another. It is difficult to manipulate people to a great degree during the first few days of a relationship, as when a freshly promoted

officer is new to a department. But as the newcomer becomes accustomed to the new milieu, this approach may become more useful.

Manipulation can be negative when it is used in a predominantly self-serving way, to aggrandize the manipulator rather than to get things done while also considering the needs of others.

Threat

Threat is the third approach. It is unlike manipulation in that in this approach the police manager goes outside the rules. Police managers use threat when they try to influence the behavior of subordinates by suggesting that the failure to comply may bring personally damaging consequences. For example, a captain may try to coerce a police sergeant to perform an unethical although not illegal act by threatening to have the sergeant transferred to a less favorable post should he or she fail to cooperate.

People who are tempted to submit to threats must recognize that they have control of their own behavior and that they must decide whether they should submit to the coercion of anyone else. People who try to use this approach to implement their power are usually recognized fairly quickly and disciplined by way of disgrace, demotion, or dismissal and a consequent loss of power.

Referent

In the referent strategy, a police manager uses the name of someone who has formal or informal power, such as the chief. The manager would imply indirectly or state directly that he or she is thereby representing the more powerful person. An example would be a captain, who strongly desires that a certain task be completed in a certain way, referring often to the police chief during a meeting about this task.

Sometimes referent power is presented in an indirect way. Consider the person who attempts to see to it that his or her office is placed directly alongside the office of the boss. In this manner people might assume, sometimes correctly, sometimes incorrectly, that this person has the total support of the chief.

Another example of the use of referent power is when one is seen with the chief as much as possible. For example, accompanying the chief to larger staff meetings or attending speeches given by the chief may give an impression of power that may be more illusory than real.

Needling

Needling is a strategy in which the police manager constantly makes suggestions or takes advantage of every opportunity to show how a decision reached by someone really is not accurately working or why his or her idea should be implemented.

A manager with certain formal power, such as a chief of police, may desire to achieve something special for his or her department. Unable to get this formally approved through the channels, the chief constantly states how the police department could be more effective if only it would be allowed to implement the original suggestion.

This technique is only successful if the person employing the strategy has a secure position. Generally such techniques tend to irritate other people and, in many instances, make enemies that are more powerful than the person using the strategy.

Coordination

Coordination is the fourth method and involves the sharing of power. It includes the involvement of other people and is the most effective use of both formal and informal power, although it is also the most time-consuming. This approach is best used in attempting to bring about changes and in resolving conflicts.

Some people see their power as limited, believing that if they delegate part of it, they will be left with less. The truth is that power can be seen as closely related to an issue such as love. The parent who has one child and then has a second does not have less love for the first child as a result; instead, the circle of love simply grows. The same is true of power. The police manager who is willing to share power with subordinates as well as superiors usually becomes far more powerful and influential within the entire community, both directly and indirectly, than one who is unwilling to share power and authority with others.

Reasons for the Use of Power

There are three basic reasons for using power: personal, social, and survival.

Although these three may seem mutually exclusive, police managers in day-to-day operations generally balance them and do not usually use their power for any one of these reasons alone. They usually follow a set of priorities, however, and will use their power primarily for one of these reasons, and less often for the others.

Personal

The manager who uses power for personal reasons is generally trying to enhance his or her own status; therefore, personal power is essentially self-serving. Although this may seem like a negative thing, it can sometimes be justifiable. For example, if the police manager recognizes that he or she may have to stand on his or her own reputation in a conflict, as with a community group or another department head, personal power may help carry out not only his or her personal goals but also those of the police department. Another example would be that of the police official who has developed an influential base in the community and therefore can effectively defend the police department against arbitrary or unjustified attacks from the media.

Social

Social power is exercised when a police manager uses his or her influence over others to achieve some common good. In this situation power is used mainly to influence people within the agency, at other levels of government, within the criminal justice system, or in the community. An example would be the police manager who is able to use his or her unique background to educate the community on the subject of crime and its prevention.

Survival

The third reason for the use of power is for survival. For example, a chief might be willing to use his or her power to implement the plans of the city manager even though he or she does not especially favor these plans. In other words, the chief "goes along" in order to retain his or her position as chief. Another example might be that of a police executive who agrees to implement performance evaluations within his or her department, even though such evaluations seem unnecessary and unconstructive, simply because he or she considers it politically risky to oppose them.

In studies throughout law enforcement agencies, it appears that most police managers do tend to place a higher priority on social power than on the other two. Personalized power usually ranks second, with survival being lowest. The only time survival power seems to come higher in the order of priority is when the chief of police feels the need to survive for a short period of time—for example, for the two or three years prior to retirement.

Data indicate that people with a strong need for personalized power seem to exhibit certain common characteristics.[1] These include (1) dominance—the desire to be in charge of a situation; (2) aggression—willingness to criticize others rather than defend their own principles; and (3) exhibitionism, or the need for personal attention. Police managers who strive for power for personal reasons usually have low needs for (1) nurturing, or caring for others; (2) perception, or understanding the reasons others behave as they do; and (3) deference—the willingness to defer to others solely because of the others' position.

Police managers who demonstrated a strong need for socialized power usually scored high in perception; achievement, or the desire to excel; and dominance. They scored low in abasement, the need to accept guilt for themselves or others' behavior, and aggression.

Police managers who sought power for survival reasons usually had high scores in guilt, nurturing, and deference, with low scores in dominance and achievement.

Conclusion

Any police manager must be skilled in the use of power. Police managers depend on the activities of other people—peers, subordinates, and superiors—as well as those who attempt to influence the operation of the department from the outside.

Power is established in a personal relationship through the ability to lead people, especially during a crisis situation. Therefore, police managers are evaluated on their professional reputations and track records and through the ideas they implement within their departments.

In conclusion, in using power at any time, either formally or informally, successful police managers are sensitive to what others might consider to be legal, ethical, and moral considerations. Police managers need a good intuitive understanding of power and influence and how their power affects other people. Successful police managers develop different types of power and are good at using the appropriate methods in dealing with various situations. They are able to take advantage of their resources and do not feel that power should be used to avoid risks. Instead, they look for opportunities that will help them to enlarge their base of influence in a prudent way. Finally, effective police managers recognize and accept the fact that they, by the role they play, influence other people's behavior.

Note

1.   Tests conducted from 1980 through 1990 by the Institute of Government at the University of North Carolina.

Discussion Questions

1.   Why must a police chief have power if he or she is to be effective?

2.   What are some techniques that may be useful in building an informal power base?

3.   Is it necessary for a police chief to have a great deal of formal power?

4.   Why do police chiefs seek power?

Civil Liability || 16

Objectives

1. The student will understand the police agency's need for protection from civil liability.

2. The student will understand issues of liability.

3. The student will be able to identify ways in which to reduce the police department's potential liability.

Introduction

The role of the police manager has been in a state of flux for some time, and although some challenges have been completely met and subdued, new challenges constantly surface to complicate the job of the law enforcement manager.

There was a time when police managers could count on exercising some degree of control over the crime rate and keeping their agencies scandal-free; this gave them a sense of security. Today, however, they have additional and more pressing problems while still having to contend with the old ones. Many of these problems have already been addressed in this text. But recently, more and more police managers are feeling troubled by the presence—very real and very expensive—of liability for the actions of their personnel and of judgments against their agencies that in some cases run into millions of dollars. But before addressing the more specific ways of confronting the liability issue, we should think in terms of the multiple layers of protection offered by policy, support, training, discipline, supervision, and evaluation. Each item will add more protection; any item alone will not offer enough protection. It is only by depending on the interaction of all these factors that the police manager can feel secure.

Another approach is to make sure that the manager selects, appoints, trains, supervises, entrusts, retains, and directs personnel so that an officer's misconduct on the street at 2 A.M. can be shown to have occurred despite the manager's best efforts. The trail of evidence that might indicate culpability should not lead to the police manager's door. If it appears that the officer acted independently, there will be no vicarious element to the

---

Chapter 16 is included with the permission of G. Patrick Gallagher.

responsibility. Liability has increased for a number of reasons; the greater the number of lawsuits in our society, the greater the scrutiny given to the actions of police officers and the greater the accountability demanded by the public and recognized by the courts.

Years ago police officers were rarely sued, but today, suits are filed almost automatically if there is any possibility that the actions of the officers fell below the standards required by the courts. Perhaps these lawsuits for "police malpractice" are a sign of the profession's coming of age.

Police managers must be familiar with current terms, concepts, and trends in the civil courts; they must keep track of the recent decisions so as to understand what is expected of them and their personnel. By monitoring the decisions of various courts across the land, the manager can learn valuable lessons and avoid potential lawsuits.

The following story concerns a question given to candidates for a sergeant's promotional examination in England:

> Q. You are on duty in the High Street when there is a large explosion, which causes a large crater in the middle of the road, a main trunk road in fact. The explosion blows a van onto its side and upon investigation you discover in it a man and a woman, the woman being the wife of your sergeant, who is currently away on a course. Both are injured. At this point two dogs, neither of which is wearing a collar, begin to fight in the middle of the road, and they are encouraged by drinkers from a nearby public house who are quite obviously inebriated and disorderly. In the confusion a car and a coach collide and you discover that the car is being driven by your chief constable and that the bus driver has taken a shotgun from his cab with obvious intentions of using it. A man runs from a house shouting for a midwife and a woman informs you that there is a fire in the large garage around the corner. You then hear someone shouting for help from the nearby canal where he has been thrown by the original explosion. Bearing in mind the provisions of the Justices of the Peace Act, the various Mental Health Acts and particularly, section 49, Police Act, 1964, what should your course of action be?
>
> A. Immediately—immediately remove your helmet and mingle with the crowd.

This is not an option for us. The plaintiff is interested in a defendant with "deep pockets." A UCLA law professor has stated: "Robbers and muggers do not have liability insurance, and they do not have assets. The job of the lawyer is not simply to find the negligent party but the negligent solvent party."[1]

The "deep pocket" theory makes it advantageous for the plaintiff's attorneys to name as many defendants as possible, from the officer who committed the alleged act to the supervisor to the chief. Therefore, the chief, as the agency head, must be able to avoid liability by proving that he or she did everything that could be expected to supervise and train the highest-quality officer.

Due to the increase in the number of lawsuits over the past few years, there are now newsletters and other publications that discuss police liability and highlight cases and damage awards. *Police Misconduct: Law and Litigation,*[2] for example, is a valuable tool for the police manager because it indicates the course of action, the points of attack, and the ease with which liability suits can be filed.

So, given the magnitude of the problem, it is necessary that police managers achieve a greater familiarity with the concepts, terms, and principles guiding the courts as well as with rules of litigation; that they have a comprehensive overview of the latest information on liability issues from jurisdictions around the country; that they glimpse a projection of future trends and issues; and that they understand the major areas of liability—civil rights violations and negligence. Finally and most importantly, managers must know how to develop liability protection programs for both themselves and their agencies. This will minimize the risk of "self-inflicted wounds," such as those from which the profession is now suffering.

Lawsuits resulting from police misconduct fall into two major categories: civil rights violations and negligent employment and supervision. Police managers must become familiar with the various ways in which causes of action under these categories can be filed and the decisions of the courts. Although not always consistent from jurisdiction to jurisdiction, these decisions should be tracked to monitor trends. The emphasis in this chapter is on the management of liability; the technical and legal aspects of civil rights and negligence will be covered in outline form only.

Civil Rights Violations

Civil rights violations, alleging the deprivation of a person's rights under the Constitution when an officer is purporting to act "under color of law," are the grounds of the most frequent complaints filed against law enforcement officers. The Civil Rights Act of 1871 gives rise to these causes of action under Title 42 of the United States Code, Section 1983. Liability under this law does not necessarily have to be based on the *intent* to violate a person's constitutional rights, because liability is based on the theory that the officer's conduct had a natural and obvious consequence and that, without intent, the officer's conduct resulted in a denial or deprivation of the person's rights.

The Civil Rights Act of 1871 provides:

> Every person who, under color of any statute, ordinance, regulation, custom, usage, of any state or territory, subjects or causes to be subjected, any citizen of the United States or any other person within the jurisdiction thereof to the deprivation of any rights, privileges, or immunities secured by the Constitution and laws, shall be liable to the party injured in an action at law, suit in equity, or other proper proceeding for redress.

The specific causes of action under this law are as follows:

- False arrest and detention
- Excessive force and physical brutality
- Illegal search and seizure
- Denial of counsel and illegal interrogation
- Denial of First Amendment rights
- Denial of medical attention
- Discriminatory or retaliatory prosecution

- Use of perjured evidence
- Verbal abuse or harassment
- Failure to provide police protection
- Misconduct resulting in death through use of deadly force

The vital points are (1) that *intention* to deprive is not a necessary prerequisite to legal action and (2) that an action can be brought for failure to prevent a violation (that is, when an officer knows that a violation or deprivation is taking place but takes no affirmative action to prevent the violation).

Negligence

To understand the basics of negligence, it is necessary to consider its four elements:

1. A duty owed
2. According to a standard of care
3. A failure to perform that duty according to that standard
4. A loss of injury resulting from that failure

The major areas in which actions can arise are as follows:

Negligent Appointment. The plaintiff alleges that the officer who injured her was unfit for appointment and that the appointing official knew or should have known about this unfitness.

Negligent Detention. The plaintiff alleges that the officer who injured him was unfit to be retained as a police officer and that the retaining police manager knew or should have known of this unfitness.

Negligent Assignment. The plaintiff alleges that the police manager assigned an officer under her command to certain duties for which that officer lacked appropriate training and experience, or which the officer was unable to perform, and that the police manager knew or should have known about these deficiencies, but made the assignment anyway.

Negligent Supervision. The plaintiff alleges that the administrator was under an affirmative duty to supervise his subordinates and that, in failing to do so, caused the plaintiff to sustain injuries or loss.

Negligent Training. The plaintiff alleges that the police manager has not trained her officers—especially in highly critical areas such as firearms, driving, defensive tactics, and first aid—and that the plaintiff was injured as a result.

Negligent Direction. The plaintiff alleges that the police manager has failed to anticipate problems arising in the field, to minimize police discretion at the operational levels, and to promulgate comprehensive written directives guiding police actions and behavior. Failure to do this is equivalent to not assuming the duty to direct personnel, and the manager is responsible.

Avoiding Liability Through Selection and Training

One of the surest ways of reducing the potential for lawsuits is to do everything possible to staff the police department with the best people possible. A systematic approach to selection and training starts with the assumption that, for the most part, the selection and training process goes on at each one of the following six steps or phases: recruitment, initial selection, psychological evaluation, academy training, field training, probation.

Recruitment. The manager selects *where* he or she recruits, *who* he or she is recruiting, and *by whom* the recruiting is done. The chief actually filters people out by the way in which he or she goes about the recruitment process. In other words, the quality of the recruits may depend in large part on the design of the recruitment program.

Selection. At this point the chief applies certain selection criteria, utilizing background checks, polygraph results, and whatever else he or she may want to use within legal and ethical guidelines.

Psychological Evaluation. The courts have recognized and accepted the use of psychological testing for police officer candidates. It is recommended that tests be administered to candidates, then scored and interpreted by a psychologist who will also interview each candidate and make recommendations to the police chief. The psychologist should be familiar with the police profession and be able to defend his or her decisions in court, present findings logically and professionally, and be willing to recommend the rejection of unqualified candidates. A final caution: psychological evaluation only gives an assessment at a particular point in a person's life. The chief cannot use the test to guarantee predictions of how a person is going to handle the job three years down the road or when unforeseen events (a broken marriage, financial problems, friction with a difficult supervisor) cause stress.

Academy Training. For many years, methods of training have not received a great deal of scrutiny, but they will in the immediate future. A proper training program for recruits is based on job task analysis and the subsequent validation of a curriculum that includes performance objectives for each block, a plan of instruction, and a training guide. Evaluation of both courses and instructors, along with simulation exercises and role-playing, should be considered essential.

Field Training. This innovation has, over the past ten years, been one of the most beneficial ways of providing officers with both training and job-related evaluations. It does much to counterbalance the "street nullification" so common in the past, and it is the best preparation for solo assignments.

One problem is with the development of supervisors. Supervisors are often trained by the supervisors they served under, who may, in many cases, be inadequate. The department may thus only perpetuate inadequacies and may not take the steps needed to improve the system. Supervisors are usually not trained prior to their promotion, and few are trained afterward. Field training programs for supervisors and managers could be very beneficial. Such programs can also reduce the effects of negligence.

Probation. This is a legal right that has seldom been employed properly, but it can challenge recruits to maintain their drive. It is during this time that the manager can make the most knowledgeable and intelligent choice of who has the potential to be the best officer in the organization. In most instances the decision to allow officers to enter career status and achieve tenure is made when they graduate from the academy; at that time, much of the information and evaluative material that is almost strictly job-related has not yet been gathered. During this period, supervisors must be conscious of their responsibility to continue the training of the recruit officers in certain one-on-one situations by critiquing their performance and offering advice.

The components of this systematic approach are not new, but taken in combination, where each part complements the others, they can help to put better prepared officers into the system and into individual police departments.

The Protection Circle

The alarm has been sounded often enough to warn police managers about the imminent dangers of lawsuits and adverse judgments. What is now needed is the description of a comprehensive liability protection program. Regardless of the level at which the manager operates, given the vulnerable areas that have to be improved and protected and the burden of responsibility on the manager's shoulders, these steps will provide a framework on which a liability protection program can be built. Simply put, the protection circle as it applies to liability consists of three equal parts or phases—direction, maintenance, and assessment—operating in three consecutive time frames (see Figure 16.1):

1. Proactive: policy and support from the executive

2. Active: training and supervision

3. Reactive: discipline and evaluation

Figure 16.1 **The Protection Circle**

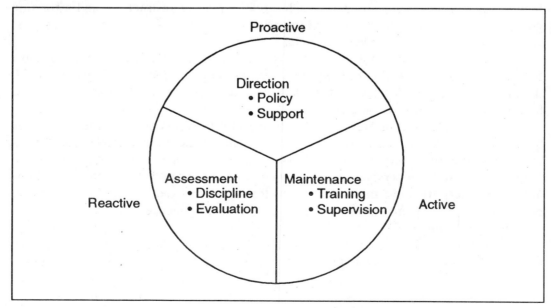

There is no way that policy can be effective without training and discipline. Each function must flow from and be consistent with the one that precedes it, because the protection circle is a combination of policies, training, and discipline integrated so that each follows, supports, and then improves the next while indicating changes necessary to improve the overall process.

To expand on the protection circle, and to lay out a series of steps that will, if followed, make it possible for concerned police managers to assess their danger and react accordingly, it is necessary to start with the chief, the top-level manager. The chief must:

1. Be knowledgeable, stay informed, keep abreast of trends and precedents, and read the literature. Identify a number of agencies that are trendsetters and regularly ask for their policies, find out what they are changing, and start a dialogue with their chiefs of police.

2. Identify the areas of greatest concern for liability, preferably after completing a job task analysis of personnel. List the areas that are producing the most lawsuits, both for the agency and for others in the area, and track the general trends from around the country. These areas might be firearms training, supervision, medical assistance, defensive tactics, arrest procedures, and pursuit driving.

3. Make an annual review of policies, practices, and procedures with respect to these areas of liability. Simple changes in policy language may be enough to avoid a lawsuit—or at least eliminate the chief from it—if they are coupled with some training and appropriate discipline. Match the areas of greatest concern—the critical tasks—with policies, practices, and procedures and ask whether all these elements are articulated adequately (i.e., what personnel must do, whether the practices are described in the manner desired, and whether the procedures are the best that the state of the art can offer). If the chief is not completely satisfied, he or she can then proceed to make changes where necessary.

4. Identify the standards of care with regard to these critical tasks. It is against these standards that actions will be judged by comparing them with recognized, accepted performance levels in both emergency and routine circumstances. Check state statutes to see what they require, the policies of other departments, the literature, and court cases and reliable experts on these various topics.

5. At this point, have available the services of dependable legal counsel—an attorney who is familiar with this topic—who can offer expert legal advice and will be able to look after the department's interests. It profits little to have an attorney who is unfamiliar with this topic work on policies. Your attorney must work on *your* policies and must be familiar with the demands of your profession, your personnel, and current legal thinking.

6. Prepare written directives for the police department, using a format that includes definitions and states pertinent policy in the clearest, most direct language, making sure that related policies are reviewed and changed accordingly where they are affected by these revisions.

7. Train personnel accordingly. Simultaneously with the training itself, document the qualifications of instructors. Do not allow someone to train just because they are "available" or "have always been doing it." Be critical of training methods and require written lesson plans, which should follow training guides developed

along with the new major policies on such matters as deadly force, high-speed chases, and medical attention for those taken into custody. Managers need to be careful that the right way of doing something is emphasized and that inappropriate or wrong methods are clearly indicated. They must be particularly careful about documenting everything pertaining to the training, such as reviewing attendance-taking procedures, whether by roll call, sign-in, or having the instructor take attendance. It is advisable to give tests (competency-based examinations) of one sort or another to ensure that the training is adequate.

8. Keep everything current—instructors' qualifications, lesson plans, and their contents, which can become outdated because of new state laws and new policies.

9. Have discipline conform to policy and training. Make sure that it is consistent and progressive. The manager must be certain that records are kept of all disciplinary actions for violations of any particular policy. Checking disciplinary records is used to review the effectiveness of policy and training. An increased number of disciplinary incidents might indicate the need for revision in the policy or for additional emphasis in the training.

10. Keep in contact with professional groups by maintaining an active membership and demanding that they provide professional assistance. The police manager can also work closely with other police departments and exchange copies of policies and procedures, thereby producing model policies or adopting uniform policies. Regional or statewide policies are easier to defend, because they indicate a more general consensus of professional opinion on what should be required; on the other hand, it is more difficult to have expert witnesses develop standards and have them imposed by the courts. The manager must realize that police agencies can no longer afford the luxury of not cooperating. As in other things, there is strength in unity. All this can be done without sacrificing autonomy.

11. Make the next year one of consciousness raising on the subject of civil liability. Lay out a plan of attack—a training plan with goals and objectives for the whole department. The plan, for example, can provide for two days of training in liability for everyone, with additional days in high-liability areas. Task forces and study groups can be formed to examine practices and procedures in the department on an ongoing basis. Incidents in the high-liability areas should be reviewed as training examples. Personnel can be debriefed on these incidents and the department can gain much value from them. Special attention can be paid to the supervisors, and it can be made undeniably clear that they have a direct responsibility for the conduct of their subordinates.

Although these steps will not eliminate lawsuits, they may help to protect the police manager from liability.

Training in the Future

Two important trends will soon make greater demands on the law enforcement profession and its training system. Although tremendous progress has been made in the past fifteen years in police officer training, too much emphasis has been placed on the quantitative process and not enough on the qualitative one. We are currently entering a time when, for a number of reasons (especially lawsuits and adverse judgments), much more emphasis will be placed on the qualitative side of training.

The courts themselves are giving the law enforcement profession credit for a higher quality of training than actually exists. In the immediate future, the courts may—in addition to a monetary damage award—order that the police agency submit a forty-hour training program acceptable to the court. It may further demand that all personnel go through this training within a certain period.

Better that the police chief understand these developments and take action to improve the local training academies (by active participation on advisory boards, by the elimination of improper techniques, by the assignment of the best personnel to the training function, and by elevating the status of training) than to have to live with the consequences of inaction.

Accreditation

The formation of the Commission on Accreditation for Law Enforcement Agencies has given rise to discussion and generated strong opinions around the country, even though the concept does not apply to every police agency. The police department itself decides whether it wishes to seek accreditation. Another movement represents an even stronger potential for the imposition of standards, and with little direct input from the profession. This development has been gaining momentum for the past several years, and it is likely to impose standards on law enforcement from outside the profession itself.

There are many examples of expert witnesses testifying that police officers violated certain standards of care in the use of their firearms, in pursuit driving, in arrest procedures, or in the use of less than lethal force. Depending on what the expert witnesses declare is the "standard," on how the jury accepts the testimony of the witness, and on the verdict, new standards can be set. As more and more cases are decided in large part on the basis of whether the officer's actions are up to the standards of care, the cases and the standards they create become criteria that the profession must adopt in order to avoid liability. This happens in the absence of uniformly agreed-upon standards accepted by broad segments of the law enforcement profession.

If the profession were to agree on certain standards and there were uniform policies and practices around the country, "standards" would exist. The profession would have the opportunity to stand together and develop its own standards, thus improving image, productivity, and cost-effectiveness.

The profession has in recent years come together and developed some standards, hammered out by professional associations that represent almost all of the law enforcement interests in this country. It is those standards that some agencies want to acknowledge, to accept for their own. Those standards and subsequent accreditation will provide a degree of protection to the agency and its managers.

Accreditation exists to make its standards available to those police agencies that want them. Furthermore, police managers should not confuse uniformity with lack or loss of autonomy. With lack of uniformity and subsequent imposition of standards from without, there is a loss of autonomy. Uniformity to a degree can lighten the burden of police managers, because they then will be able rest assured that broad segments of the profession will have similar standards. Uniform policies, standards, and accreditation are ideas whose time has come, and they will go a long way toward helping police agencies in the courtroom.

Conclusion

The police manager's ability to manage liability is the direct result of his or her knowledge of the accepted standards and the initiation of liability protection programs in the police department. Nothing can prevent managers from being sued, but managers can take steps to protect themselves and their department from liability.

Liability can be seen as both an enemy and an ally. It can be a moving force for great change, which might not take place were there not the danger of liability. It can exert tremendous leverage on the system and, if properly countered, can be a force that helps to initiate needed change and increased professionalization of law enforcement. With the proper resources, it can be managed.

Notes

1. *Time*, June 13, 1984.
2. *Police Misconduct: Law and Litigation*, Chicago, IL: Clark Boardman.

Discussion Questions

1. Will liability become a greater issue for the typical police department in the future?

2. What can police departments do to avoid civil liability in the future?

3. Why should the average police officer be aware of the rules of civil liability?

4. How can the protection circle best be applied to a small police department?

Labor Management || 17

Objectives

1. The student will learn why police unions have grown in the last decade.

2. The student will understand the preparatory steps necessary prior to the opening of collective bargaining talks.

3. The student will understand what assistance is available to police managers on the issue of labor management.

4. The student will understand "management rights" as defined and used in collective bargaining.

5. The student will understand techniques that may be used to avoid the formation of police unions.

Introduction

Police employee organizations, whether called unions, benevolent associations, or anything else, have risen both in number and in power since the mid-1960s. This has created a new issue—collective bargaining—with which police commanders must be able to deal in devising their management systems and implementing their programs.

At present, not all states have collective bargaining. Therefore, the individual police manager must first review the laws within his or her jurisdiction concerning this issue. A typical example is the situation in Dade County, Florida, where collective bargaining had been carried out for several years before the state of Florida enacted enabling legislation (in 1974) requiring all police agencies to become involved in collective bargaining. In states such as Illinois and Maryland, state legislation does not exist; however, individual municipalities engage in collective bargaining with police employee associations or organizations representing the police officers within that municipality. Some states, such as North Carolina, have no collective bargaining law or even ordinances enacted at the local level.

When police officers organize, a fundamental shift occurs in internal relationships. What may have been a "one team" police department embracing both senior and junior police officers can begin to divide, and these two groups may become respectively "management" and "employees."

Before the appearance of collective bargaining in police agencies, there were few encroachments in the area of management policy. This is now starting to change, and police officers are beginning to win an increasing voice in policy formulation. As this transformation continues, changes cannot be ignored; they must be recognized and adopted by the police manager as soon as possible.[1]

Proactive management is no guarantee against the emergence of a police union. Peer group pressure, family background, and examples set by other public and private sector labor organizations are some of the factors that may also make police receptive to unionization.[2]

Hopefully, prior to either the formal or informal recognition of a police officers' group, the police manager will have certain policies established, including a selection and placement program, a promotion program, a classification and pay program, grievance procedures, a fringe benefit package, and personnel policies, to mention but a few of the major areas that must be developed.

Growth of Police Unions

Today police agencies in some instances are overmanaged, and in many instances, overcontrolled. Police officers currently do not appear ready to accept the rigid control that may be imposed on them; nor are they likely to accept it in the future. They may resort to overt acts of retaliation, sometimes amounting to outright sabotage of the police department and its efforts to achieve law and order. Typical examples include deliberate misuse of departmental equipment or resorting to the tactic of the "blue flu" to emphasize their power and achieve their demands.

Once police officers have experienced the freedom to participate in problem solving and decisionmaking, as they do in their homes, schools, and other areas of life, they begin to demand those same rights in their jobs. The granting of more or better fringe benefits, or the provision of special equipment does little to settle the unrest that exists at the bottom level of many police agencies. Police officers today are not always willing to make personal sacrifices for the economic security of belonging to a police agency if this personal sacrifice does nothing to provide self-fulfillment for them as individuals.

This feeling of restlessness, anger, and sometimes even hatred has come from the rules defined for police officers that provide no challenge or variety and from supervisors and managers who are inconsiderate and autocratic in their leadership. The new breed of police officers has doubts about the ideals of efficiency. They are unwilling to exchange the loss of personal pride, the monotony in the performance of mundane tasks, and the stress of working for poor managers in return for the high wages.

To many police officers today, the idea of success involves some kind of self-fulfillment and is not geared specifically to material rewards. If these needs are not satisfied by management, another organizational structure within or parallel to the police department begins to take form. In many instances, this turns out to be a police union.

Preparation for Collective Bargaining

Police managers must know about collective bargaining laws, their budget, and the relationship between their department and other agencies within city or county government. They should have a fairly concise and accurate idea of the city's or county's political stability as they enter into bargaining.

The next issue police managers must face is whether to develop in-house negotiators or to hire outside consultants to do the collective bargaining. The police chief must recognize that collective bargaining is a time-consuming process.

There is divided opinion as to whether the chief of police should be a part of the talks conducted at the bargaining table. Most city managers and police chiefs seem to agree that their role is not one of actually conducting the bargaining but rather of being aware of what is proposed and agreed upon. The police chief, therefore, should try to get help from people who have experience in negotiating management contracts, whether that experience be in dealing with police or governmental unions. Such assistance can be an asset to the chief whether he or she decides to participate in the negotiations personally or to leave this responsibility to other managers in the department.

Some of the strong reasons why a chief should not be on the bargaining team include the fact that he or she may have risen through the ranks and may strongly identify with the rank and file, thereby prohibiting the bargaining team from presenting a unified front. Furthermore, it is the responsibility of the chief of police to implement any contract agreed upon. If the contract negotiations were strained, the chief's role as the manager of a department could be hampered. There is no question, however, that a commander within the department, a personal representative of the chief, should always be a part of the bargaining team.

The police chief should, after making a decision as to whether or not he or she will be a negotiator, develop a negotiating team that will represent his or her points of view. This team could be made up of personnel from within the department, such as top commanders and middle managers. The chief must also decide whether an outside consultant should be brought in to assist. If there are experienced and qualified negotiators within the police department, there is no need to bring in an outside consultant. This is especially true if the managers have been carefully trained and clearly understand the legal and political implications of collective bargaining. If a department's management staff has not received such training, outside consultants can provide a tremendous amount of assistance for at least the first negotiating and contract session.

Whether the police chief elects to partake in the bargaining or whether this is delegated to his or her commanders, the chief must recognize that he or she has to give the necessary authority to his or her commanders to participate in the bargaining and to make binding decisions.

There is no magic number as to how many should be on the management team. However, members of the team should be able to understand the demands being made by the police union, the role of the police officer within the community, and the needs and desires of the chief of police as to the amount of control he or she feels is necessary in operating the department. They should be aware of the budgetary restrictions placed on the department. The team should know the laws governing the bargaining session, the contract, and the arbitration that may be necessary. To ensure that these matters are handled properly, outside consultants may be called on to assist. Sometimes these consultants are attorneys who bring with them expertise in bargaining as well as knowledge of the law. Other management teams are made up of police department managers and representatives from other city departments, such as finance or personnel.

Once the bargaining team has been formed, it must collect and analyze information in advance of any meetings with the union representatives. It must also develop (in close conjunction with the chief of police) the management demands that will be made during the bargaining sessions. This is where such issues as the management's "rights clause" and what it means are agreed on by the management bargaining team.

In its initial meetings, the team should establish certain criteria to be used in reaching decisions about all key issues. Once identified, these issues can then be analyzed and discussed one at a time. A simple planning form such as that shown in Figure 17.1 can be used. This form lists the topics to be discussed, what management is attempting to secure within each topic, what its initial position will be, its fallback position, its final position taken, and any remarks that may be necessary for the management team to analyze as it begins bargaining with the union representation.

It is generally agreed that members of the governing board should not be part of the bargaining sessions or the management bargaining team.

Whoever is on the bargaining team, the team surely should include at least the following people: an attorney, a financial expert, a representative of the chief of police, a representative of personnel, and a chief negotiator who is a labor-management relations expert. If this negotiator comes from within the police department, it would help strengthen the bargaining team. The chief negotiator must be open and honest and create a feeling of trust between both sides as the negotiations continue. Usually when the police department hires a professional negotiator, the police union is inclined to do the same. In situations in which the police department does not hire an expert, the police union will not normally do so.

Figure 17.1 **Planning Form for Collective Bargaining**

Team Leader—

Team Members—

Topic	Objective	Initial Position	Fallback Position	Final Position	Comments
Contract length					
Wages					

The following checklist of items that should be researched prior to negotiations is from the Management Information Service of the International City Management Association.[3]

1. Anticipate union demands and prepare counterproposals.

2. Review contracts and awards that have been negotiated in police agencies within the general area.

3. Review department policies and procedures in this regard.

4. Review any literature that has been prepared by the police union and distributed to their members to determine what promises, if any, have been made.

5. Be thoroughly briefed and familiar with all local and state legislation regarding collective bargaining and management's rights.

6. Keep complete and thorough records of all grievances, because many times these grievances will become the demands of the unions.

7. Review any previous contract talks and analyze what notes were made and what issues were dropped, compromised, or held on to in each of the prior meetings.

8. Review the recommendations of first-line supervisors or middle managers as to the feasibility of proposals that have been developed by the top managers in the police department.

9. Have information readily available concerning the present work schedules, fringe benefits, and any other data that may be discussed during the bargaining session.

10. Review economic and labor market information for the current cost of living and trends that may be developing.

11. Compile information on officers in general, including their average age, length of service, turnover data, absenteeism, overtime, and the actual dollar cost for the present fringe benefits being given to police officers.

12. Insist on receiving proposals from the police union in writing.

13. Formulate objectives for each of the union's demands.

14. Establish ground rules for determining when negotiations will begin, what information will be released and when, whether the bargaining talks will be open or closed to the public, who should make the press releases, when the negotiations will be held and where, and what shall be on the agenda.

With these kind of agreements reached in advance, there will be few surprises at the bargaining table.

Assistance Available to Police Managers

If police departments, with their employees represented by various police union organizations, are to function effectively in collective bargaining, police managers must be able to develop the skills of union leaders. They must feel confident that they are on a par with those they face across the bargaining table. In administering and developing a contract between the police union and the police department, the management team must be able to show knowledge and techniques equal to those of the union bargainers. To achieve this result, the police manager must be aware of the political, social, and legal ramifications of the decisions reached. Education and training hold the key to the police manager's successful fulfillment of this additional role.

Educational institutions must be advised by police managers of their needs in this field. Academic courses, special seminars, and workshops can assist police managers in developing necessary skills. In-house training programs should be conducted to provide information to management teams that are responsible for representing the police department at the bargaining table.

Through the National Criminal Justice Reference Service the police manager can keep abreast of the latest journals and newsletters as well as the special labor relations training programs available at different times and in different parts of the country.

Reference material is available from the International Association of Chiefs of Police through their publications *The Police Labor Review* and *The Public Safety Labor Reporter*. The annotated bibliography *Police Unionization and Bargaining*, published by the Traffic Institute of Northwestern University, could also be an asset to the police manager.

Management Rights

"Management rights" is perhaps the only clause that, if properly structured, truly represents the police managers' interests and rights under a collective bargaining agreement. Such a clause provides protection from having an outside arbitrator rewrite the contract because of a lack of specific language, reserves certain operational rights, and has a psychological impact on the police union when demanded in writing.

A list of the most significant rights to be preserved by the police manager is as follows:

1. The right to hire and fire.
2. The right to determine the size and composition of the individual organizational units.
3. The right to allocate work assignments.
4. The right to determine geographical assignments of officers.
5. The right to determine the level of service and the types of service to be offered by the police department.
6. The right to discontinue operations or discontinue performance of operations by the police department and police officers assigned to those functions.
7. The right to establish and change schedules and assignments of police officers.
8. The right to transfer, promote, and demote police officers consistent with personnel regulations.
9. The right to discipline police officers for violations of departmental policies, rules, and regulations consistent with the procedures established within the department to handle such matters.
10. The right to develop and enforce policies, rules, and regulations.

11. The right to schedule and assign overtime based on needs and situations that face the police department.

This list is not intended to be exhaustive but is offered only as a guide to help the police manager review existing agreements and develop a new agreement with a police union.

The key concern of police managers should be to protect the police agency's ability to offer the required services to the public in the most effective manner. A good management rights clause enhances the police manager's flexibility. Protection of operational authority should be one of the police manager's primary goals during a collective bargaining session and during the term of an agreement between management and the police union.

Avoiding the Development of Police Unions

One way to prevent the formation of a union in a police department is through good management. If police officers are pleased with their present benefits and feel that they have a good rapport with management, they are not likely to feel a need to unionize.

Many unions are created because the police officers believe that through the union organization they can relieve their feelings of frustration and boredom and achieve some prestige and recognition. If the police chief using systems management techniques achieves this same result—that is, of decreasing the frustration levels within the department, decreasing the level of boredom or number of mundane tasks assigned to police officers, and giving officers a chance to achieve personal satisfaction and recognition— the chance of unions developing will be very small.

The police manager must strive strongly to develop confident leadership qualities so that subordinates, although they need not feel personally close to the manager, respect and trust his or her judgment as their leader. The police manager does this by keeping open communications, by meeting as often as possible with the police officers—whether it be on a social basis, at monthly meetings, by roll calls, or just by making his or her presence seen and known by walking through the building and talking on an informal basis with the officers.

Some of the things that the police manager can do to avoid the creation of a union is to see to it that the police officers receive fair treatment from their immediate supervisors. If they believe that their immediate supervisors and the management team are sensitive to their needs and will protect their rights, police officers generally will not seek any outside type of assistance to reach these objectives. The police chief should attempt to give as much personal recognition as possible to police officers. He or she should see to it that the officers do not doubt their job security but have adequate benefits, wages, and fair personnel policies and benefits. All of the above should be clearly spelled out in some form of written directive and should be known by each member of the department.

Another technique that has been found to be successful by police managers is for all key managers in the police department to take an active part in the basic or recruit training program and any in-service programs that may be conducted. The police manager, by his or her presence in the recruit program, allows the issues and doubts raised by the new recruit to be answered directly by management. This is an effective manner of dealing with rumors that the recruits may have heard during their formal training or during any type of "on-the-job" training they receive during this basic training program.

All in all, the police manager who treats people fairly and equitably, is open and honest with them, and develops the qualities listed earlier in this text will probably not be faced with dealing with a union.

The police manager must recognize, however, that even with effective leadership skills, he or she might possibly be required to deal with a union because of ineffectiveness on the part of superiors or of the governing board. If this is true, it is the obligation of the police manager to show to these people the effect that they are having on the police department by not recognizing the worth of the individual police officer and by not meeting the professional standards established by the police manager for his or her agency.

Conclusion

As in any other successful operation, effective collective bargaining—which includes careful planning, rational decisionmaking at the bargaining table, and fairness and honesty—will not only assist police management in achieving its objectives, but also help police officers to build a unified police department. Police managers need not fear police unionization, nor should they take the opposite view—that the police union should fear them. If a police union is voted in, police managers must accept that fact and be willing to work within the framework of careful preparation, bargaining, and implementation.

In each stage of the collective bargaining process, different roles are played by various individuals. These roles must be played carefully and well. If they are not, the whole process fails in its objective and strife ensues. Separate roles exist on both sides of the bargaining table, and seldom does the ability to play these roles come naturally. The requisite skills must be learned and practiced if they are to be used effectively. Learning by trial and error is dangerous for the police manager, because errors in the bargaining process may be of such magnitude as to place the police manager at a severe and lasting disadvantage. Any police manager who has a role in collective bargaining should become familiar with the extensive literature on the subject. He or she should discuss tactics at length with others in the field of collective bargaining and, if at all possible, observe the collective bargaining process before becoming a participant.

This chapter has not been designed to teach the police manager how to go about collective bargaining with officers' associations but is rather intended to give a broad overview of the issue. Much has been written in this field; each police manager should study this literature, review the legal requirements within his or her jurisdiction, and work closely with a legal advisor, the city or county attorney, and the city or county manager.

Notes

1. Jim Morgan, "Impact of Collective Bargaining on Law Enforcement" (St. Petersburg, FL: Public Safety Research Institute, 1976).

2. Molley H. Bowers, "Police Administrators and the Labor Relations Process," *Police Chief Magazine*, (January 1975).

3. "Police Unions," *Management Information Service Report* (Washington, DC: International City Management Association, March 1976).

Discussion Questions

1. Are police unions good or bad for the police profession?

2. What are some positive features of police unions?

3. What are some negative features of police unions?

4. In your opinion, has police unionization reached its peak or will we see further unionization in the future?

5. How can the police union be an effective management tool?

6. What, in your opinion, is the role police unions will play five, ten, or twenty years from now?

7. Should all members of the department, excluding the chief of police, belong to the union?

8. Should all members of the department, including the chief of police, belong to the union?

9. Should any special privileges be given to the union president?

10. How can a police chief use the union as a positive force?

Ethics for the 1990s ‖ 18

Objectives

1. The student will understand the different theories of ethical system.

2. The student will be able to relate an ethical system to an effective leadership style.

3. The student will be able to develop a principle, define an action, and relate the answer to an ethical system.

Introduction

Police managers are drafters, designers, and implementers of the ethical standards of their departments. By their behavior they establish norms that become standards within the department. Because other police managers are influenced throughout the profession, they are able to raise the ethical standards of the profession itself. These standards become the basis for making decisions, hiring personnel, judging daily actions, and demonstrating the example of the police department's values, beliefs, and principles. High standards will continually raise the level of professionalization.

Ethics are defined as a principle of right or good behavior. It is the standards governing the conduct of the members of an agency, of a profession, of a community. It is, in essence, a contract between the police manager and personnel within the police department, the city government, and the community.

There are numerous purposes for developing strong ethical standards. High standards bring outcomes of credibility to the individual police agency. As a result, all members of the police department—sworn and nonsworn—are suddenly accepted by the community as helpers, protectors, and advisors. In many instances people from the department become leaders within city government and the community. High standards produce social good for the community.

By having a set of professional ethical standards, the police agency learns to be trusted and learns to trust.

As mentioned in Chapter 2, there is a difference between ethical and legal standards. Legal standards are those that are defined by the law. Ethical standards are those that are defined by a profession, a community, or an individual police manager in his or her leadership role. There are moral standards that are standards established on an individual basis, which may or may not have anything to do with the agency. Finally, there are performance standards. The police manager is faced with an attempt to prioritize these four sets of standards. In his or her role as a law enforcement official the implementation and adherence to legal standards always come first. Then there is the opportunity for the individual police manager to prioritize ethical, moral, and performance standards. In this chapter, we will discuss the different theories of standards of ethics and the way in which each of these theories has an effect on the role of leadership and how power is used to gain the specific outcomes desired by the police manager.

In the leadership role the police manager is influenced in his or her ethical conduct by a series of factors. The behavior of his or her superiors plays an important role in determining the limitations of behavior that can be attached to any standard. In addition, in many instances the professional ethical standards of other department heads can play a role. For example, if the personnel department believes that people should be promoted with a strong emphasis on race or sex, and police executives believe that the best qualified people should be appointed to supervisory and management positions, a conflict arises as to which ethical standard should apply to the police department.

The practices of the law enforcement community in the police manager's region have a strong influence on the standards that the police chief may be able to establish. For example, if the police chief wants only college graduates as police officers and yet he or she is the first chief in that geographical area to impose such a standard, there will again be a conflict, especially if the department is not able to attract a sufficient number of qualified college graduates to meet its needs.

The moral climate of the community also affects the ethical conduct of the chief. For example, some communities believe that having police officers act as school crossing guards is important. However, the police department may find that such a standard is not cost-effective and is an inefficient use of personnel. The same might be true of walking beats in a downtown area. However, because of the influence of such groups as parents or business owners, the agency might be ordered to perform these tasks.

We now will examine five ethical systems: (1) utilitarian ethics, (2) rule ethics, (3) social contract ethics, (4) justice ethics, and (5) personalistic ethics. Figure 18.1 shows the relationship of these systems.

Ethical Systems

Utilitarian Ethics

The utilitarian ethical theory was developed by Jeremy Bentham in 1789.[1] The rightness or authority that the police manager would use is to concentrate on the consequences of his or her behavior. Police managers who emphasize utilitarian ethics determine whether the action of themselves or others is right or wrong by concentrating on the consequences of the behavior. Any action taken by members of the department from this ethical point of view is valid if the sum total of its outcome produced by their behavior is

Figure 18.1 **Ethical Systems**

Ethical Systems	Proponent	Rightness Is Determined By	Leadership	Power	Decision-Making Strategy
Utilitarian ethics	John Stuart Mill (1806-1873) Jeremy Bentham (1748-1832)	Considering its consequences	Manipulator	Coalitions through conning	Test for results
Rule ethics	Immanuel Kant (1724-1804) John Locke (1632-1704)	Laws and standards	Bureaucratic	Position in agency	Test for procedures
Social contract ethics	Jean-Jacques Rousseau (1712-1778)	Customs and norms of a particular community or group	Professional	Knowledge and experience	Test for organizational values
Justice ethics	Aristotle (384-322 B.C.) John Rawls (1921-)	Ensuring that all receive opportunities and fair share of output	Team	Coalition by groups, associations, employees	Test for agreement of others
Personalistic ethics	Martin Buber (1878-1965)	One's conscience	Transforming	Empowerment	Test for personal conviction

greater than the sum total of negative effects produced by the action itself. This ethical system emphasizes the role of happiness. In theory, if someone desires to do something that will bring happiness to themselves and others, they are acting in an ethical manner.

Rule Ethics

Rule ethics was developed by Immanuel Kant around 1800.[2] The rightness of some-one's behavior is determined entirely by laws and standards. For example, if there is a law demanding that the police department do certain actions, then under rule ethics there is no room for compromise. In a larger legal theoretical sense, industry is not necessarily governed nor does it need specific authority to bring about changes. Industry is free to undertake many endeavors unless in some way it is constrained by the law—for example, the need to be licensed or to be open to certain kinds of inspections. Government, on the other hand, can only operate when there are specific laws that grant authority to that facet of government. For example, the police department could not operate unless there were specific state statutes granting cities, towns, and counties the authority to form police departments, and each police agency must be formed by a specific law passed by the county commissioners, city council, or town board. As a result, in government we find a heavier emphasis on rule ethics because of this philosophical approach to the need for laws and standards prior to the undertaking of any large government endeavor, such as police, fire, or public works.

The negative feature of rule ethics is that too much emphasis can be placed on very definitive rules, and as a result, freedom of judgment is taken away from members within the police department. If the city council adopts a rule that says police officers are to work certain shifts, it has taken away from the discretion of the police manager the assignment of personnel to different shift schedules to meet the goals of the department. The same holds true if the chief of police designates that personnel within the agency must reach certain decisions such as shaking doors on the midnight shift or the manner in which equipment must be kept in the patrol units. This takes away the freedom of choice from the individual officers. Sometimes police chiefs correctly view the need to pass rules in order to provide for an ultimate goal of safety. An example would be mandating the wearing of bullet-proof vests by all department personnel whenever they are perform-ing their assigned functions in the public arena. This would include not only sworn offi-cers, but also commanders, investigators, and possibly even support personnel such as crime scene technicians.

Social Contract Ethics

Social contract ethics is based in the theory of Jean-Jacques Rousseau, which he developed about 1760.[3] According to social contract theory, the rightness of behavior in policing is determined by the customs and norms of the department, the city or govern-ment, and the community itself. In many instances, under social contract theory, guide-lines are not in any written rule or procedure, but become *custom,* which may be an unwritten but strongly supported tradition. For the individual police manager this may include such issues as which civic groups are important for the police leader to join and how to contribute in some effective manner. Under this theory of ethics each person must act under the authority of the general will of all people. For example, if the agency has a strong tradition of police executives attending or not attending shift parties and a new chief or a newly promoted executive decides to attend the next shift party, his or her presence in one instance would be viewed as a positive act, but in the other he or she may be viewed as breaking the custom and therefore may be viewed as having negative intentions. The general will of people within the police department will serve as the ultimate standard for determining what actions the individual officers should take. Sometimes social contract ethics come into play when the question of responsibility of an individual officer to advise superiors of improper conduct by a fellow officer is raised.

Justice Ethics

Justice ethics was first taught as a theory of ethics by Aristotle in approximately 340 B.C. According to this theory, the rightness of any behavior is determined by ensuring that all persons receive opportunities and a fair share of whatever resources might be available. Police managers who espouse this theory of ethics may believe strongly in seeing to it that all people receive basically the same dollar amount in a specific pay raise or may demand that if certain personnel have special privileges, such as a take-home car, then all personnel within that class of employment (for example, sworn members of the department) would also be assigned a take-home vehicle. Justice ethics in many instances is defined as a democratic principle. That is, it is a responsibility of government to provide some kind of service to all persons within the community. As a result, the police executives may find themselves having to allocate resources to geographical areas of their city or county even though there are very few calls for service or crime is very negligible in those areas. In some communities, police departments are obligated to have walking beats at each shopping mall solely because there is a crime problem at one mall and if something is done for one, it must also be done for all others.

Personalistic Ethics

Personalistic ethics was first espoused by Martin Buber in 1930.[4] The rightness of any behavior under this ethical system is determined as adhering to one's conscience. This theory emphasizes the truth solely in the eyes of the beholder, and it is based on human existence, not necessarily on knowledge of what may be provided. Individual personal convictions serve as the ultimate standard for determining what the individual police manager should do. The police chief who may strongly believe that it is a waste of taxpayers' dollars to put walking beats in the malls and downtown area may be willing to be dismissed solely because of the principle of effective use of taxpayers' money. Police executives are faced with dealing with people who emphasize personalistic ethics over rule ethics. Police officials must protect abortion clinics regardless of what their personal feelings are concerning the issue of abortion; they must emphasize adherence to the law. The people who are demonstrating may be relying on personalistic ethics and place what they personally consider their conscience to be above the law. As a result, there is a confrontation and it is almost impossible to convince such people that the law is the guide that should be adhered to in such demonstrations. As a result, the police official must be aware that personalistic ethics may not only create a conflict, but also require the use of special resources and tactics to resolve the issue as the demonstrators may have a strict reliance on their own individual conscience.

Leadership and Ethics

Leadership styles may be emphasized differently depending on the ethical system employed.

Utilitarian Ethics

Utilitarian ethics provide a leadership style consistent with the autocratic manager. This individual may use manipulation to achieve the results that he or she demands. Manipulation in and of itself is not always negative. It means the ability to influence someone else's behavior without disclosing the true intent. For example, the police executive may personally decide that certain officers should attend certain training programs. He or she then brings these people into the office and explains the benefit that could be achieved by attending such a program, for example, the first-line supervisory program at the local community college. However, one of the major intentions behind this executive's move is to see to it that certain personnel that he or she has selected in advance will do better in the promotional process and as a result, he or she would be viewed as an effective leader.

Generally speaking, people who emphasize utilitarian ethics in their leadership role test for results and concentrate on such results. Therefore, the outcome that they achieve may be positive in one area but may hold numerous negative outcomes that the police manager has not prepared for. To the manipulator, the most important requirement for success in the police department is power. They believe that without power there can be no authority, without authority there can be no discipline, and without discipline there can be difficulty in maintaining order and systems goals and in producing effective decisions on a daily basis. As a result, police managers who emphasize utilitarian ethics maintain this ethical stance by the development of support prior to the implementation of a decision.

Another example of leadership in this ethical system is when an investigator decides that it is proper to give immunity to someone who has committed a breaking-and-entering offense so that the investigator may solve a robbery case. The investigator may believe that his or her superiors will not support the decision and therefore will manipulate the decision by going first to the people of higher command who would be responsible for assisting in such decisions later on. An example would be a discussion with the local district attorney or state attorney. As a result, the investigator presents the proposal to the police supervisor or manager with an emphasis on having already spoken to the prosecutor, who was solidly behind the proposal.

Rule Ethics

Police leaders who emphasize rule ethics relate very much to the avoidance style of management. Most of what they say or do depends on the principles of a good bureaucracy. They believe that the police department's organizational structure should emphasize control over coordination or communication. They rely heavily on the position that they hold within the police department to establish an ethical standard. Think of the police chief, who, working his or her way up through the department for many years, never said much about a dress code, yet on being promoted to the position of chief of police immediately passed a general order establishing a very strict dress code within the department. Police executives who follow this ethical system make decisions based on written procedures. If an officer behaves in a way that is inconsistent with the department's norms or customs, the officer is not disciplined, but instead, a new rule is written so that the next person who acts in the same way can be disciplined because of the new rule that has been established.

Police executives who support rule ethics usually emphasize a system of promotion in which seniority and past achievement are weighted heavily and rewards such as salary should be granted based on the position that the people hold within the hierarchy and not based on the contribution they make to the overall goals of the police department. They would, for example, demand that salaries of nonsworn personnel never be higher than sworn personnel of equal status within the department, thereby always guaranteeing that sworn personnel are considered more important to the agency. The emphasis here is based on rules and regulations, not on the ability or contribution of the individual.

Social Contract Ethics

Police managers who emphasize social contract ethics are sometimes referred to as implementing a "professional" style of leadership. Much of the principles underlying this ethical approach were later espoused by Peter Drucker in his numerous texts on management. The principles that the professional police manager strives to achieve are the department's objectives and goals through the effective and efficient deployment of all resources including money, people, and materials. Police managers who emphasize social contract ethics rely on knowledge and experience but do not limit this knowledge and experience to themselves. In fact, they have a tendency to seek additional knowledge and to emphasize other people's knowledge and experience in both the establishment of purposes and the action to be taken. There is a heavy emphasis on department values in such a police department, and as a result the police executives, in deciding the evaluation of individual actions, will rely on the intent of the action as opposed to the rule that may have been violated. Police executives who follow this system would praise an officer who bypassed a rule to achieve a stated principle. An example would be an officer who orders the immediate replacement of the front door of someone's home who accidentally or through error had been served a search warrant. As a result, the citizen feels good, and the department—although rules may have been bypassed—evaluates such an action based on the positive intent that the officer had in performing his or her duty.

Dress codes that exist within police departments in many instances arise out of social contract ethics. When personnel dress in a professional manner, even though a specific rule, such as the wearing of a hat, may be violated, the personnel are supported for their behavior, and in many instances the rule, which may have been unenforced over the years, is finally deleted from the procedure manual. One of the features that police managers may find negative in following this system is how to deal with personnel within the department who believe that some of the rules and traditions should be changed. Obviously, when a police official believes strongly in the system he or she will allow personnel to speak and to be supported in that right. In many instances police officials who use this system emphasize a compromising leadership style.

Justice Ethics

Police managers who emphasize justice ethics rely heavily on team management practices. They acquire authority and power by involving numerous groups in the overall purpose of the department. This coalition, which is formed by integrating numerous purposes, can be an effective way of bringing about an improvement in the ethical standards of a police department. This democratic principle can be seen in many instances by the manner in which city councils designate their budget or in the way a department will be required or not required to emphasize an affirmative action program so that all minorities such as females, blacks, Hispanics, and Orientals are included within the department. The negative feature of an emphasis on this ethical system is that sometimes pressure groups become powerful within the department itself. An example might be if the Police Benevolent Association or Fraternal Order of Police start dictating what the overall policies or ethical standards of the department might be. Police managers, in implementing this ethical system, rely on testing for agreement from those groups who are responsible for implementing ethical standards.

Personalistic Ethics

The main principle behind this form of leadership is to allow people within the agency to become better human beings. They emphasize transforming themselves and others into becoming better people than they originally thought they could be. Police managers who implement personalistic ethics rely on a relationship between themselves and others within the department. The personal contact and adherence to the leader's high standards for the department are strictly enforced. This leader receives great joy from the successes of others and takes every opportunity to praise the personnel of the police department. The police chief who is thinking of implementing a new personnel allocation system under personalistic ethics would involve the men and women of the department who must implement the process and be committed to its objectives. The negative feature is that the manager empowers other people, some of whom may not be able to respond effectively to the new degree of authority and responsibility placed on them; however, the police leader would give such people time to develop, provide them with the necessary knowledge, and be tuned to their specific desires for personal growth and how that personal growth affects the overall growth of the police department.

Conclusion

Each type of leader uses power differently. The manipulator develops coalitions that are not necessarily out in the open. The bureaucratic police chief relies on his or her position in the department. The professional police manager relies on knowledge and experience in the principles and methods of effective management. The team leader relies on his or her relationship with other groups that affect the ethical standards of the department. Finally, the transforming leader relies on the empowerment of others. Each of the aforementioned styles makes a significant contribution to the overall development of ethical standards.

In some instances the results are extremely important. In other instances adherence to the laws and standards would tend to solidify the growth of the department. In yet other instances, customs and norms should be honored whenever possible and only changed on agreement with those affected. When all people receive opportunities and fair shares in how the department operates, they too raise their level of commitment. And finally, when individuals are able to go home at the end of each workday and be satisfied that their behavior is consistent with their individual conscience, you begin to have highly successful, happy, and productive police officers.

Sometimes people seek a simple set of guidelines in helping them to be considered ethical people or police managers. A simple set of guidelines have been developed and used by Lou Holtz, Notre Dame head football coach, for many years. He has three very simple guidelines: (1) do what is right, (2) give it your best effort, and (3) treat others with dignity and respect. These three guidelines answer the three major questions that every police officer and employee will have of his or her manager. When you do what is right, you have answered the question, "Can I trust you?" When you do your best, you have answered the question, "Are you committed?" And finally, when you treat others with dignity and respect, you have answered the question, "Do you care for me?" Although these guidelines appear simplistic, in reality they work very effectively.

One way to help determine the ethical standards of the individual police manager, and the police department, is to see how he or she deals with some very specific issues. The issue of accountability is first. Are members of the agency held accountable for their behavior? Think about the police middle manager who has been ineffective in his or her position for years and yet no one holds this individual accountable for poor performance.

The result is that the individual establishes a low standard that becomes the new standard for the police department. The second issue or question that is answered is, "How much public scrutiny are we willing to allow?" Police departments that emphasize an openness to the public very rarely are asked to provide or to support a civilian review board. On the other hand, when departments attempt to hide from public scrutiny, there seems to be a much stronger emphasis, especially from the news media, on getting the police department to be more open in every way. As a result, stronger influence is brought for the establishment of some form of civilian review.

The third issue deals with liability. Does the department support its personnel when they are right or does it automatically agree that there is liability just because someone makes an accusation against the department itself? And, finally, how does the department deal with people who gripe, complain, and "blow the whistle"? If people bring forth ideas or a grievance that clearly shows that the department is operating in an inefficient or ineffective manner, is that individual chastised or praised?

The important answer to all these questions is that they allow any police department to be carefully evaluated as to its minimum and maximum ethical standards. We judge police leaders by their actions, not by their statements of intent. If their actions are unethical, then they cannot stand public scrutiny. By the same token, if they act consistently with high ethical standards regardless of the system, they become leaders in the department, profession, and community.

Notes

1. Jeremy Bentham, *An Introduction to the Principles of Morals and Legislation* (Oxford, England: Oxford Press, 1789).

2. Immanuel Kant, *Lectures on Ethics* (New York: Harper and Row, 1963).

3. Jean-Jacques Rousseau, *The Social Contract* (New York: Hafner Publishing Company, 1947).

4. Martin Buber, *Between Man and Man* (Boston, MA: Beacon Press, 1955).

Discussion Questions

For each of the following sets of facts, develop a principle (from Chapter 2), define the action to be taken, and identify the ethical system used in your answer.

1. People in your department are not allowed to exceed a certain number of overtime hours because of budget constraints. Your officers are so dedicated that they have been working more than the maximum but not putting in for them.

2. You read in the paper that an officer in a neighboring community has been arrested and charged with showing pornographic literature to a minor. The arrested officer states that he has been having a homosexual affair with your Officer Jones. You ask Jones and he admits that he has practiced homosexuality and intends to continue

this behavior. You determine that Jones had nothing to do with the showing of pornographic literature to the minor. You find that Jones' work is average to above average, he is never late, and he has never created any problems within your agency. About half of your officers come to you about Jones, fifty percent of those stating that they do not like the idea that they have to work with a homosexual, but the other half say that it doesn't bother them in the least.

3. Your captain, after securing your pledge of confidentiality, confides in you information that makes you realize that the city/county is violating its affirmative action responsibilities under the law. When you point out the problem, the captain says that politically you and he have no choice in the matter.

4. The established working hours are 8:30 to 5:15 with 45 minutes for lunch. You notice that people in one unit are leaving between 4:45 and 5:00 every day. You check on the work output of that unit and find that it is on schedule and of excellent quality. Other unit heads have mentioned the early departure pattern to you as an observation without saying whether they thought it was good or bad.

Assessment Center Process ‖ 19

Objectives

1. The student will be able to recognize the advantages and disadvantages of using an assessment center in the promotional process.

2. The student will be able to recognize the eight steps to be included in the development of an assessment center.

3. The student will recognize and understand the most common exercises used in an assessment center.

4. The student will recognize and understand the use of different rating scales in an assessment center.

Overview

Through an assessment center, candidates for promotion can be observed and evaluated over a specific period, such as one or two days, during which they undergo a series of exercises designed to test specific characteristics. In some situations, assessment programs can be used to guide career development, to select new personnel, to determine supervisory and management candidates for the future, and to identify training needs. The assessment program process allows individual candidates to be evaluated on the basis of their observed capabilities and behaviors. Exercises are geared specifically toward real-life situations within the agency and the dimensions are related to the position being sought.

Assessment centers have proven to be effective for promotions to management positions. However, when numerous candidates seek first-line supervisory positions in medium to large police departments, assessment centers can get caught up in a cumbersome bureaucratic process, and this may fail to produce the desired results. They appear to be more effective in testing candidates for management positions. Overall, assessment programs can be useful in filling executive positions, but they become less practical as one moves down the line in the organizational structure.

In running an assessment center, the police manager must be aware of the question of trust between agency personnel and the assessors. That is, it may be necessary to use outside assessors until such trust is developed. Usually, in the first few assessment centers, police managers have a tendency to use a combination of inside and outside assessors. It is advisable to use at least one inside assessor on each exercise in order to deal with special policy questions as well as to clarify the exact meaning of phrases that may be unique to the individual police agency. Prior to the implementation of an assessment center, it is important to train both assessors and candidates and to conduct a job analysis from which criteria can be established.

Many police departments use aspects of the assessment center approach for promotional testing to the positions of first-line supervision and full assessment centers for mid- and top-level management positions. The assessment center concept combines a various array of performance tests, both written and oral, with evaluations by human observers. That is, this center includes the observation of actual behavior and is considered more job-related than many traditional methods.

There are benefits to be derived both by the participants and by those conducting the evaluation. Normally, a promotion made on this basis—as opposed to the more traditional written test and oral interview—can be made with greater confidence.

One major issue to be overcome by large police agencies, especially in first-line supervision, is how to select the candidates for an assessment center. The issue is still open for debate, and many agencies are in the process of testing different devices. The most common method involves a written test followed by a short oral interview by a board made up of personnel from within the department. These exercises are scored, and the top twelve to fifteen, depending on the number of open positions, are included in the assessment center itself. If this does not produce enough candidates for promotion, follow-up assessments are conducted.

In many instances the assessment center approach benefits the assessors as much as or more than the candidates. Many industrial agencies, such as General Electric, believe strongly that the benefits of assessor training are great; they therefore increase their assessor participant ratios in order to expose more personnel to the experience. Among the benefits to assessors are improved interviewing skills, broadened observation skills, increased appreciation of group dynamics and leadership styles, new insights into behavior, strengthened management skills through repeated exposure to case problems and situations, a broadened repertoire of responses to problems, the establishment of standards by which to evaluate performance, and the development of a more precise vocabulary with which to help describe behavior and feedback processes on a day-to-day basis.

Assessment centers offer benefits to all officers regardless of whether they are promoted. The two major benefits for a police department that develops an assessment center are (1) the identification of management potential and (2) the development of the candidates' skills. Most assessment programs help the candidates—those who are promoted and those who are not—to recognize their individual strengths and weaknesses. This gives the candidates insight into how their management potential can be enhanced.

If the procedure is to aid the individual candidates significantly, they must behave in a certain way. For example, they need an opportunity to talk with those who evaluated their behavior. This is normally done in the feedback process. There is a need to be honest and candid when isolating weaknesses and strengths, and candidates need to seek ways in which they can improve their conduct or behavior patterns.

In any promotional process, it is extremely rare to find a single individual who greatly surpasses all other candidates in every facet of an assignment. This is also true of the assessment center. Normally candidates have a tendency to score well in some parts and poorly in others. Such evaluation of an individual officer's strengths and weaknesses prior to promotion gives the police chief an opportunity to see which areas may require more intensive, personal attention. Thus, the chief can be more effective in helping a new commander to become an effective member of the management team.

Sometimes consultants work closely with an individual police department in helping it develop its assessment program. Usually the personnel department sits in on meetings in which the consultants play the role of facilitators. Questions are raised, examples of how to deal with issues are addressed, and eventually an assessment center is put together. The consultant plays an advisory role for the first assessment center, in many instances participating as an evaluator. Once the first assessment center has been completed, the consultant helps by evaluating the program itself—whether its purposes were met and how future programs might be made more effective. After the first couple of assessments, the police department usually conducts its own programs. Sometimes outside evaluators are called on to sit as individual assessors, but normally they have little to do with the development of additional centers for the police agencies.

In many instances, police departments will use psychological testing as part of their assessments. These tests are designed to assist the newly promoted candidate and the supervisors or managers to work better in the future. They carry no weight in terms of the assessment itself. The most common tests used include the Myers-Briggs Type Indicator, the Edwards Preference Test, and the Styles of Management Inventory. If these tests are used, the candidates are given either group or individual interpretations of the results.

Advantages of the Assessment Center

On the positive side, an assessment center approach is usually seen by police personnel as a "fair" system. Therefore, its results are more easily accepted not only by those promoted and those who did not receive promotion but also by other members of the agency. A second positive feature involves a process by which the officers receive feedback about their strengths and weaknesses. Just as important, top-level managers and the chief receive feedback concerning what might be serious issues that need immediate attention. For example, it may prove that some candidates for assessment resent the performance evaluation system more than the department's top managers had realized. Upon being informed of this, the police chief may be able to check out the process more thoroughly and make immediate changes if such are necessary. Solutions offered during the exercises may produce useful ideas for the police department. In this way, even unpromoted candidates sometimes get to feel that they have a stake in the growth of the police department.

A third reason assessment centers are popular in government is that they are generally accepted by the courts as being legally fair.[1] This allows police chiefs to implement affirmative action programs and meet other legal requirements.

Disadvantages of the Assessment Center

Like any management tool, the assessment center contains negative features. It is time-consuming. A promotional process that involves only a written examination can be conducted in a half-day to a full day; assessment programs may run anywhere from two to five days. This does not include the time necessary for preparation, training of assessors, or final evaluation and analysis.

A second problem is that of locating good assessors. Experienced assessors are not common because of the newness of this approach. As more assessment centers are implemented, qualified assessors are becoming more and more common.

A third negative consideration is the cost. Assessment centers can be expensive, especially in comparison with more traditional methods. Usually the cost of the first assessment center includes that of the consultants who help to develop it. It may, in some instances, require a job analysis, which is used as a basis for the development of dimensions. In many areas assessors are paid honorariums or at least are reimbursed for their expenses. As a result, the overall cost can rise. But when agencies in a general area tend to train assessors and share such personnel, the costs are reduced.

Experience shows that assessment centers normally provide highly detailed feedback to the police chief. This information is developed and presented in a few days, sometimes short-cutting years of informal feedback.

An assessment center approach may help avoid lawsuits that require a police department to defend its present practices. In essence, assessment centers are more likely to be realistic in demonstrating that they actually test for the abilities a candidate will need in his or her new position.

Assessment centers are used to help enforce departmental policy. For example, in agencies that believe in encouraging the personal growth of their employees, the assessment center can serve as a tool to test such growth. Individual plans for personal growth can be developed with the help of the assessment program. In one police department, the police chief recognized the strengths and weaknesses of each of the candidates after conducting an assessment center. The chief offered each candidate the opportunity to develop his or her strengths and overcome weaknesses.

Assessment centers tend to identify training needs, especially in the human systems approach to running the police department.

The personnel department should be involved in implementing and developing an assessment center by providing job analyses and developing adequate dimensions that are consistent with personnel practices. Personnel departments may bring about community involvement, either through input prior to the actual assessment center or by providing people from within the community to act as assessors.

Personnel departments can assist in the physical arrangement of an assessment center. They also play a key role in coordinating it, taking care of the numerous details such as housing for assessors and outside candidates, providing meals, and, when necessary, providing role-players.

Although an assessment center approach might be expensive, it tends to reduce the chances of promoting people to positions for which they are not qualified. As a result, the cost of the assessment center tends to be far outweighed by the quality of personnel promoted.

Developing the Assessment Center

There are eight steps to be taken from the stage of early discussion to final completion. These include (1) performing a job analysis, (2) developing dimensions, (3) creating a matrix, (4) developing guidelines, (5) developing exercises, (6) training assessors and candidates, (7) conducting the assessment center, and (8) ensuring feedback.

Performing a Job Analysis

In this first step, either a formal task analysis can be performed or personnel from within the agency can be called together to carefully discuss the behavior and traits required by the sought-after position. In general, agencies have a tendency to bring together personnel of the rank of police captain or deputy chief to discuss what these people perceive to be the more important characteristics of their positions. These characteristics then become the job analysis. Consultants who have experience in the development of a task analysis study for police departments are also available. The expense incurred, however, is sometimes prohibitive, especially for smaller agencies. In many of the larger police agencies, a continual job analysis is performed by the personnel department, and its findings often serve as a basis for the assessment center.

Developing Dimensions

In the second step, dimensions are developed. Dimensions are the behavior traits to be examined during the assessment center. These dimensions fall into four broad areas. General dimensions may encompass commitment to handling responsibility and authority as well as command presence. The second area includes technical skills such as work perspective, handling of complaints, and career development. The third general area includes rational skills, including the ability to handle written communications, decisionmaking, management of time, planning, fact finding, and control. In the final area, human skills, the candidate is observed and examined for characteristics that are necessary for personal development as well as to foster growth in others. Human skills are usually the main category. These include such dimensions as leadership, oral communication, interpersonal sensitivity, stress management, the handling of people, and team development. An example of a list of dimensions is included in Figure 19.1.

Once dimensions are agreed on, they must be prioritized. It is impossible for an assessment center to test for all possible dimensions the candidate may need to perform his or her assigned job. Realistically, the dimensions that can be tested in an assessment center number between twelve and fifteen. Once the dimensions are prioritized and the most important ones are established, it is possible to move on to the next step.

Figure 19.1 **Assessment Center Dimensions**

1. General
  a. Command presence
  b. Commitment to service
  c. Handling of responsibility and
     authority
 	
2. Technical skills
  a. Work perspective
  b. Technical and professional
     knowledge
  c. Career development
  d. Handling of complaints
  e. Dealing with rumors
 	
3. Rational skills
  a. Communication (written)
  b. Judgment
  c. Decision-making skills
  d. Management of time
  e. Planning and organizing skills
  f. Fact-finding skills
  g. Control skills
  h. Delegation skills
  i. Problem analysis
  j. Follow through
	4. Human skills
	  a. Leadership
	  b. Emotional maturity
	  c. Oral communications
	  d. Interpersonal sensitivity
	  e. Assertiveness skills
	  f. Adaptability
	  g. Fairness
	  h. Flexibility
	  i. Attitude toward development
	     of personnel
	  j. Stress management
	  k. Attitude
	  l. Handling of people
	  m. Power
	  n. Enthusiasm
	  o. Patience
	  p. Integrity
	  q. Intuition
	  r. Team development
	  s. Stability
	  t. Organizational climate

Creating a Matrix

In the third step a matrix is drawn up that lists the dimensions on one side and the possible exercises across the top. Normally each part of the assessment center will test for six or seven dimensions. It is possible for dimensions to be tested in more than one exercise. The more important dimensions are tested in three out of a possible four exercises. In some assessment centers a dimension may be tested once; for example, command presence in the role-play situation.

Figure 19.2 shows an example of a typical evaluation matrix for an assessment center for a police department.

Developing Guidelines

Once the matrix and exercises are agreed on, guidelines are developed for each part of the assessment center. The guidelines include the purpose, a brief definition of the individual dimensions, and examples of behaviors that should be considered positive and those that should be considered negative. In the guidelines, specific behavior patterns for the individual police department are given so that assessors can understand which behaviors would be rated high and which might be rated low. For example, in the dimension of written communication, high grades might be given for complete sentences, conciseness, and correct spelling. Low grades may be given for poor spelling, poor organization, or incomplete sentences.

Figure 19.2 **Evaluation Matrix for Assistant Chief**

		Project Development and Presentation	In-Basket Exercise	Leaderless Group Exercise	Oral Interview	
1.	Work perspective		X	X		(2)
2.	Command presence	X			X	(2)
3.	Oral communication	X		X	X	(3)
4.	Written communication	X	X			(2)
5.	Interpersonal sensitivity	X		X	X	(3)
6.	Decision-making skills		X	X		(2)
7.	Stress management				X	(1)
8.	Control skills	X	X			(2)
9.	Emotional maturity				X	(1)
10.	Delegation		X			(1)
11.	Planning and organizing	X	X	X		(3)
12.	Flexibility			X	X	(2)
		6	6	6	6	

Developing Exercises

In the fifth step, each exercise is developed in great detail. In the oral interview panel, the assessors are selected and questions that are common for all candidates are developed. In the role-play situation, a role-player is selected. Instructions for the role-player as well as the candidate are prepared. It is also decided whether to use audio or video equipment. Video can be used for two purposes. First, it can allow the command personnel of the police agency to identify the behavior patterns of each candidate after the completion of the assessment center. Second, and just as important, it is a way to give individual feedback to candidates on how they were graded and how they appeared during their part of the assessment center.

Special instructions for each exercise should contain as much detail for the assessors as possible. For example, in the in-basket exercise, instructions may include even the fact that the name should be placed on envelopes. Instructions should be read carefully, and if extra answer sheets are needed, assessors can provide them. For leaderless groups, the instructions might include the fact that the assessors should provide name tags and solicit questions prior to the actual beginning of the exercise.

Instructions are provided for each exercise. One set of instructions goes to the candidates. In a role-play situation, the instructions may designate the information to be provided for the candidate. They may say that the candidate is to play the position of captain and that he or she is going to interview a disgruntled employee who has received an attached performance evaluation report. In addition, instructions are provided for the assessors. These are usually one or two paragraphs in length and are concise, so that the assessors understand their role in the process.

Next, the problem is defined for each exercise. The written plan problem may be extensive in its detail. It may include pages of data from the department's annual and monthly reports. In another instance, it may contain information from other facets of the department, such as memoranda from the chief and policy statements. The last part is the scoring form, which is necessary to help assessors complete the scoring as consistently as possible and in the terms and manner in which the police department deems most effective.

Training

In the sixth step, assessors and candidates are trained. In assessor training, it is a common practice to hold a short meeting with the assessors for each exercise, usually the night before or a few hours prior to the beginning of the assessment center itself. In some areas of the country, a general pool of assessors is trained at a community college; they then are called on by individual agencies within a general area as they are needed. Usually this short-term training program is conducted by giving an overview of the assessment center and then going through the guidelines for the individual parts for the assessors in great detail. Emphasis is placed on the assessor's understanding of his or her role and of the definitions of each dimension as it applies to that individual agency. In most assessment centers, one assessor is assigned the responsibility of playing the lead role. Usually this is the more experienced assessor, especially for that individual exercise. In this step some agencies have taken the opportunity to prepare individual candidates for an understanding of the assessment center approach. This training usually takes a maximum of five hours and involves explaining the meaning of the dimensions and how candidates will be graded.

Conducting the Center

In the seventh step, the assessment center is conducted. It takes place in a neutral locale and the coordinator does not take part in the exercises. The coordinator is responsible for seeing that candidates are on time and that assessors' questions are answered. One of the major tasks for the assessors is to get together at the completion of the center and meet with the police chief to give their personal views of each of the candidates. This kind of feedback is not designed to qualify any candidate but only to give to the police chief the personal impressions of the assessors. This feedback is given after the center has been completed and all scores have been tabulated. In this way, scores or rankings cannot be adjusted and the integrity of the assessment center approach is not compromised.

Ensuring Feedback

The eighth and final step includes giving feedback to the individual candidates. This is done within two weeks of the completion of the center. Each candidate must receive as much information as possible, avoiding comparisons but simply helping candidates understand their performance and what steps they might take to improve it in the future.

A common approach of feedback is for a single assessor to receive comments from other assessors, study the individual scoring forms, and then hold a personal interview of about thirty minutes with each candidate. In some police agencies, candidates are required to appear before a departmental assessor from each exercise. In this manner the candidate has four feedback sessions with separate assessors as opposed to one summation. Either method is satisfactory. The important factor is that the candidate is provided feedback within a reasonable time.

Components of the Assessment Center

There are numerous exercises available to police chiefs who wish to implement an assessment center. The most common exercises include oral interviews, leaderless groups, in-basket problems, role-play situations, oral presentations, a written plan, and scheduling.

Oral Interviews

In the oral interview phase there are three assessors, although many times a fourth is also included. Three is usually the more effective number, and two tend to make the interviews not inclusive enough. Four, on the other hand, can create a situation in which the issues are discussed only superficially. Three assessors, however, generally have enough time to let each one ask specific questions. Time frames are extended for top-level management positions. For example, for the position of police chief, the time might range from one and one-half hours up to as many as three hours. For positions such as first-line supervisors, for which there are many candidates, the times are shortened to 45 minutes. A minimum of 30 minutes for each interview is normally needed to obtain the necessary information.

An additional quarter hour should be allowed to give the assessors a chance to score the candidate immediately after the interview. The interviewing process, although very common in police departments, is not necessarily the most effective measure of future behavior patterns. Usually the interviewing panel is made up of one member of the department, another member of city government, and a third member with a special skill, as in psychology or a technical area relevant to the specific position.

Each candidate must receive the same questions in oral interviews. Sometimes candidates are given as many as ten to fifteen questions, which is too large a number to permit answers of any depth. When the questions are restricted to four or five, they can be open-ended. An example of such a question would be the following: Assuming the police chief asks you your opinion on a certain issue such as the color of vehicles, would you state your honest opinion? At this point the questions continue, regardless of what the answer might be, leading the candidate through his or her approach not only to the chief but also to other managers, fellow supervisors, and subordinates. The real issue is at what point the candidate is able to distinguish the priority of two values—loyalty to the police department and honesty toward subordinates and superiors.

In the oral interview, it is advisable to develop specific questions to which the police agency requires answers. For example, if the police department is facing an affirmative action program, questions dealing with how such a program might be implemented would be important. If change or dealing with conflict are other important issues, then questions geared to them should be developed. It is not advisable to have stock questions that have no clear-cut relevance to the examining police department. For example, a question such as "Do you believe in professionalization?" does not really help the assessors to discover how the candidate would behave in the new position.

Sometimes questions asked in the oral interview have no special value to the grading process but are designed to provide feedback for the police chief. Such questions may focus on what the candidate may have done to prepare for the position, what he or she perceives the position to include, and how he or she would rank the individual candidates. This last question provides the police chief with feedback about how the candidates perceive one another and who they think is the best within their group.

Leaderless Groups

Leaderless groups are designed to test an individual's ability to work in a small group. The minimum number needed to make such an exercise effective is usually five. The maximum number is eight. There are two approaches to the kinds of questions to be asked within a leaderless group. The most common method is for the police department to develop one large issue or a series of small issues that are important to the present environment. For example, policies that are presently under study can be presented for discussion by the leaderless group. Such policies might include off-duty work, the use of firearms, or reorganization. In some instances, more than one problem is given. For example, three small issues might be (1) whether the department should accept gifts at Christmastime; (2) whether the agency should issue press releases, and if so, on what incidents; and (3) whether cars should be assigned to personnel on a permanent basis.

Sometimes fixed problems that have nothing to do with the police agency are also used. Examples include group problems such as "Lost in the Desert," "Lost in the Arctic," or "Man on the Moon." In these exercises, some answers are recommended by experts; however, the purpose of this part of the assessment program is not to elicit the "correct answer" but to see how the candidates work together.

A third approach involves asking each member of the leaderless group to play a specific role. For example, persons seeking the position of assistant chief of police may be asked to role-play other department heads, and the issue may be how to best reduce the citywide budget. This may give each person the opportunity to show some understanding of how other agencies have to deal with problems similar to those within the police department. Some departments restrict the role playing to positions within their own agency. Of the many types of problems available, this seems to be the least effective, because it restricts the individuals involved. It therefore is not necessarily used when a large amount of information is to be analyzed during a leaderless group problem.

The leaderless group problem usually lasts 45 minutes to one hour. To add additional stress, sometimes the assessors will collect the answer, have a short discussion among themselves, and then advise the group that the solution it has produced is not adequate. They then ask the group to continue to work on the exercise for an additional 15 minutes. Usually this additional time tends to place people under high stress, so that they begin to show behavior patterns that may not have been evident before.

In-Basket Problems

The in-basket exercise is considered an especially effective one, because it explores the candidates' ability to set priorities and their understanding of departmental policies, rules, and standards.

In most police departments, a series of real-life memoranda are gathered approximately 60 to 90 days prior to the assessment center. Copies are made—changing names and dates—and most of the items in the exercise are then based on them.

The most common approach is to bring all the candidates together in a room and present the in-basket at that time. The answers are written on pieces of paper, and each candidate, upon completing them, places them in an envelope. The envelopes—one for each candidate—are then returned to the assessors. In some instances, names are excluded and candidates are judged only by assigned numbers. In this format, the only knowledge the assessors have is through the written documents provided by the candidates.

Another approach has the candidates complete the in-basket problem in 45 minutes. They are given the memoranda, asked to prioritize them, and required to describe briefly what they would do in each instance. Upon completion of this task, they present their written answers to three evaluators. The assessors read the answers and then take approximately 20 to 30 minutes to question each candidate concerning any issues they may feel are not totally resolved in the written responses. This allows a wider range of information to be evaluated.

In the in-basket exercise, the departments provide a priority list and model answers. Priorities are listed as those that should be handled within eight hours and those that could wait 24 to 48 hours. Model answers are usually one or two sentences at most, and these serve to guide the assessors as to the direction that the correct answers should take.

Role-Play Situations

In these exercises, individuals are asked to play a specific part dealing with an individual role-player. The most common example involves the use of a disgruntled officer who is objecting to his or her performance evaluation report. In some instances, women play the role of complainants of sexual harassment or blacks complain about discrimination. Sometimes a combination is used to focus on more than just one issue. For example, a black sergeant might complain to the candidate, who is role-playing a captain. The sergeant complains that the performance evaluation report is not fair—that it is based predominantly on racially discriminatory attitudes on the part of his lieutenant. In such situations, the same role-player must be used in each instance.

A police department can use a role-player from within the agency. This individual may play the part of a captain with candidates seeking the position of assistant chief. The role-player may be accused of taking something from the scene of the crime, and it is up to the assistant chief to conduct an interview to determine whether the accusation had any merit. In some instances two role-players, both of whom are professional actors, can be used. They role-play the parts of two employees, subordinates to the candidate, who are involved in a conflict concerning the best way to implement a certain project. Each takes an opposite point of view and, during the role-play situation, both indicate severe stress by raising their voices, standing, and pacing about the room.

In another instance, the candidates seeking the position of police captain might be brought into a room and advised that they are to give a speech to the chamber of commerce within ten minutes. A specific issue is presented—one on which the candidates already know the department's point of view. They will also already have the data they would need to deal with this issue as police captains. Each candidate is asked, after ten minutes of preparation, to present a ten-minute speech and role-play the situation as if he or she were speaking to members of the chamber of commerce. The evaluation would include not only the role-play presentation but also the candidates' handwritten notes.

Usually the role-play situation is limited to 30 minutes. Assessors are given an additional 15 minutes to discuss their ratings.

Oral Presentations

In the oral presentation, the candidate is given a specific question and is asked to respond within a short period, such as five to ten minutes. Oral presentations include such issues as, "Why do you seek this position?," "What do you feel are your personal qualifications?," or "How do you view your strengths and your weaknesses?" The weight given to this part of an assessment program is usually small, as it does not require a tremendous amount of forethought on the part of the candidate. Because of the nature of the questions and the amount of time provided, an in-depth analysis is not required of the assessors.

Some police agencies include an oral presentation in conjunction with a specially developed personal qualifications appraisal task. A series of questions and tasks are given to prospective candidates at least 30 to 45 days in advance. For example, the candidates may be asked to interview people in their professional and personal life, summarize what they have learned from these people, and supplement such knowledge with their own perceptions of themselves. They may be asked to write a short scenario about where they would like to be in their personal lives in five years. This would include such issues as lifestyle, vocation, organizational life, family, and free time. They are also asked to write an outline of their expectations for the police department within the next five years. During the oral presentation, they are given 15 minutes to explain their written document and are granted an additional 30 minutes in which to expand on their plan on the basis of questions provided by the assessors.

Written Plan

In the written plan exercise, candidates are given from 90 minutes to three hours to prepare a written document concerning a specific issue within the police department. The problems are varied, depending on the nature of the position sought. For example, in one police department, because the position being sought was in management, the problem involved planning for a rock concert at the civic auditorium. Other written plans have included broad issues such as (1) what promotional system should be implemented within the police department, (2) how the department should go about recruiting additional women and blacks to meet the requirements of the city's affirmative action program, and (3) how to develop team management practices.

The police department may give candidates approximately 45 days in which to develop a five-year budget plan for the police department. The budget documents are submitted at the end of that time. The assessors are then given approximately two weeks to read through these documents. Each candidate is given ten minutes to explain additional information and then an additional 30 minutes during which to answer questions from the assessors. Only after all of this information has been gathered is the written plan evaluated.

The police chief should recognize that a written plan is a good exercise only when the position being sought requires people to write such plans. For example, a police department that has a Research and Development Unit should not necessarily demand a long written plan from every candidate for a supervisory position. Only for those seeking posts in the Research and Development Unit would such an assignment be appropriate.

Scheduling

In the scheduling exercise, the candidate is given the personnel roster of a given unit and asked to allocate the time of these people—that is, to develop a scheduling system—to achieve the overall goals of the police department. To create stress, the problem may be complicated by introducing additional information halfway through the 30-minute exercise. For example, individuals may resign, call in sick, or need to be scheduled for training programs. In this way, flexibility and the ability to make decisions under stress can also be analyzed.

Rating Scales

Numerical Scales

There are different ways in which scoring scales can be developed to evaluate the individual candidate during the assessment program. In most cities, a specific numerical value is assigned to each exercise. For example, an oral interview might be worth 40 points; an in-basket exercise, 30 points; a leaderless group, 20 points; and a role-play situation, 10 points. Each candidate, upon completion of the assigned exercise, is rated individually by each assessor. Once the individual ratings are completed, assessors discuss the ratings and come to a consensus as to the final numerical score. After all candidates have completed an exercise, the raters examine final consensus scores given to each and make any adjustments necessary to clearly show differences that may be greater than originally agreed on. For example, suppose that candidate A received 28 out of 30 points, and candidate B received 26. The assessors may later agree that candidate B was not 2 points but 3 points behind. Thus, the second person's score might be changed to a 25.

In using numerical ratings, it becomes difficult to show large differences between the candidates, especially when the maximum score is below 20 on any exercise. When numerical ratings are used, each exercise should be graded on a score of at least 30. The total scores of all exercises can be computed to reflect an overall grade of 100 percent. For example, if there are four exercises, the first might contain 30 points, the second 40, the third 50, and the fourth 60, for a total of 180 points. This score can easily be computed to a scale of 100 percent. (Divide the applicant's score, say 120, by the total of 180, for a final grade of 66.6.)

Strengths and Weaknesses

A second approach is to use a rating form that discusses the strengths and weaknesses of each candidate. Under this form of rating, however, no numerical grade is given, and the police chief receives feedback on the strengths and weaknesses of the individual candidates in each of the dimensions in each of the exercises. The final judgment as to the value of strengths and weaknesses is left up to the person responsible for the final promotion.

Composite Graphs

The third method is to develop a composite graph. Here points are given to each dimension instead of each exercise. For example, if decisionmaking is examined in three of the four exercises, then the number of points given to decisionmaking is placed on a bar or line graph denoting the score for each exercise. In this way, the person responsible for the promotions has a composite graph from which to analyze individual scores on each dimension and where dimension scores may appear the strongest and the weakest. Again, using decisionmaking as an example, an individual may be an effective decisionmaker in a one-to-one situation such as role-playing during an oral interview process, but he or she may not have exhibited strong decision-making skills in the leaderless group. Thus, the police chief has an understanding of how the candidate will behave in different situations.

Forced Choice

Another approach is to have assessors rate the candidates on a forced-choice scale. They have to rate candidates first, second, third, and fourth during each part of the assessment center without giving assigned weights. This system has not proved to be effective in giving an overview of the candidate's behavior during the total assessment center.

Consensus

In the rating process, individual assessors must rate the candidates prior to any discussions between themselves. Once they have completed their individual ratings, the assessors discuss them and come to an overall consensus. All the scoring is given to the candidate during the feedback process. In this way, the integrity of the assessment center is maintained and more data can be analyzed before the final consensus is reached.

Conclusion

In conclusion, police chiefs must recognize that assessment centers will not solve all promotional problems. They are designed to serve as a tool in police agencies where such tools may be useful. History has shown that the assessment center approach may help to pinpoint quality candidates and, more importantly, lend a sense of fairness to the promotional process. These are both important criteria, especially in government agencies. The assessment center must be recognized as only a tool; therefore the belief that this approach always produces "the best" is not necessarily justified. Police chiefs must recognize that they must personally be strongly committed to anyone who is promoted to a key management position. Assessment centers can help to develop that commitment by identifying the strengths and weaknesses of persons to be promoted. This tends to reduce the amount of time it takes a police manager to learn about key managerial personnel. Conflicts are thus reduced and working relationships develop more quickly and effectively.

Although assessment centers may not be the final answer, they are certainly helpful in identifying the assets and liabilities that a candidate may bring to a new position.

Note

1.   *Kirkland v. New York State Correctional Services*, 711 F.2d 1117 (1983).

Discussion Questions

1.   Do you believe an assessment center is the best approach for making promotions within a police department? If so, why?

2.   What are some issues that could be addressed in a typical assessment center?

3.   Why do you believe assessment centers are perceived as fair by the candidates?

4.   Is there a better and more effective way of promoting personnel in a police department than the assessment center approach?

Afterword

The Future

The word *future* brings up ideas reminiscent of science fiction. It suggests a world of fantasy and evokes dreams that may eventually lead to action. The future cannot be predicted precisely, but without an anticipatory vision, it may seem frightening and unmanageable.

The future belongs to those who have the foresight to plan, the intelligence to implement their plans, and the courage to take personal risks in order to bring about improvements on the present.

The police leader of the future will deal with critical choices on a daily basis. His or her decisions will be basically positive but will also have negative potential. In short, every leader must have the capacity to apply the lessons of the past to the problems that are yet to be faced.

A major issue for the police leader of the future will be the amount of control required to operate the individual agency. There are two areas in which, if a police leader loses control, he or she will no longer be able to direct departmental operations: finance and personnel. It is therefore incumbent on the leader of the future to attempt in all ethical, legal, and moral ways, to gain control over the financial resources of the department and over its personnel practices. In bureaucratic situations, trade-offs that call for compromise may be required, as when the demands of law enforcement must bow to a level of equality with other agencies of city or county government. If law enforcement is really to reach its highest level of effectiveness, this must be done in other ways than by attempting to place law enforcement agencies on a par with all others. The law itself has recognized that law enforcement officers are required to operate at a higher legal standard than other members of government. This is because of the ultimate responsibility and trust placed in each officer at each moment of his or her life. If officers are to be accountable and if chiefs are to be accountable for the officers' behavior, then they must be able to implement the high standards required to bring about what is considered to be truly professional law enforcement.

Successful Police Agencies

In their book *In Search of Excellence*, Thomas J. Peters and Robert H. Waterman, Jr., studied a series of successful American companies and found that certain common factors tended to create an effective organizational culture and allowed the company to achieve its goals. These same criteria can generally be applied to a police department.

Typical Factors

For years theorists have stated that the critical success factors included zero-base budgeting, management by objectives, matrix organization, the use of computers, strategic planning, and management science techniques. After looking at law enforcement agencies throughout the country, the author has found that poor police departments use all of these strategies. However, good police departments also use these strategies. They are basically techniques that can be purchased or installed, much as a tire can be placed on a car or a stereo system in a home, without necessarily providing all the requisites for departmental effectiveness.

Effective Factors

The following factors seem to be characteristic of police departments that are successful in reaching their stated goals and in developing a climate in which people are committed to their work. The first and major factor is a bias on the part of the police chief toward some form of action. Phrases such as "we must delay" or "it may not be the right time" are not used in these departments. Instead, the emphasis is on performing now and the willingness to take risks to achieve the department's important goals. Police leaders in the future, therefore, should have a bias toward such action.

The second factor is that effective police departments are usually simple in their organizational structure. They have a lean staff—that is, a small ratio of staff to line personnel—which requires line-assignment members such as patrol and investigations to make many decisions that affect the activities of the entire department. Personnel within the department are keenly aware of the leader's role, personality, and goals.

A third factor is that such departments are oriented toward productivity, and such productivity depends on the improvement of the people within the agency—not just on mechanical devices such as computers or equipment. This is not to say that computers and other equipment are not important, but only to say that they do not determine the level of productivity. Only when each individual within the department develops the highest possible capability does productivity reach great heights. In such departments, people are treated as individuals regardless of whether they act in an individual or team capacity. In such departments, commanders of units are not told how to do their jobs but rather what they are expected to achieve. For example, a patrol shift may be told to reduce the number of armed robberies being committed in a certain area of the community during a certain time against a certain target, such as convenience stores. The manner in which this goal is reached is left up to the people who are responsible for the actual implementation. Thus, they become autonomous and accountable. Individual officers know where they stand and also how well they are doing with the ideas that they have generated and put together as a group.

There is also a fourth factor. The police leader emphasizes a few key goals and does not burden the department with so many rules and regulations that the big picture is lost. Instead, three to five goals are defined, such as reduction of the crime rate, quicker response time, and development of department personnel. The role of the leader is to see that these purposes are achieved. Almost every action that follows—whether initiated by police officers, supervisors, or middle managers—is geared toward the achievement of the three major goals. An example is the McDonald's Corporation, which stresses that (1) its stores are to be kept clean, (2) people are to be kept moving in and out, and (3) each outlet is to sell its food at prices equal to or lower than those of other fast-food chains in the area. These three basic guidelines have helped to make an idea grow into a multibillion-dollar business.

In a similar way, a highly effective police department might stress that (1) requests from the public are to receive the fastest possible response, (2) all police officers are to do their utmost always to be courteous, and (3) the law is to be justly enforced.

Finally, although the police leader should have controls to see that work is completed, he or she should also be willing to loosen these controls when possible and to spend extra time attempting to coordinate activities and communicate purposes. "Loose but tight" controls include the ability to allow personnel and the department to make judgments at any time to do whatever is best in a given situation. Rules therefore are viewed not as rigid controls but rather as guidelines. They may be observed most of the time, but people can still feel free to come up with new solutions to special problems so as to do whatever is best for the department and the community. This requires a police leader who can be both flexible and consistent—flexible in day-to-day operations but consistent in the overall direction of the department.

What, then, does all this suggest about the police leaders of the future? It would seem that police leaders will not be able to hide behind traditional practices. They will not be able to find easy acceptance by defining activities, such as the number of arrests or miles driven. These leaders may have to play a much stronger role, having to take and defend strong stands. They will have to build imaginative police departments that can continue to grow, develop, and help bring about a better life for all.

Personal Characteristics

Police leaders of the future must realize that they do not necessarily have any special insight—no special credentials that will guarantee their total success. Instead, they must possess certain characteristics. In examining law enforcement agencies for over twenty years, the author has come to the conclusion that effective leaders implement three major characteristics on a daily basis: attitude, courage, and enthusiasm.

Attitude

Attitude is defined as a position assumed for a specific purpose. The police leader of the future must assume the position of being a winner for the purpose of achieving. A winner is one who shapes the world; nonwinners are those who accept the world as it is; and losers are those who proceed to set impossible goals or no goals at all, thereby depriving themselves of success and guaranteeing failure. To develop this kind of attitude, police leaders must constantly seek the truth and must have the necessary skill to use this truth. Their attitude should include the strong commitment to implementing the truth, thereby guaranteeing the success they seek. Police leaders of the future need to recognize that they are whatever they think they are. If they firmly believe they can win, they will. If they believe that they are going to lose, they will lose.

Police leaders of the future can test their attitude, especially when they come face to face with an obstacle. If they stop behind the obstacle and stay there, committing all their energies only to complaining about the presence of such an obstacle, they will probably lose. If, on the other hand, they have a winning attitude—the ability to go through the obstacle, around it, over it, and in some instances even under it—they will win. A winning attitude defines the purposes of the department as more important than its rules. If rules present an obstacle to the achievement of these purposes, rules can be changed.

Leaders with positive and winning attitudes do not say things like "They made me do it" or "We can't make it." They never use the words "I can't," because this can bring about failure in the present and in the future. Police leaders recognize that a positive idea is unbeatable. Their attitude is one of accepting responsibility and being accountable for their individual behavior and the decisions necessary to run the agency.

Courage

The second important characteristic, courage, is defined as the inner strength to preserve one's legal, ethical, and moral values. These values must first be established; their importance must be prioritized. For example, will it be more important to be honest with people or to be tactful? Will it be more important to be honest and admit one's mistakes or to try to avoid criticism? Effective leaders have the ability to be honest, to trust others and themselves, to implement their attitudes with courage, and to practice self-discipline. Self-discipline is the ability to eliminate the parts of one's behavior that serve no useful purpose. The police leader who can speak to large groups and does so in an effective manner is not necessarily practicing self-discipline. However, such discipline is shown by the police leader who may feel uncomfortable in such situations but is still willing to take part in them, practices, and does a good job.

A police leader who achieves courage has the ability to believe in the personnel of the department. The leader will have the courage to share ideas, set goals, and produce loose but necessary controls to see to it that ideas are effectively realized. He or she also has the ability to be open and honest with all people. Courage is the ingredient that allows the leader and others to be accountable for their individual behavior.

Police leaders recognize that they have three separate aspects: goals, joys, and individual behavior patterns. There is what they want to be, their potential for the future, and what others think they are. This latter part is nothing more than an approximation of the truth. Effective police leaders do not waste time and energy trying to impress people but rather press forward to achieve their potential. They are willing to be what they really are.

It takes courage to deal with others in a police department. Police leaders of the future must express such courage. They must attempt to praise people in the department and not spend time criticizing. Leaders will walk the halls and speak both to people who report directly to them and to anyone else in the agency. Leaders will take a few minutes each day to develop others' self-esteem. They must be willing to be honest and recognize that personnel of the department hunger for the truth and for the opportunity to tell the truth. They will want to share their opinions, their judgment, their feelings, and their knowledge. Such steps demonstrate that they are satisfied with the present but are looking forward to a more productive future.

It takes courage, but police leaders of the future will recognize that, in dealing with people, their true impressions must be reflected in their actual responses—otherwise they will come across as insincere.

Enthusiasm

Enthusiasm is defined as a strong, positive sense of excitement and anticipation. It allows us to grow. It is the leadership quality on which all others depend. With it, the police leader has everything; without it, he or she has very little. People with enthusiasm demonstrate it by the sparkle in their eyes, the swing in their walk, and the energy with which they implement their plans. Police leaders who develop alibis and excuses are usually dooming themselves to a life that lacks enthusiasm and to an eventual loss of respect and trust.

To possess and demonstrate such enthusiasm the leader must try to do things differently than they may have been done in the past. For example, when a person feels down or depressed, they act in a depressive way that then makes them even more depressive. However, effective leaders begin to act enthusiastically about any project, about the work environment, about the people they work with, and about the opportunity to spread ideas and see people and projects grow. Once one begins to act in an enthusiastic manner and to feel enthusiastic, one continues to do so. The loser has a tendency to place actions on top of feelings, the winner has a tendency to place the feelings on top of the actions.

Effective police leaders are winners when they practice attitude, courage, and enthusiasm. It is rare to find an effective leader who was ever an enthusiastic loser. Instead, enthusiasm gives one the ability to win.

Effective law enforcement did not really begin until people possessed the kind of enthusiasm that grew and made their departments the realities of their dreams. An enthusiastic police leader is possessed with a spirit that allows him or her to go further than others. He or she is a driving force that no power can overcome. It is the choice of the leader of the future to accept life enthusiastically, enjoy it, and change it for the better or to accept the world and follow the direction of others.

Police Chief, City Manager, and Council

Police Chief to City Manager

Every police chief who reports to a city manager will eventually become aware of the role that he or she must play with the city manager. The police chief, therefore, must understand the city manager's point of view—that is, what the city manager may expect from the police chief, what the city manager may expect from the council or commission, and, finally, what commissions or councils usually expect from their city manager.

In the first instance, the city manager has certain expectations from the chief of police. The chief must recognize that he or she is but one department head and in many instances can only spend a few hours on a weekly basis dealing with the city manager. In some instances, such as in large communities, this contact may consist of only formal staff meetings and informal sessions over lunch. What, then, does the city manager really expect from the chief of police?

The average city manager expects the police chief to give professional advice and to know law enforcement. Although the city manager might not expect the chief individually to be able to answer all questions, he or she expects the police department to provide the office of the manager with a solution and other alternatives as well. The chief of police therefore must be able to effectively communicate to a nonpolice person, the city manager, in language that the city manager can understand.

A city manager expects the chief of police to present the police department's point of view. It is incumbent on the police chief to know the department and the views of the police officers. The police chief is not expected to play games with his or her manager or to use highly technical arguments when the real problem may be nothing more than a difference in points of view or an understanding of differences of opinion. Police chiefs should attempt to make themselves understood and, whenever possible, not become involved in highly emotional discussions, thereby creating feelings of anger on the part of one or the other.

The manager expects the police chief to understand the broader point of view. The manager will expect the police chief not only to recognize the need for budget restrictions within the police department, but also to understand and analyze the budgetary problems that face the city as a whole. It is incumbent on the police chief to learn something from other department heads concerning their priorities and—just as important—what they consider to be necessary to serve the citizens of the community effectively.

The city manager expects the police chief to be a manager and to assume the necessary responsibility to take initiative and be accountable. Normally, a city manager would expect the police chief to make recommendations and not continually ask the city manager what he or she, the manager, wants done. The police chief should, therefore, have his or her information carefully analyzed before discussing any serious issue with the city manager. The police chief is expected to be candid with the city manager about what the manager needs to hear in order to pass information to other department heads, administrative personnel, and the council or commission. The police chief must keep the city manager advised of serious issues such as high absenteeism or the effect of poor equipment before the city manager finds out about such issues by reading about them in the newspaper or listening to criticism from the council. It is usually better for a police chief to provide more information than less. When important facts are left out, these facts may come back to haunt both parties, not only in dealing with that issue but, more importantly, in dealing with the long-term issue of a relationship of trust.

The chief of police must attempt to be as understanding as possible about disagreements. The chief of police should not to attempt to place a city manager in a corner so that he or she has but one alternative. Under all circumstances, the police chief should share the information so that there are no big surprises for the city manager that could make him or her feel locked in a corner.

In summary then, it is incumbent on the city manager and chief of police, through day-to-day contacts, to develop a relationship of earned respect and trust in which honesty plays an important role.

City Manager to City Council

A city manager has expectations of the council or commission. He or she normally expects the council to advise him or her of what it expects the manager to accomplish. The manager expects the council or commission to give the city manager feedback, especially when any problems exist. The city manager expects the council to observe behaviors within city government, including those of police officers, and report on those observations. The manager further expects that when such issues arise, they are brought to the city manager's attention rather than directly to department heads.

The city manager expects the council to bring employee issues such as tardiness, sloppiness, or ineffective work habits to him or her for possible action. The city manager expects that the council will support the manager in increasing service levels, in reducing costs, and in improving the image of city government in general. Overall, the city manager expects the council to be supportive and positive not only in the program area but also in helping to develop new directions, so that the major purposes of city government can eventually be achieved.

City Council to City Manager

The police chief must also be aware that the typical city council or commission has certain expectations of the city manager. In many instances these expectations can only be fulfilled by a close working relationship between the city manager and the police chief.

Most councils expect their city managers to keep them as informed as possible as to what is going on. They expect their manager to be abreast of problems, especially those that become public. For example, if there were a series of newspaper articles concerning the promotional process within the police department, they would expect the city manager to be aware of how the police department was dealing with these issues.

Councils expect the city manager to explain to them what the manager needs to perform his or her duties effectively. They expect the manager to make specific recommendations as to how an issue—such as the image of a department or the reduction of employee dissatisfaction—can be resolved.

City councils expect to evaluate the important key positions within city government. Normally this includes the position of chief of police. Therefore, the chief of police, in sharing as much as possible, is able to guarantee that the council itself will gain further knowledge of the performance of the police chief. A council expects the city manager to keep it abreast of any legal actions that may be brought against the city. For example, if a police union refuses to accept the promotional testing process and intends to file a lawsuit, it is incumbent on the city manager to keep the council advised from the moment of possible rumors until the conclusion of any lawsuit.

In general, the city council expects the city manager to perform in a timely fashion, at a low cost, and without disrupting service to the citizens. Obviously this is a very difficult task. However, the police chief can help the city manager to achieve a high degree of success. Finally, the city council expects the manager to be in good health. Therefore, the police chief must share the workload, not only running the police department but also helping to run the entire city government. Otherwise, the city manager's job may become one in which burnout is prevalent and the manager becomes ineffective after a short time on the job, thereby adding to the problems of the chief of police.

Final Thought

What, then, can the police chief of the future do first as a leader? As a department head, he or she can strive to develop individual responsibility and accountability in every member of the police department and as much as possible in every member of the community. He or she can see to it that the police department provides a positive role model for the entire community. This applies to the areas of honesty, service, and commitment. The police leader can develop feelings of self-esteem, self-worth, and confidence in his or her subordinates to the point at which they will have freedom and at the same time be responsible. The police leader can develop the rational and human skills needed to implement these standards.

The police leader can also lead the community. He or she can help develop opportunities for the enrichment of citizens' lives by letting the department participate in cultural, recreational, and developmental programs that will help make the community the best place to live. Through leadership, the police chief can foster strength, spirit, and community involvement in the law enforcement endeavor. This can be done through openness with the news media, special community work projects, and public appreciation days.

The police leader can help the community by making a determined effort to bring together those who need help and those who can help. A police department can develop volunteers and services that will help young people in times of stress. One of the greatest positive role models for youth is an effective police officer. Walking the beat, although not popular, is effective because the individual officer gets to know the individual citizens and each plays a role in making the other feel important.

The police chief can further provide citizens and groups of citizens with easy access to information about how the department operates and how the resources at the police department can be utilized. The development of a simple hot line to answer questions and offer help can go a long way toward meeting this overall purpose. In the area of crime reduction, the police chief can attempt to make citizens aware of their roles in crime prevention through school programs and encouragement on the part of all citizens to report anything suspicious, especially any time they become the victims of crime. The leader can further encourage the public to utilize the crime-prevention programs generated by the department.

Both police and fire personnel can assist architects and builders in planning and designing structures so as to discourage crime and increase public safety. By making crime prevention a strong consideration in the designing of buildings, cars, and public areas such as airports, the leader of the future can affect the entire community.

In the future the police leader may need to involve the courts and correctional agencies in crime prevention. The police leader can take the attitude that everyone within the criminal justice system plays a role in the prevention and reduction of crime.

The role of the leader in the future may appear complicated, but it is challenging and rewarding.

The future belongs to those who are willing to accept its challenges.

Index